Angels and Others

This is a work of fiction. Names, characters, illustrations, and other material are the product of the authors' imaginations Any resemblance to actual persons, living or dead, events, or locales is entirely coincidental.

First Printing, August 2025

ISBN 978-1-0686941-6-5

Angels and Others

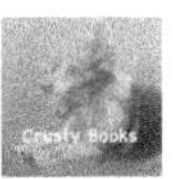

1

ANGELS GOOD & BAD

We most probably associate Angels with
heavenly choirs and/or good deeds.
We are not saying that is wrong,
but there is another side to these delightful winged creatures.
Let's face it Angels can be Bad!.
It is interesting to study human interaction with Angels,
and we have on the whole showed situations
where men (particularly) are rather aggressive.
Perhaps it is just a way of covering
their confusion and embarrassment.

LANDING ANGEL

Beware if you're an Angel
In a State that is not free
The Authorities will chase you
And never let you be
If you have a little problem
And you need to take a rest
Departing from your flight plan
Makes you liable to arrest
If you overfly the city
And your route is not so high
They see you as a traitor
Or perhaps a foreign spy
So cover up your assets
Just so they do not try
To enjoy this bit of heaven
That has fallen from their sky

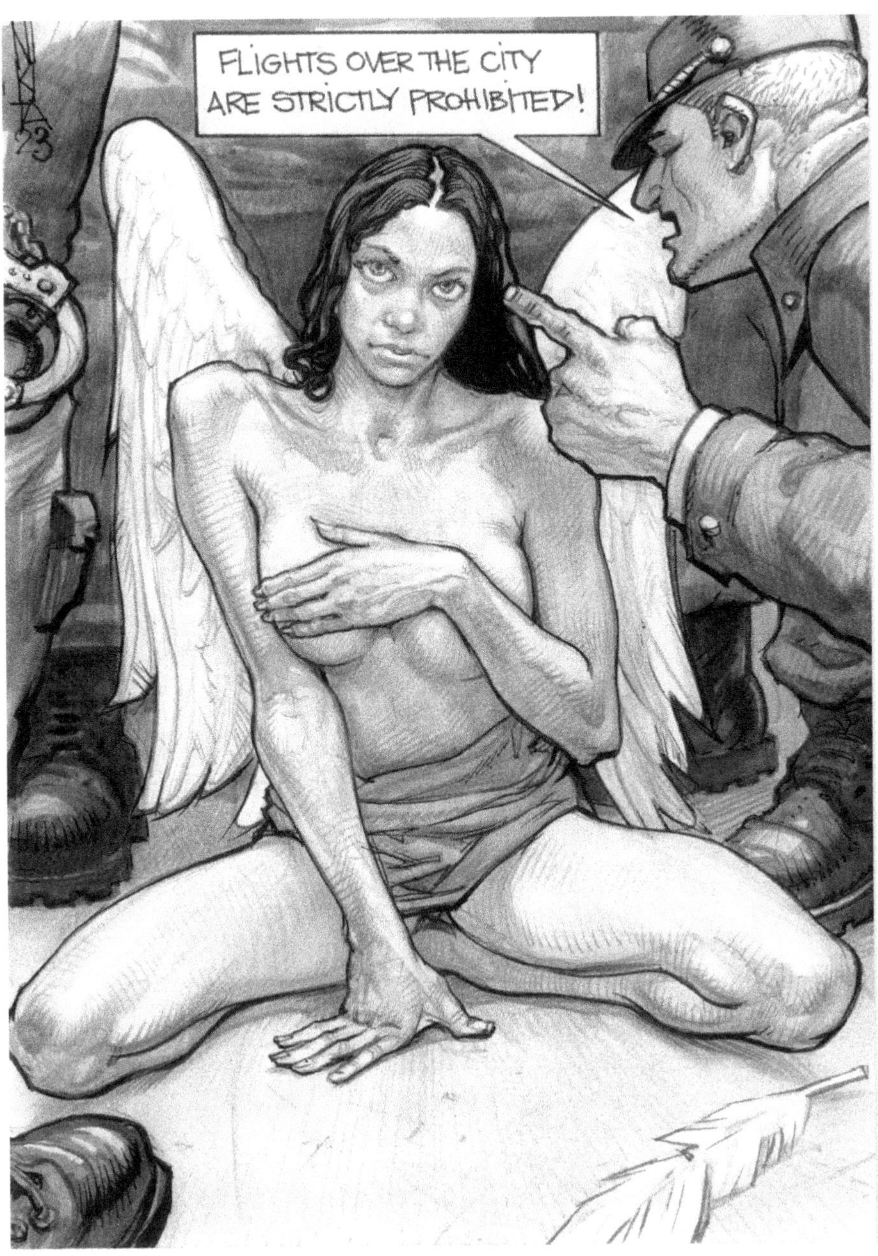
FLIGHTS OVER THE CITY
ARE STRICTLY PROHIBITED!

CRASHING ANGEL

Suddenly we fall
My love
Suddenly
We fall

For a heart-splitting moment
We stand
Poised on the knife-edge
Of indecision

And then the balance swings
And with increasing
Momentum
We crash headlong
Into the eternity of certainty

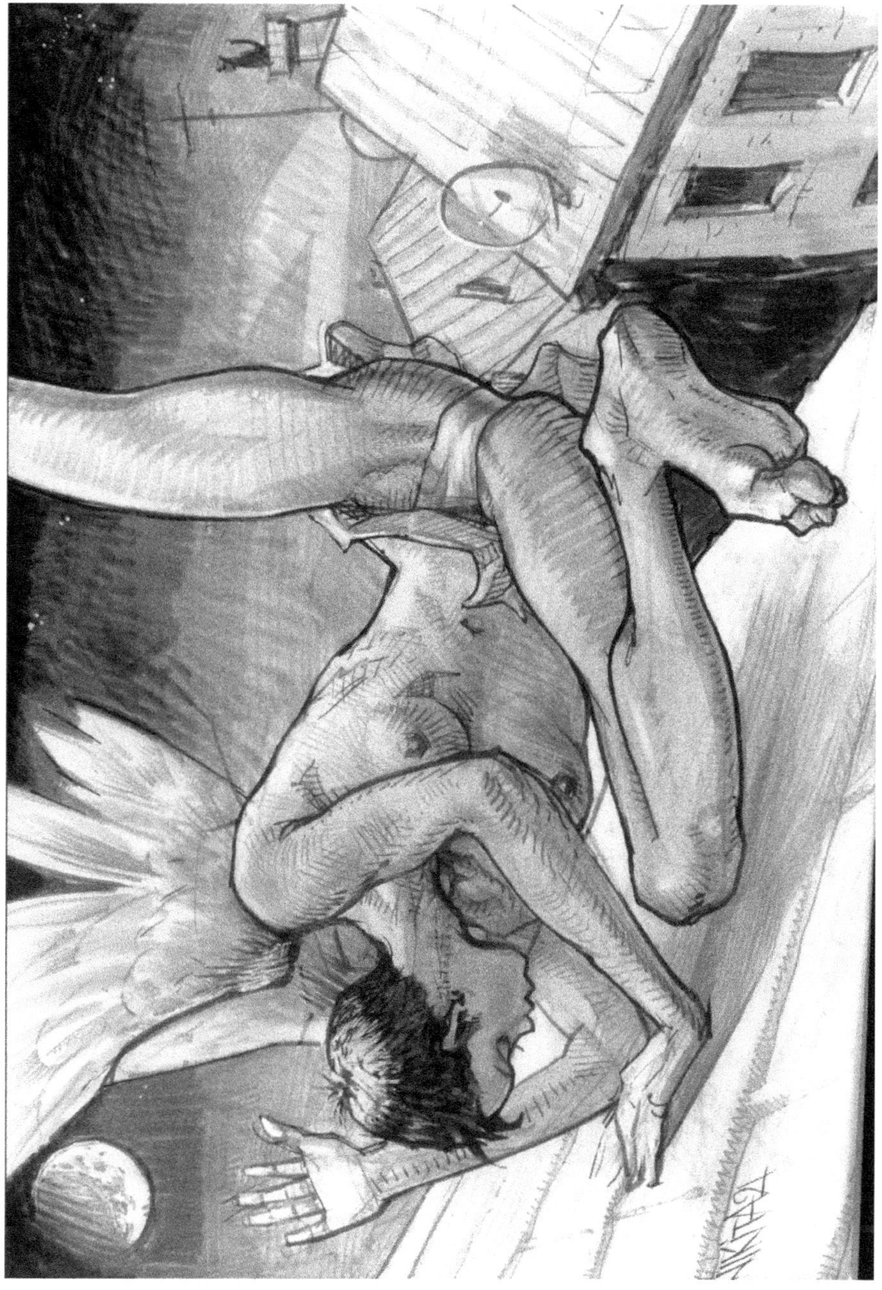

ROOFER

Angel
Pure Perfect
Hover Guard Love
Wings Doom Earth Heaven
Banish Revile Deny
Fallen Evil
Devil

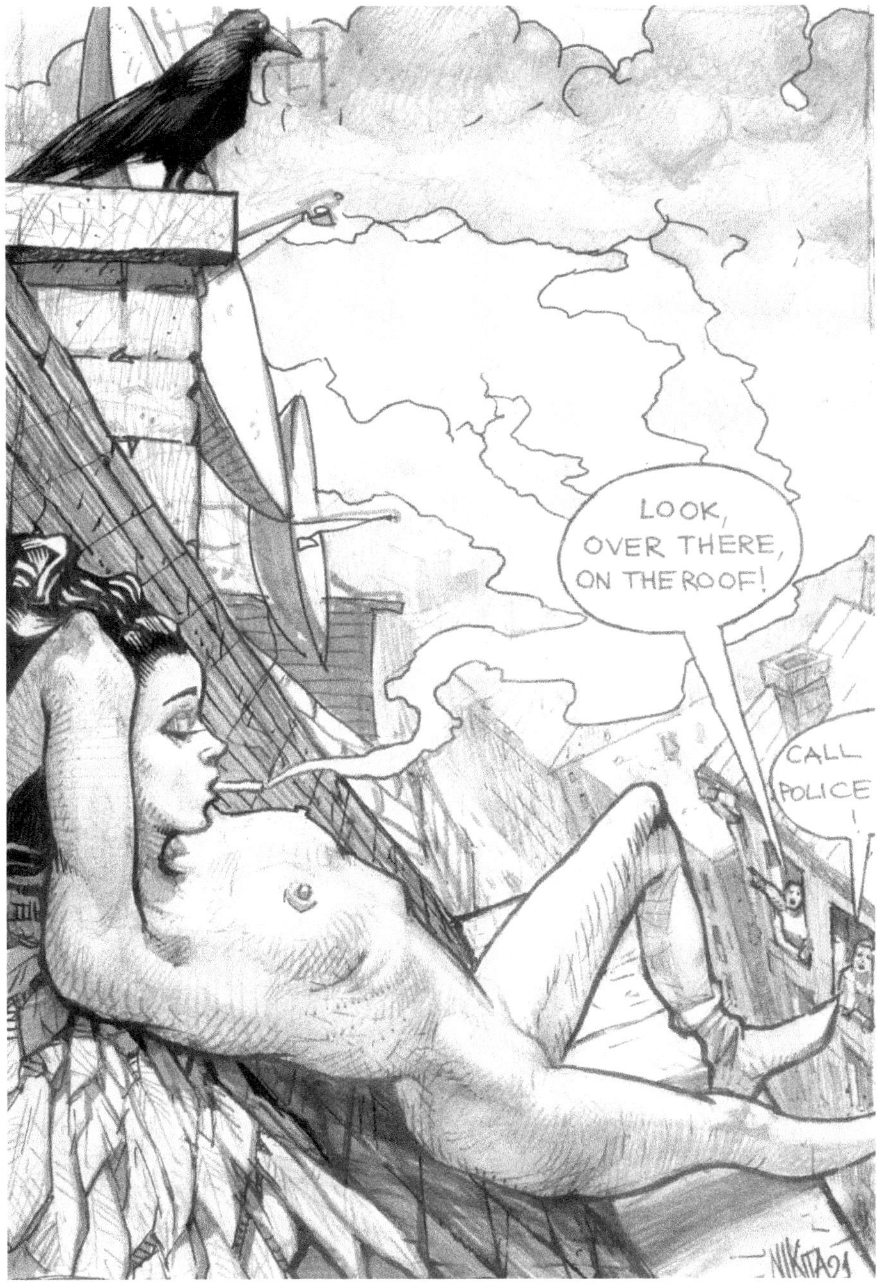
LOOK,
OVER THERE,
ON THE ROOF!
CALL
POLICE
!
NIKITA21

CAPTURED ANGEL

.

There once was an Angel - so pretty
She fell to the earth in the city
They pinioned her arms
And photo'd her charms
Whilst showing her no kind of pity.

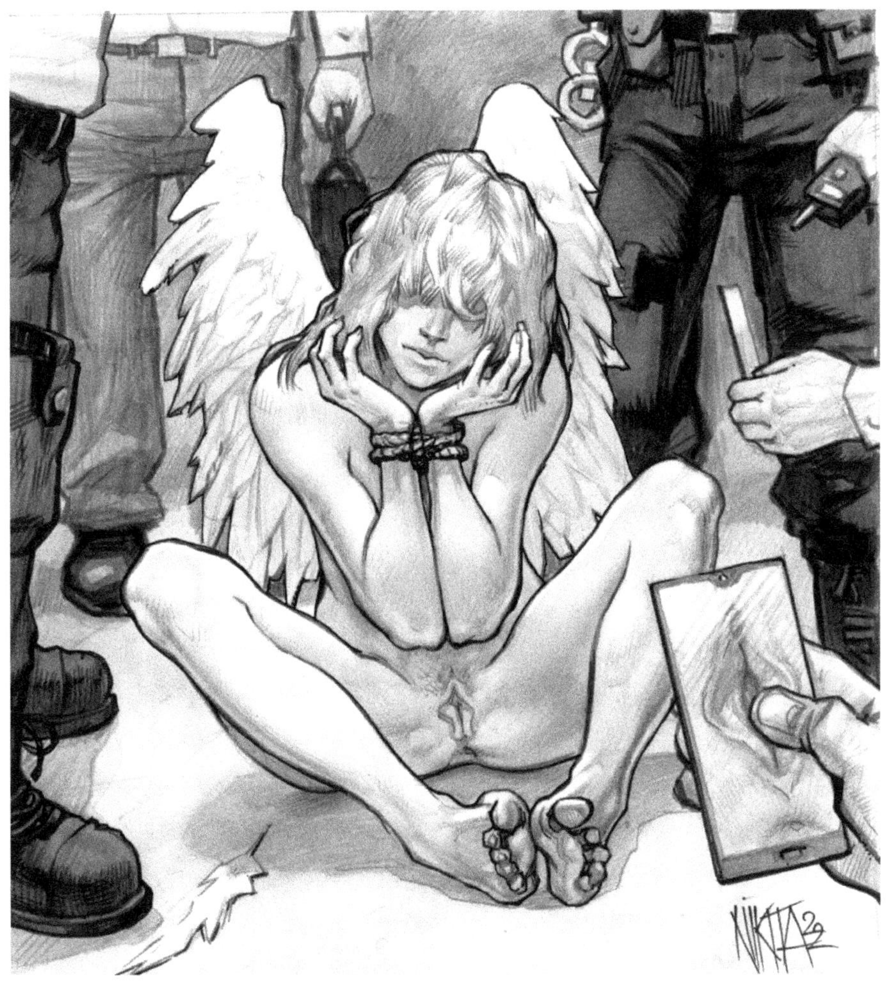

NAUGHTY ANGEL

There was a young Angel called Mabel
Whose naughtiness was quite a fable
When told to be good
She'd said that she would
But found that she just was not able.

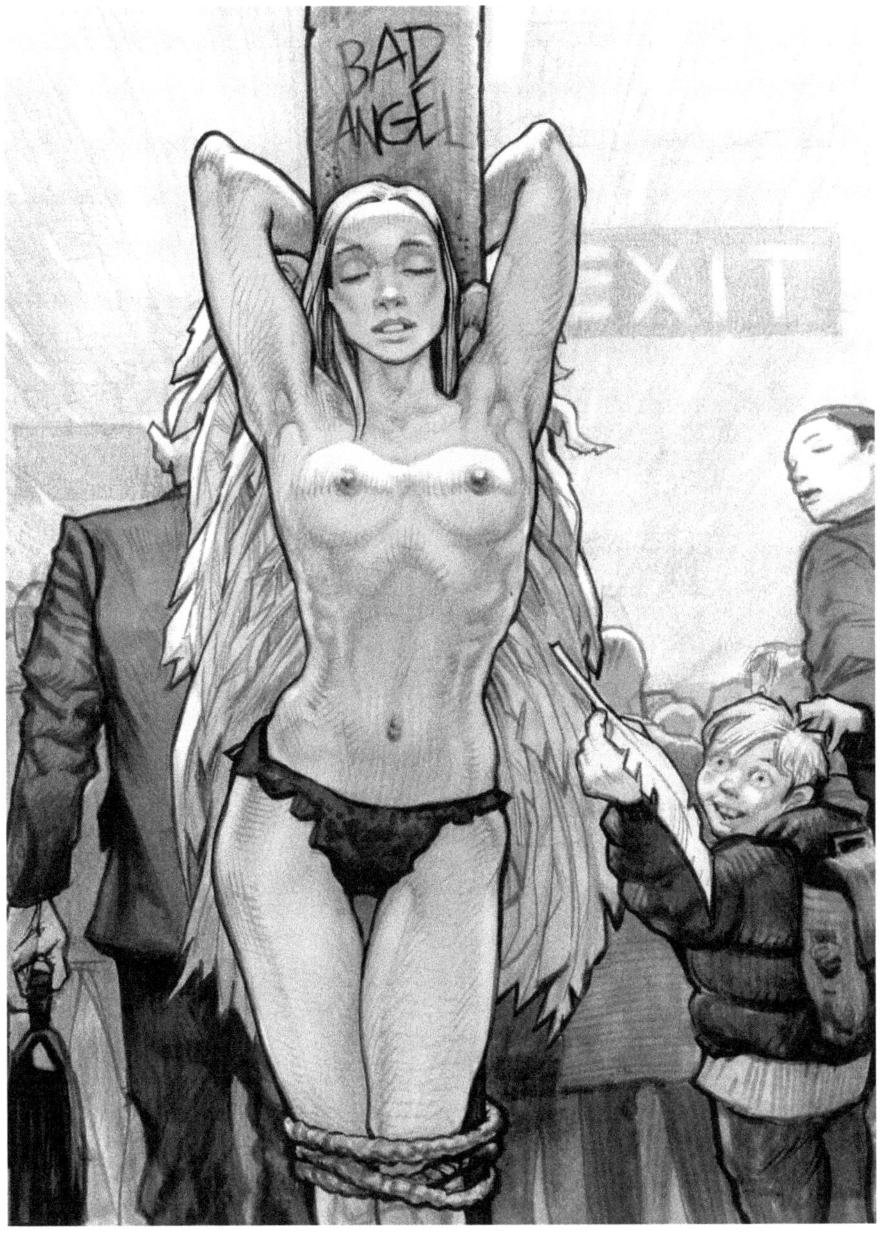
BAD
ANGEL
EXIT

JUST ARRIVED

In a poor war-torn nation
In an inner-city slum
Where hope was long forgotten
An Angel has just come
She strides with clear intention
Through alleyway and street
Amidst human desolation
A semi-naked treat
So will this new arrival
Save us from our fate
Or has angelic intervention
Sadly come too late?

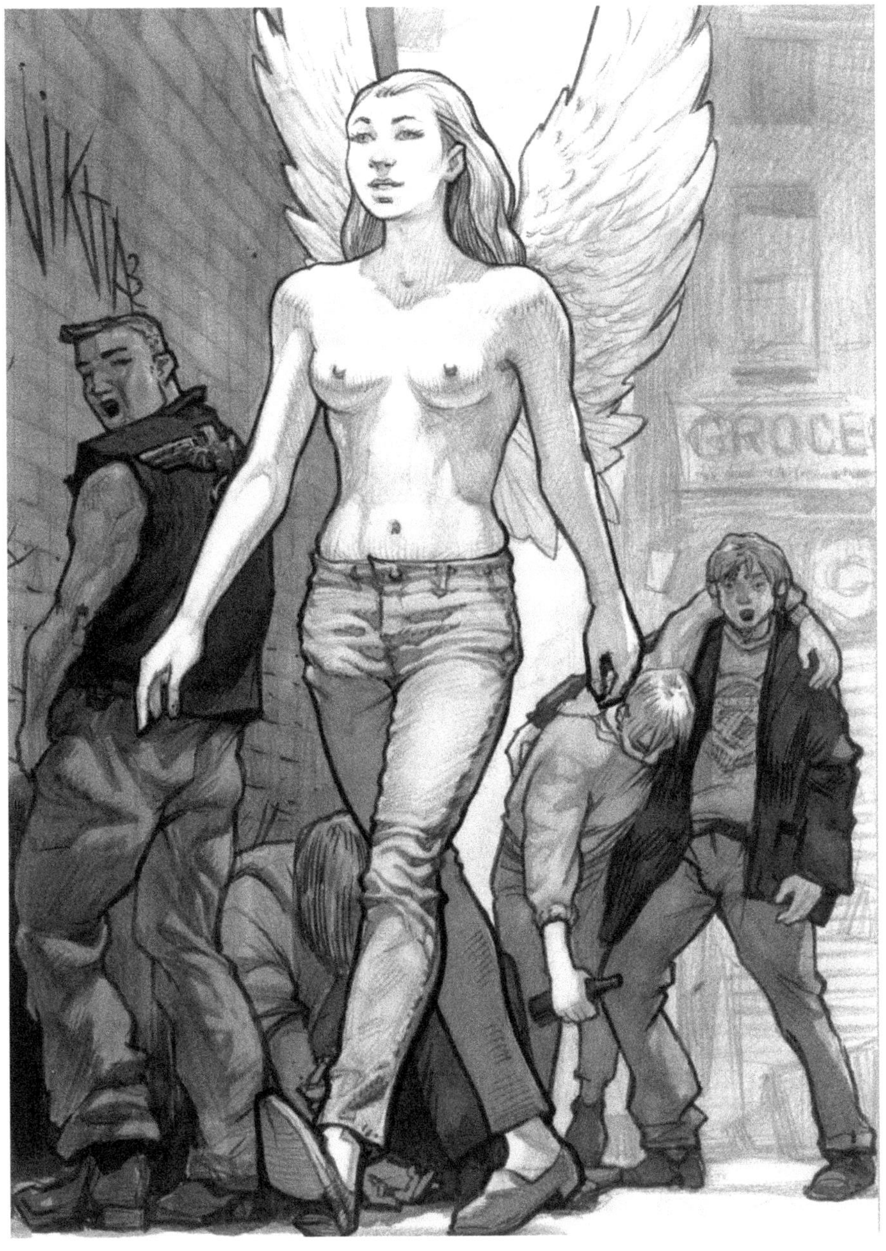

REFUSAL

A naughty young Angel they say
Simply would not obey
When her dad said 'come here'
She said 'no bloody fear
'Cos on Earth I can party all day. '

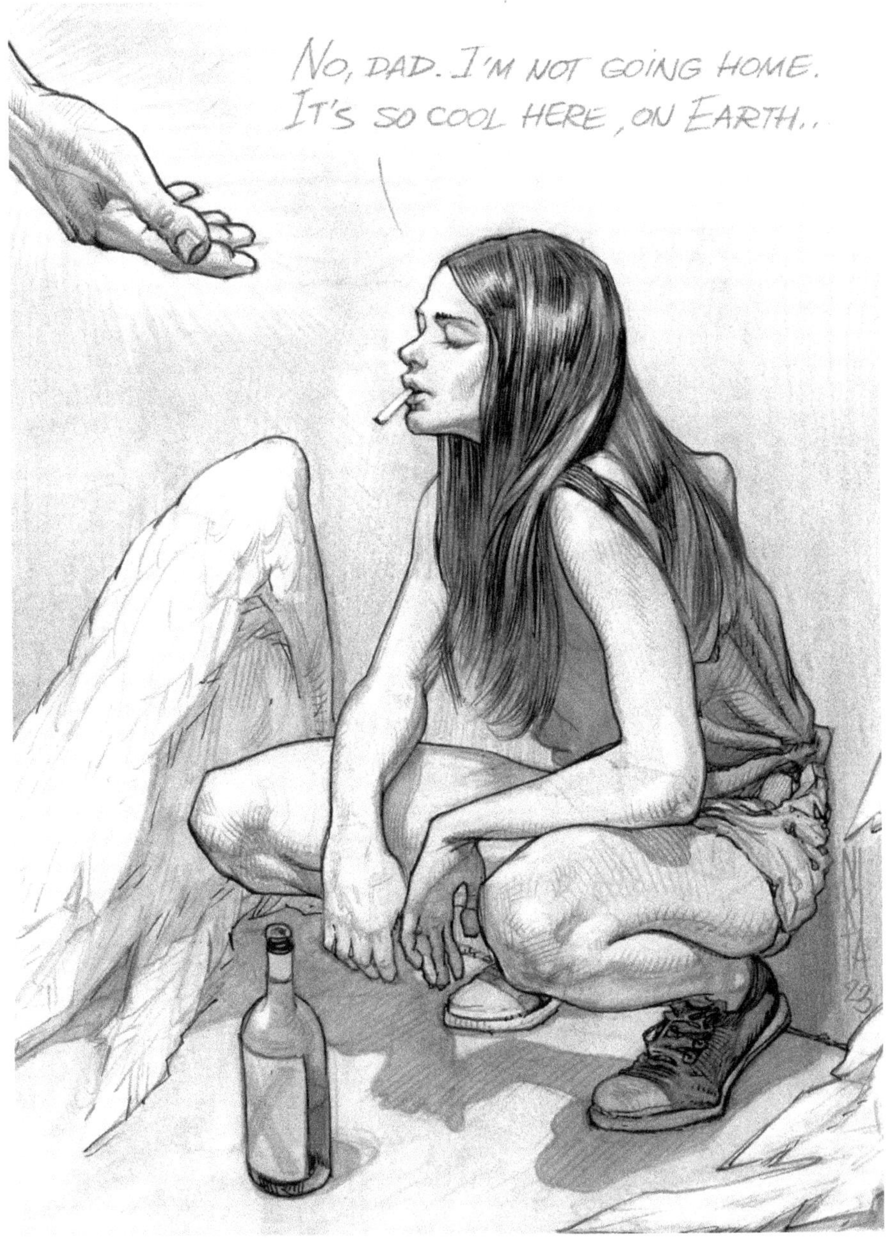
NO, DAD. I'M NOT GOING HOME.
IT'S SO COOL HERE, ON EARTH..

ANGELS' SAUNA

If you feel the need for a scrub
And you find a good sauna club
You must take off your wings
And the rest of your things
And give yourself a good rub
The problem for Angels must be
That voyeurs, just like you and me
Will disturb their ablutions.
So their only solution 's
To offer their services free!

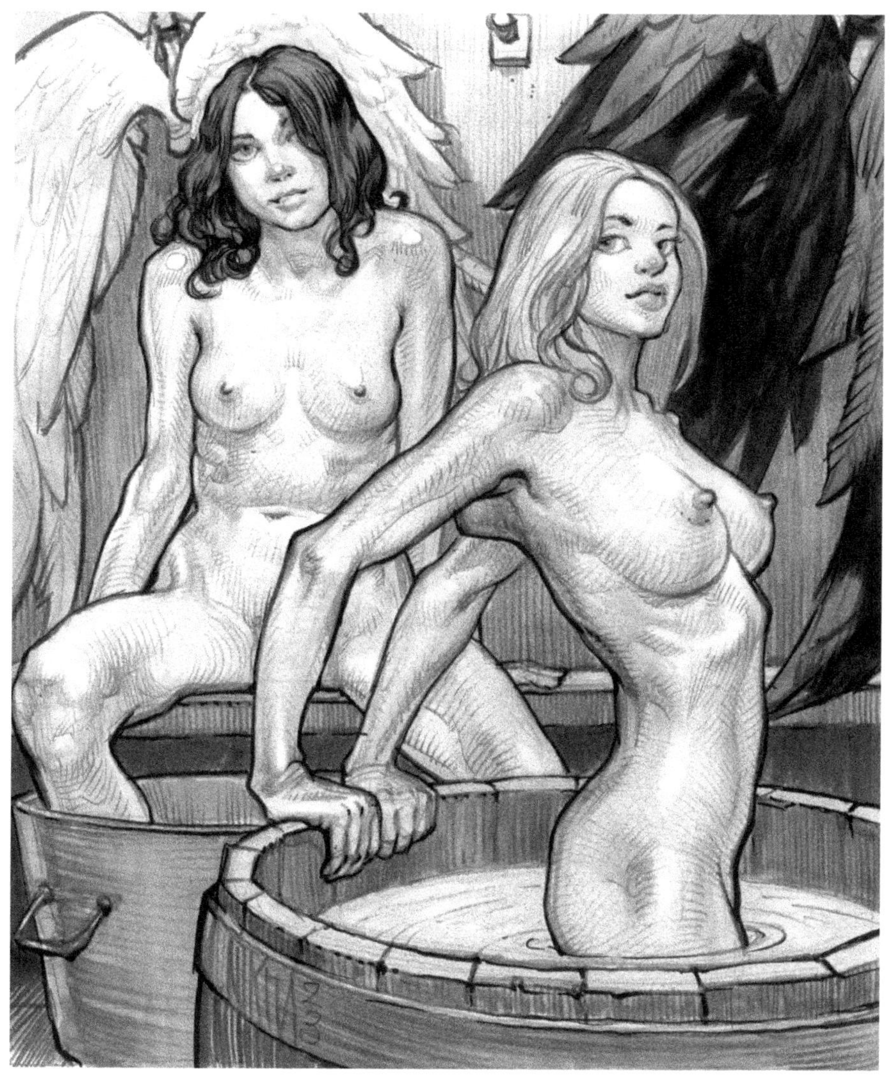

BATHING ANGELS

First remove your wings,
Then your clothes. Get in the tub.
Now pleasure yourselves

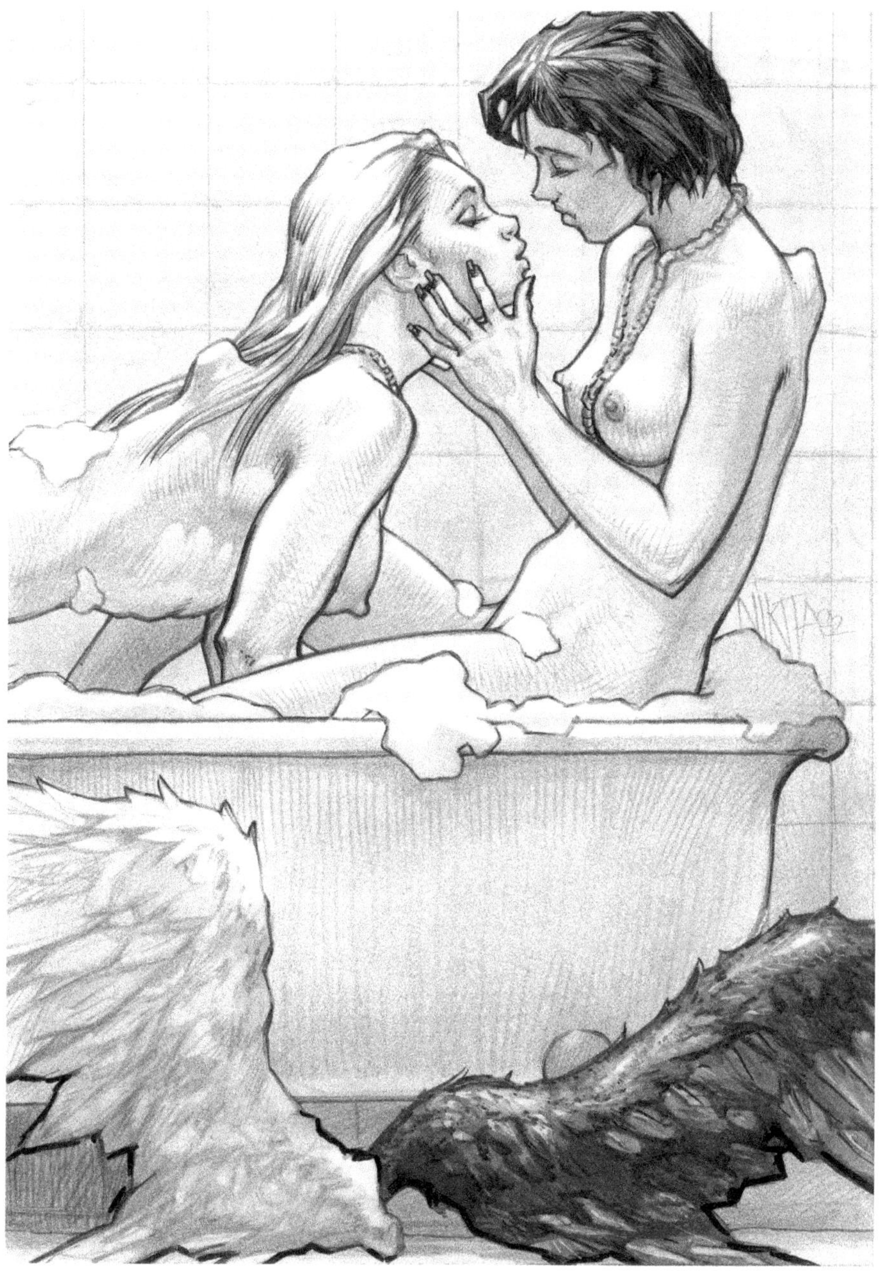

2

LOVE & HATE

Human emotions can be all-consuming
and this is most particularly true of love.
There is only one word in the English language
but in Greek there are six words
used to define the emotion.
On the other hand we have Hate.
Not that these two 'opposite' emotions are
that far apart - and that makes them
particularly dangerous.
Perhaps the best antidote to an excess
of either love or hate is
a really good dose of humour!

DOG TRAINER

I once knew a lady called Kate
Who named her two dogs Love and Hate
She said it was fun
Deciding which one
Should accompany her on a date

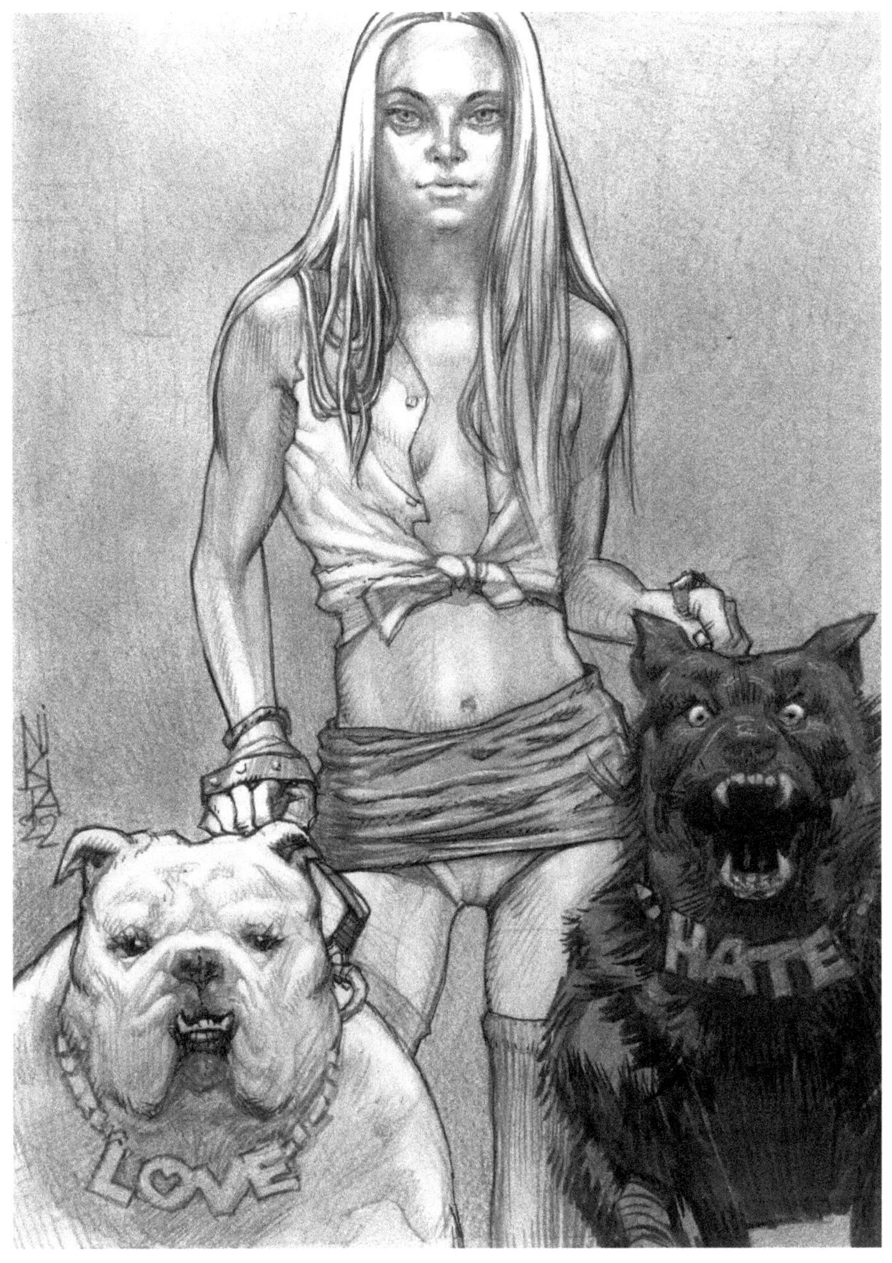
HATE
LOVE

BLACK DOG

I am The Black Dog.
I purport to offer love
To have the wings of an angel
But don't be fooled, I am always with you
On social occasions,
Or in the workplace,
Or during intimate moments
I will haunt you and belittle you,
I will not leave you.
No one sees me, except you
It is you that they mock
That they sneer at
That they bully
That they call incompetent.
But you see me
You know me
You fear me,
Because I am your deepest
Depression

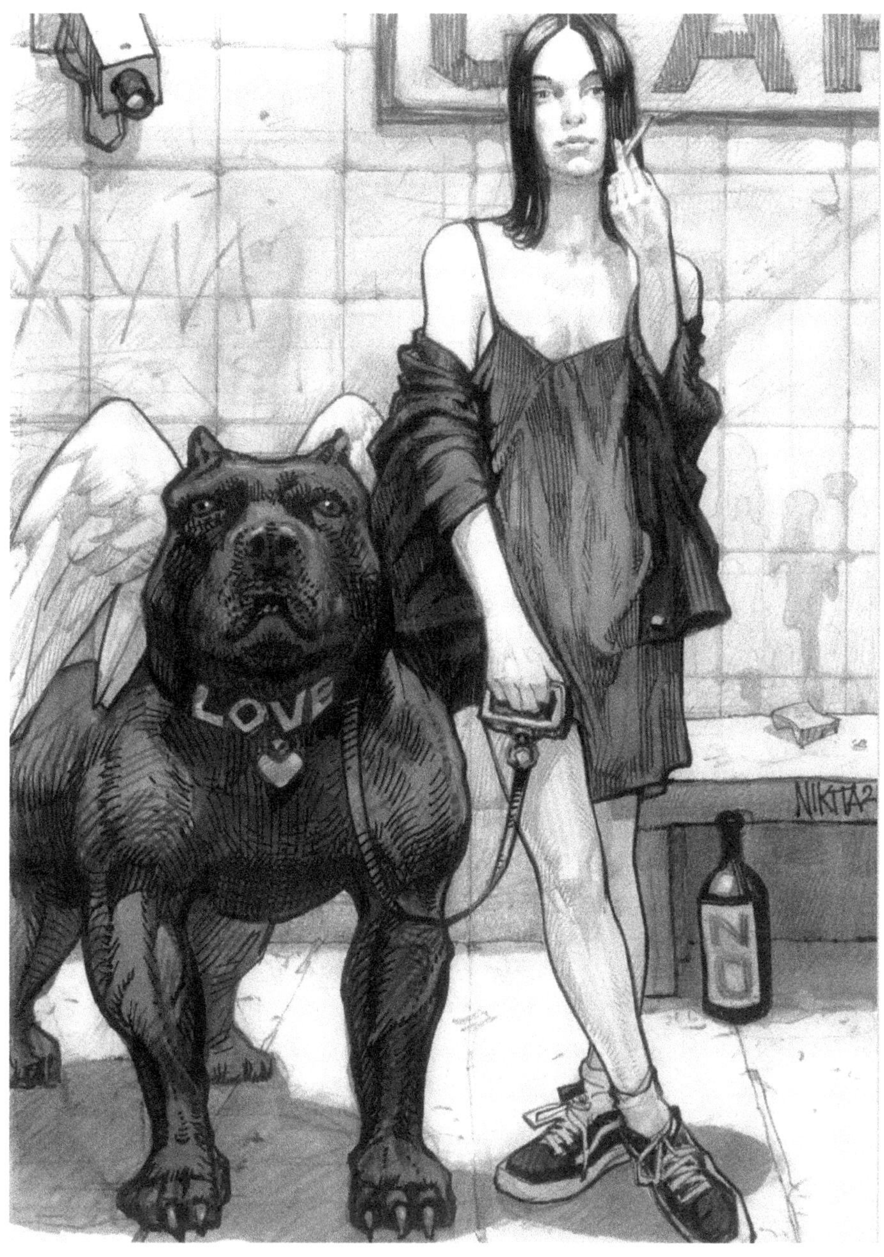
LOVE
NO

ATTRIBUTES

We toads are relaxed.
We enjoy the good things
That life heaps upon us
Like booze and fags
And the occasional wife.
Although others might
Consider us gross
I think 'portly' might better
Describe our physique
And whilst you might think
That sylph-like maidens
Would be repulsed
By our knobbly skin
And bulging eyes
That is far from the case
For we have attributes
Oh yes, attributes
Such attributes as motivate
Beautiful women to strip naked
And slip into a bathtub with us
Oh Bliss!
I suppose it might
Give rise to jealousy
Amongst those who do not
Possess our attributes
But whoever heard of anyone
Being jealous of the attributes
Of a toad!

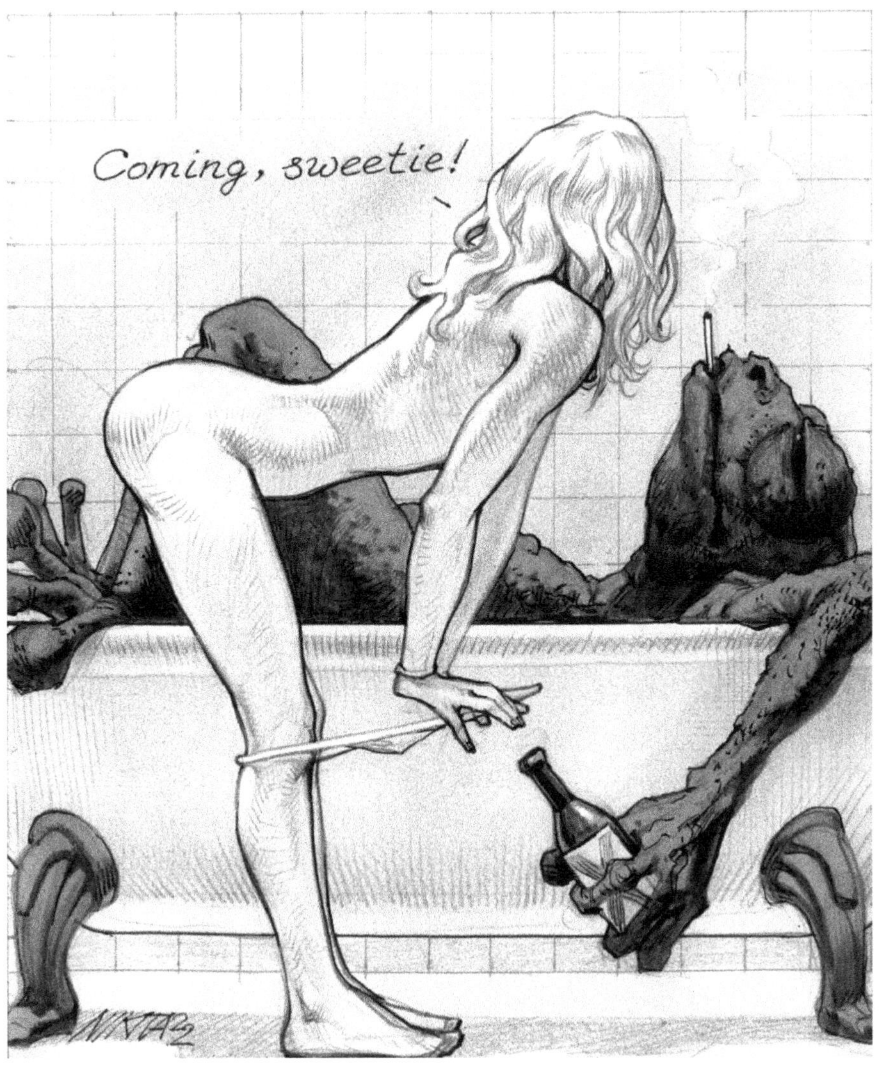
Coming, sweetie!

BATHING

There are Things
That lurk
In the most mundane places.
Whilst some Things
May conceivably be
Relatively harmless
The evil majority
Are just that.
You must exercise
Extreme caution at all times
But most especially
When you are at
Your most vulnerable
Such as when
You are naked and
Just swinging your leg
Over the rim of the bathtub.
A lusting, drunken degenerate
Could be reaching out
To grasp you in
Its powerful slimy grip.
Such Things may not be
Immediately visible
To virgins and other innocents
But virgin or not
It is always best
To be wary at bath-time

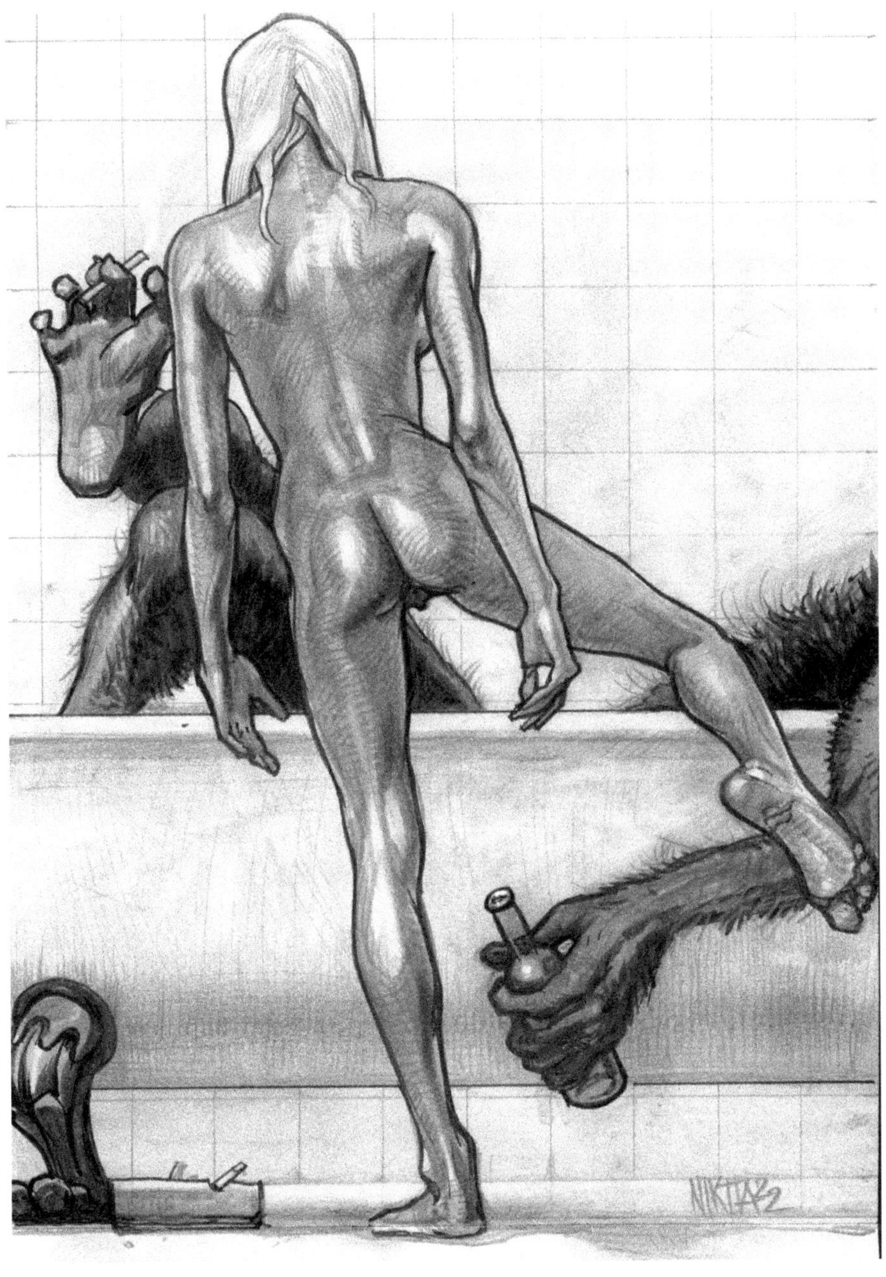

EGGS & BANANAS

It was Thumbelina's own suggestion
To solve Toad's chronic indigestion
She thought bananas might suffice
And if mixed with eggs they would taste nice
But waitress service was out of the question.
As it came at too high a price!

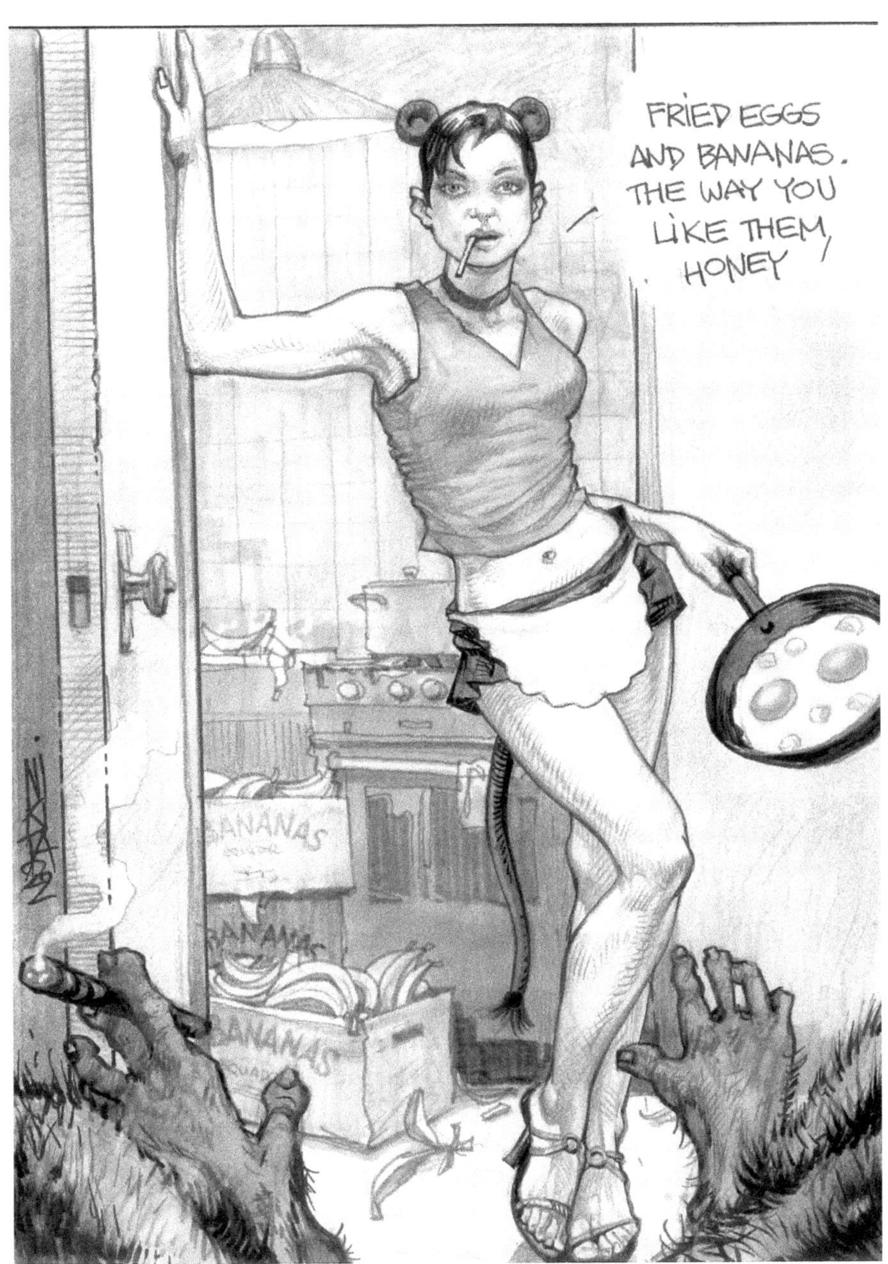
FRIED EGGS
AND BANANAS.
THE WAY YOU
LIKE THEM,
HONEY
BANANAS
BANANAS
BANANAS

BREAKFAST

A certain young lady called Jill
Thought that she knew how to thrill
But her man just ignored
This stark-naked broad
So she let all his coffee go spill!

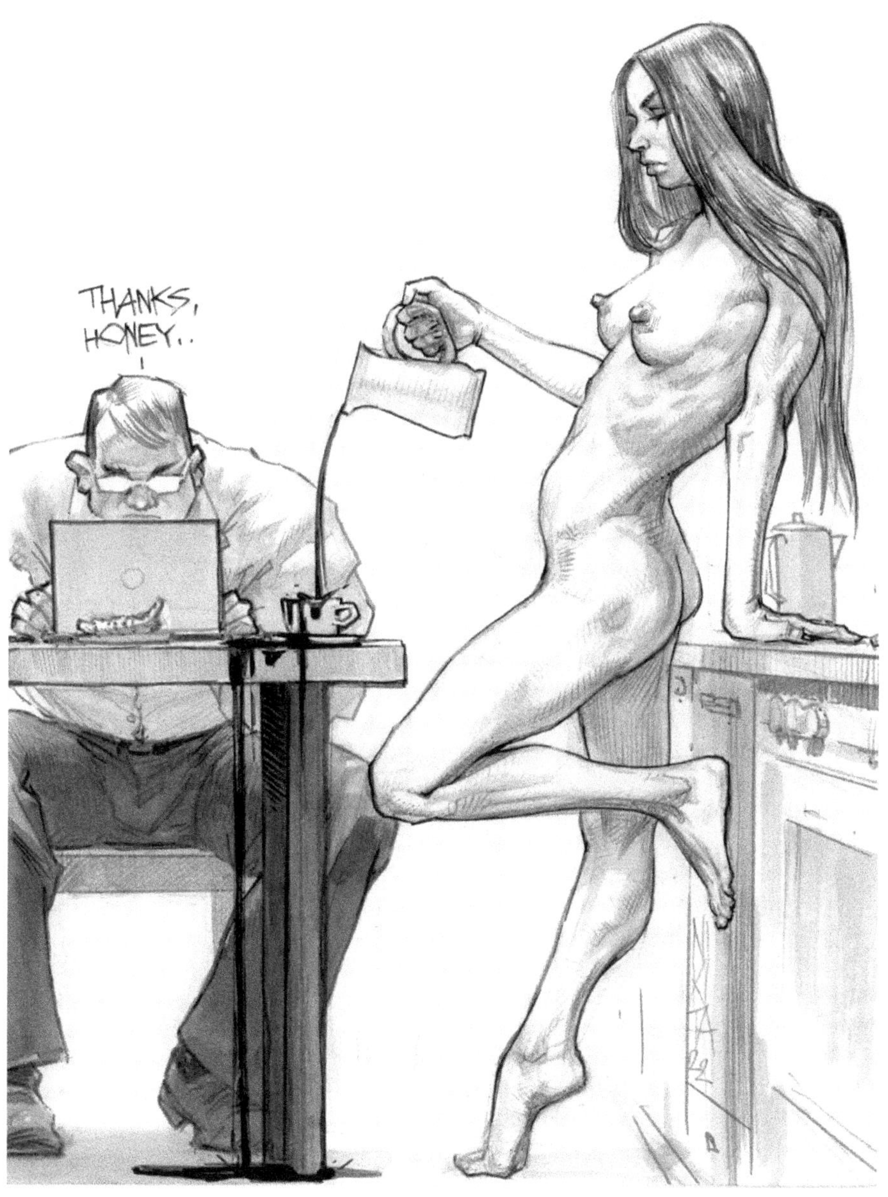
THANKS, HONEY..

RESCUE

on a
rope ladder
I say
it is
in the
best interests
of you
& me
as we
are swinging
on it
to try
to be
very sensible
as we
may not
be at
the very end
of it
at all

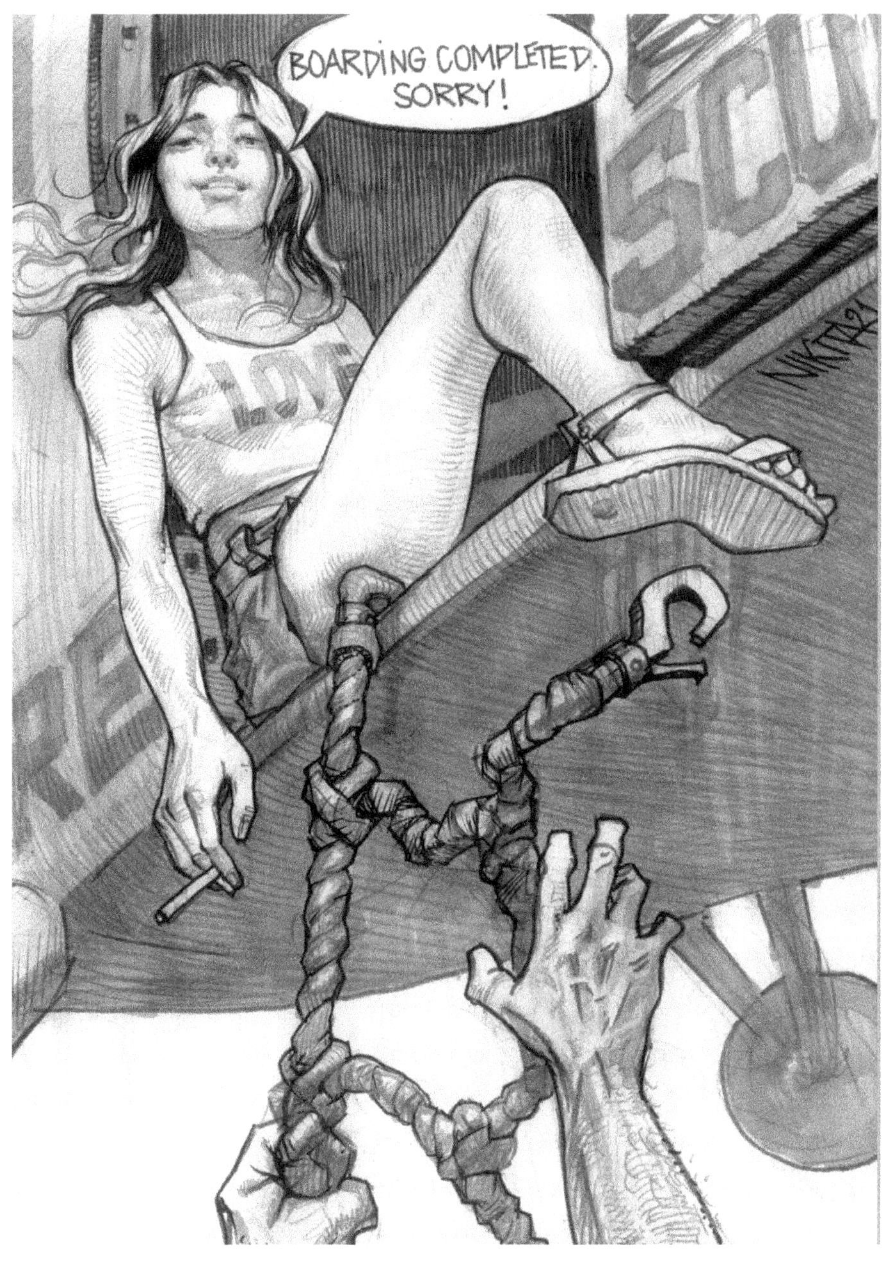
BOARDING COMPLETED. SORRY!

MUTUAL ENVY

When it strikes
The green-eyed-monster
Shows but little mercy
For unlike rage
Or sadness
Or love
This subtle emotion
Rarely bursts to the surface
But works its ugly evil
Inside our heads.
It is clever. Oh so clever,
Because we do not want
To speak of it.
To admit to it.
To reveal that we have failed
Even if only in our own eyes
Envy is about inferiority
About a gut-wrenching
Certitude that we
Are not as good as the other.
Which may be why
Here in Greece when we
Compliment someone
We then turn and spit.
Thus warding off
The Evil Eye.

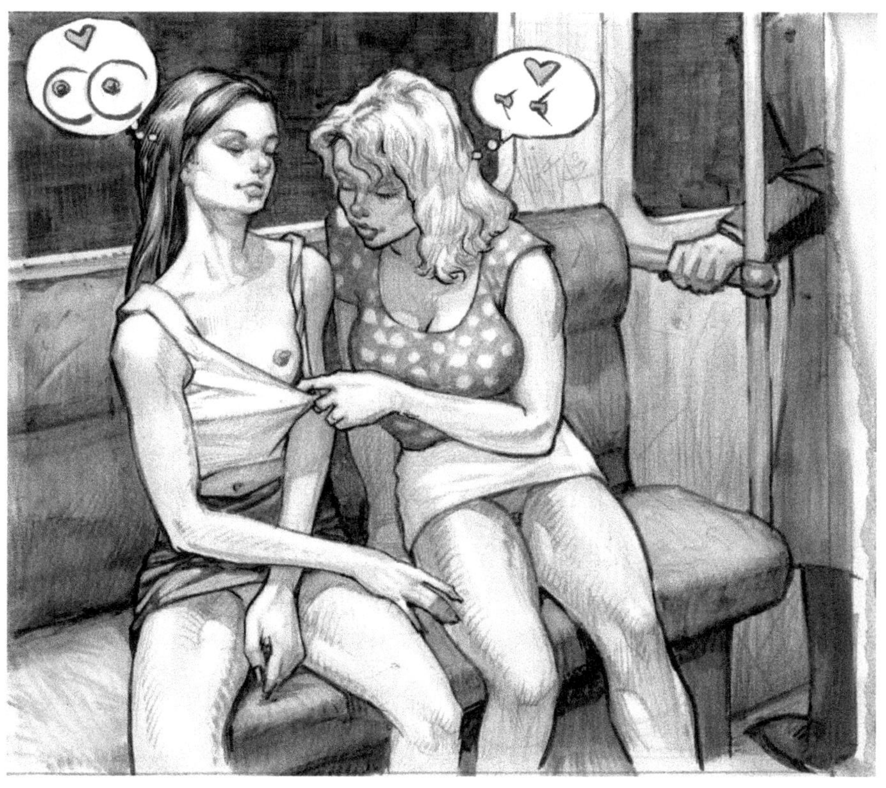

LOVE

In English there's one word for Love
And for the English that might do,
But since ancient times the Hellenes
Knew that one was way too few
Agape, is the selfless love
An unconditional bond
Or *Pragma* the enduring love
For a spouse of whom you're fond
A warriors love for his friend,
That's *Philia,* manly and strong
But *Philautia*, the love of self,
Is a type of love gone wrong
The playful love called *Ludus*
Is an absolute delight
As is *Storga,* the collective love
That holds the family tight
Mania is destructive love
Uptight and obsessive
But there is one more, that's hardly love
Harsh, selfish and excessive
I talk of that, where *Eros* stalks,
Afire with genital flame,
Unmentionable, unquenchable
At his urgent lustful game

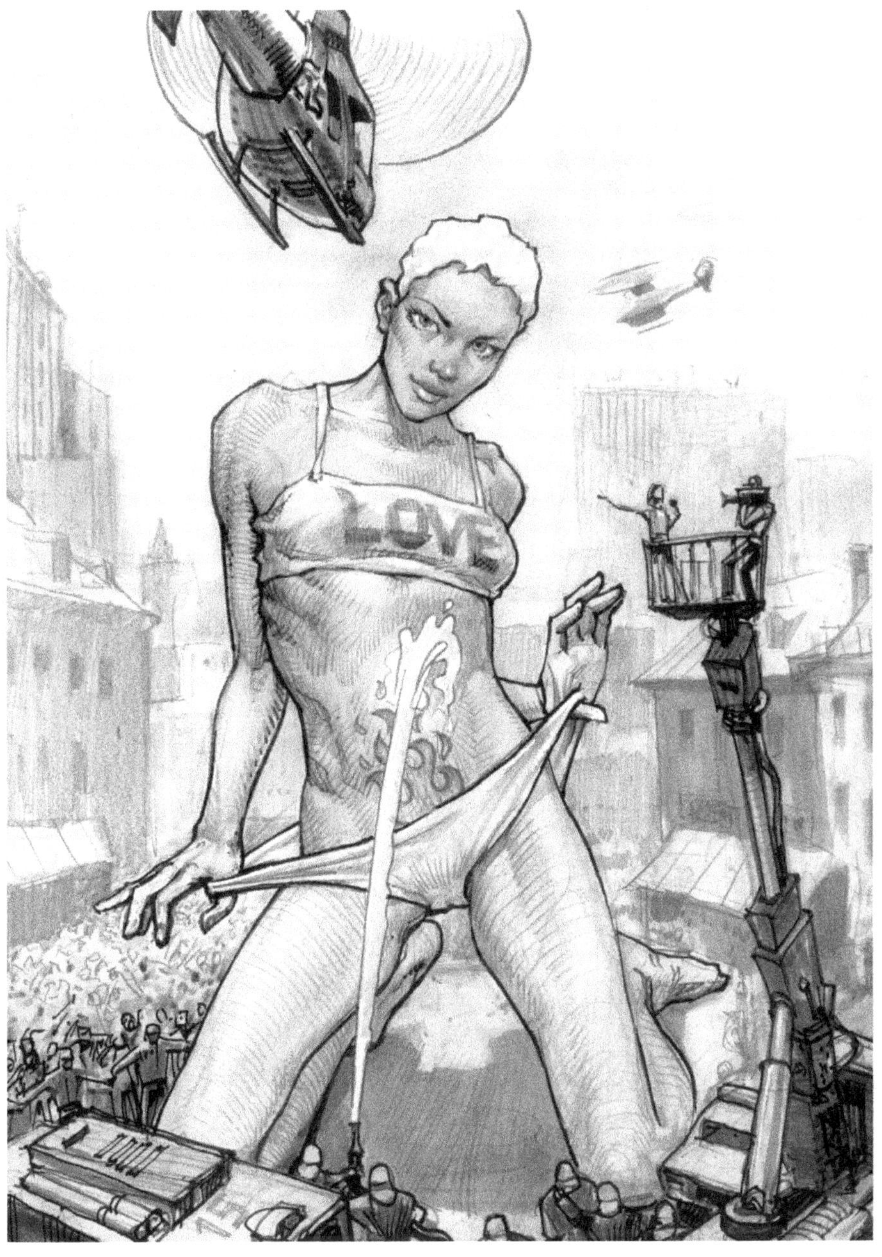
LOVE

CONFESSION

If your life's in a mess
Then it's best to confess
To wash all your sins away
If you have not been good
Then it best that you should
Get down on your knees and pray.
The confessional priest
Will, at the least
Give you a penance to do
But it's worth it you know
For your sins will all go
If you say a Hail Mary or two
If you are a believer
And you want to receive a
Pass for the Pearly Gates
You can sin all day long
And do everything wrong
Because absolution awaits
But woe betide those
Who do not suppose
That this system works very well
For with no one to say
Their sins are okay
Their final account is with Hell.

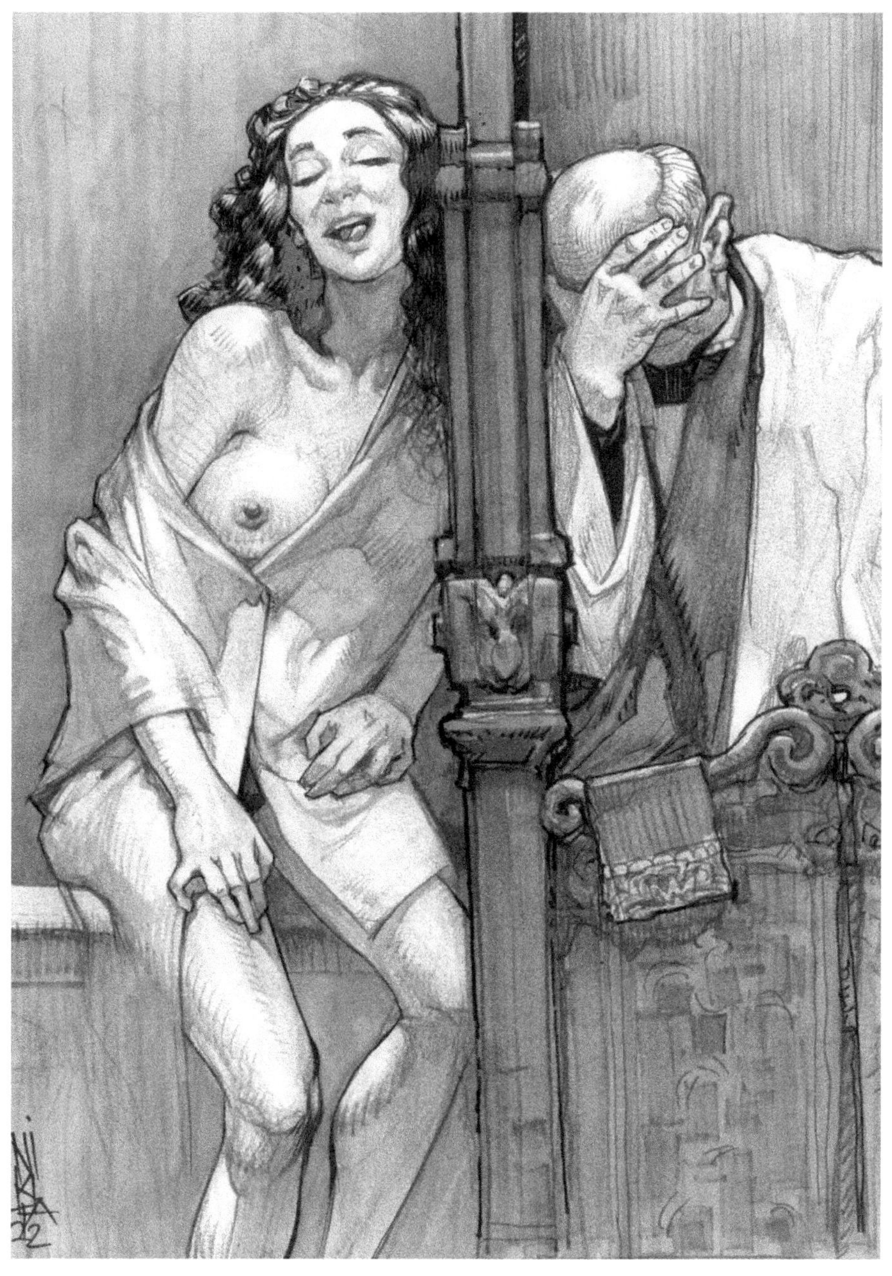

LUNATIC

The unfettered mind
Reaching vainly for the moon
Finding the Psyche

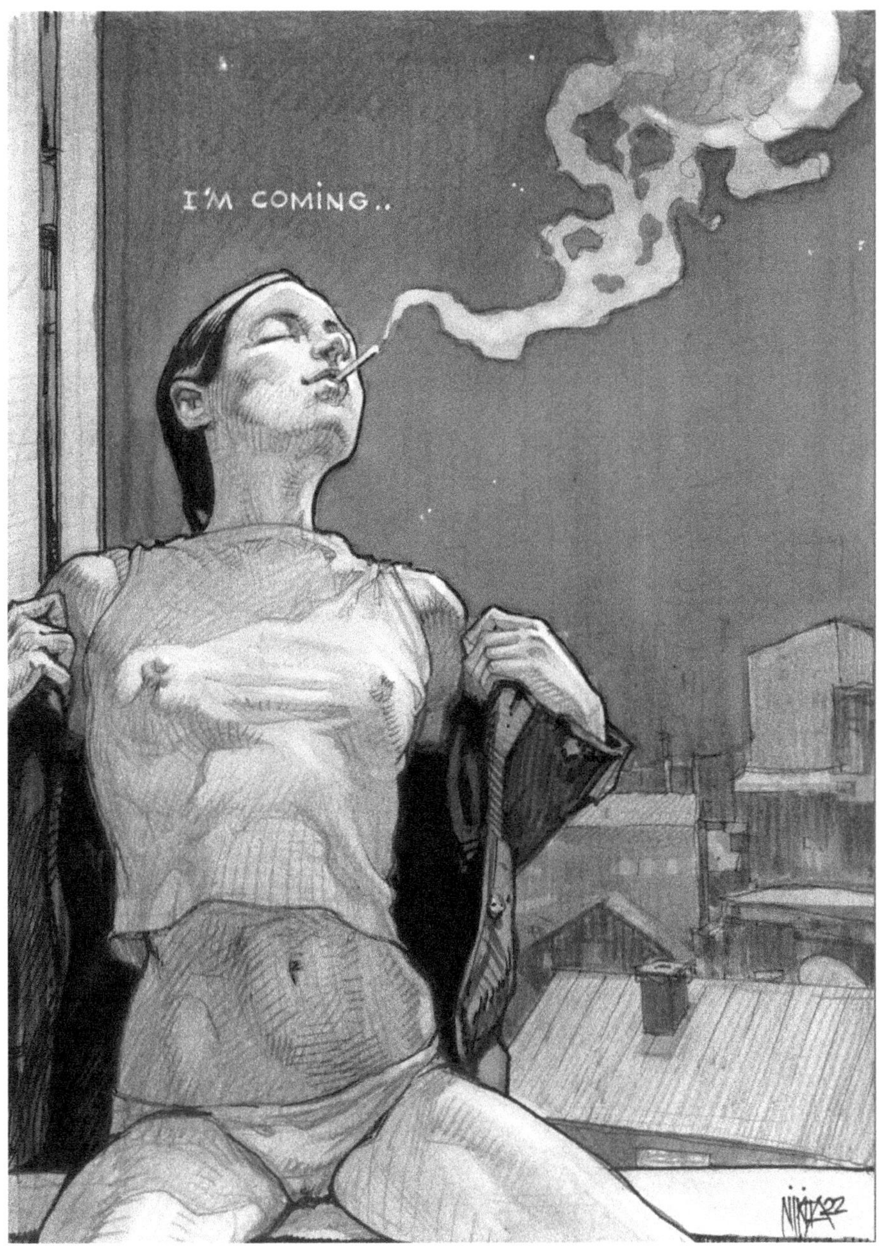
I'M COMING..

UFO

We treasure them
We rely on them
We confide in them
We help them
We laugh with them
We cry with them
Sometimes we wait for them
For a long time
We do so patiently
They are our friends
We wait for them
However weird they are!

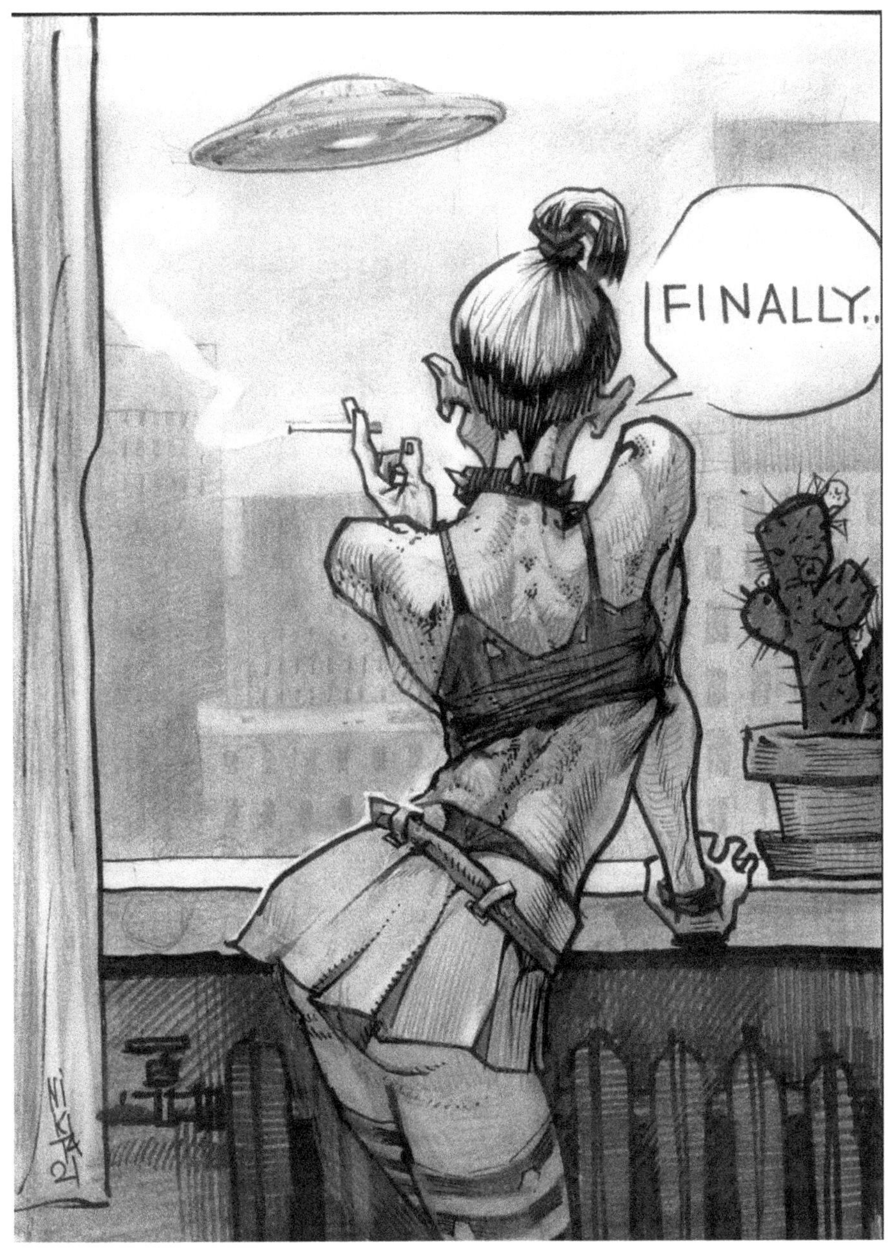
FINALLY..

TANK MAN

There was a young lady - Marlene
Who imagined a hunk in her dream
But she could not remember
If the size of his member
Was enormous or merely obscene

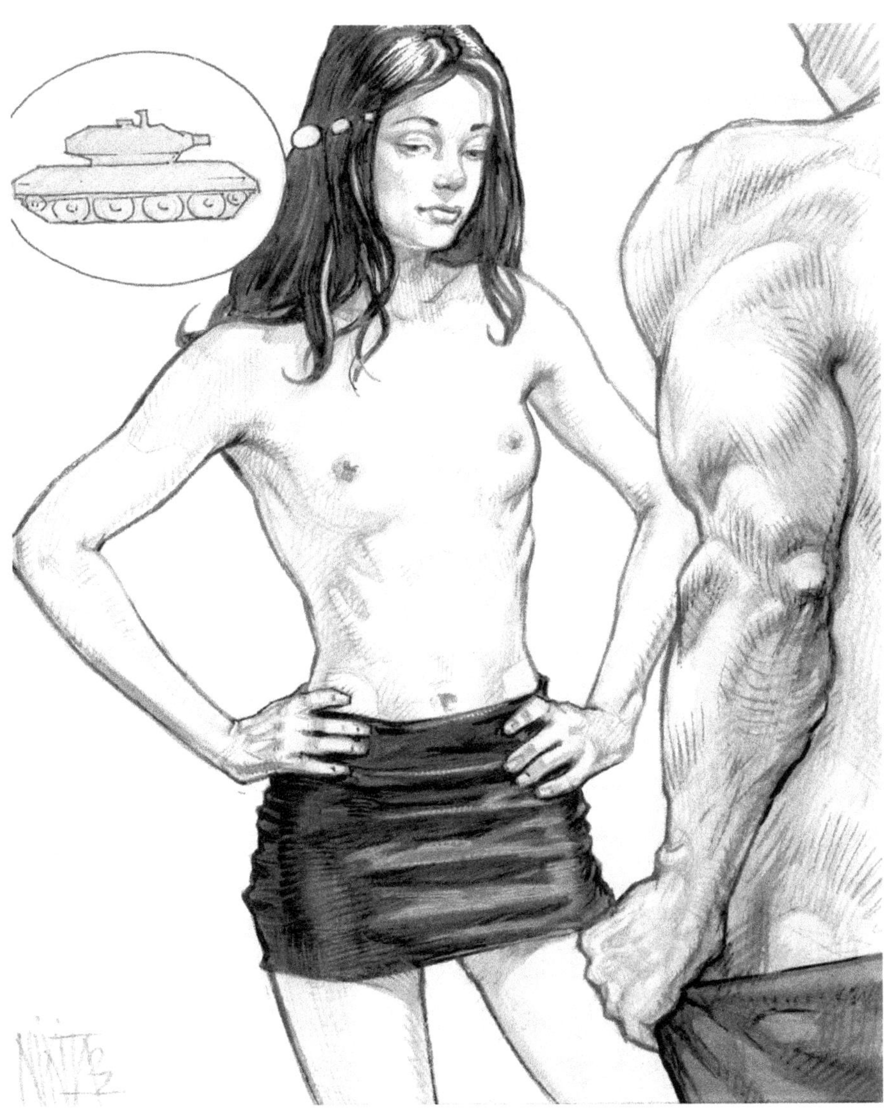

LAOKOON'S DAUGHTER

Why Laocoon's two sons
Should be made to suffer
The fate of their father
Is somewhat perplexing.
After all it was he, and only he,
Who incurred the wrath of the Gods
For fucking his wife in the temple.
And now there is a further anomaly
A previously unsuspected
And sexually teasing daughter,
Whose very own snake seems
Less of an existential threat
And more of a sinuous complement
To her highly sensual body.
Since their appearance
In The Garden snakes
Have had a bad reputation
So is this a warning to beautiful girls
About their corruption by evil things
Or a caution to boys regarding
The duplicity of gorgeous girls.
It is indeed a conundrum.
What we do know is the old man
Got what was coming to him
And his sons had a very raw deal!

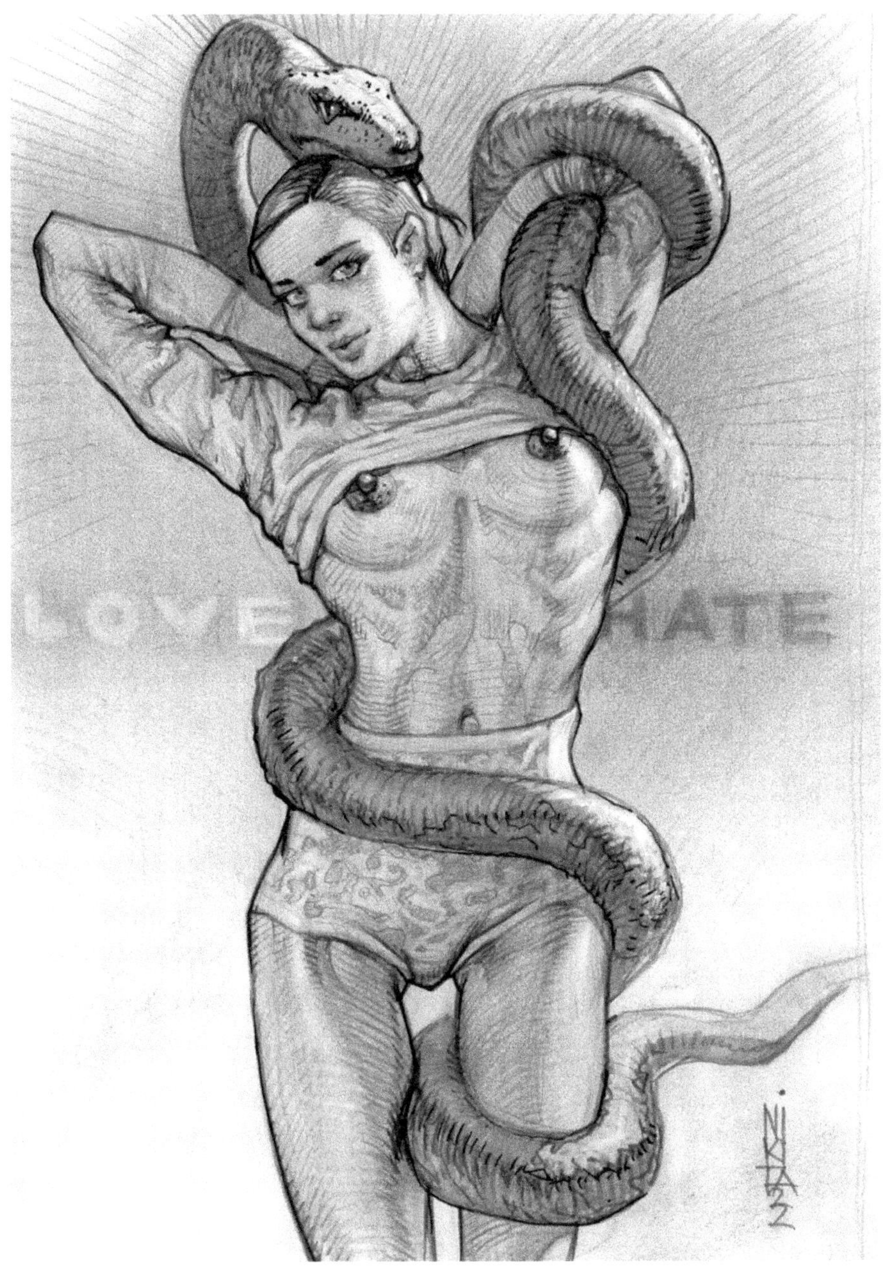
LOVE
HATE

WOLF

Wolves are never easy
To meet at a fancy-dress ball
In fact they are a problem
To find at a party at all.

You may find this disturbing
If you expected an introduction
'Cos the genuine wolverine feeling
Is you really ought not to meet one.

However if you're insistent
That your lupine experience lacks
Then for goodness sake be cautious
'Cos the buggers hunt in packs

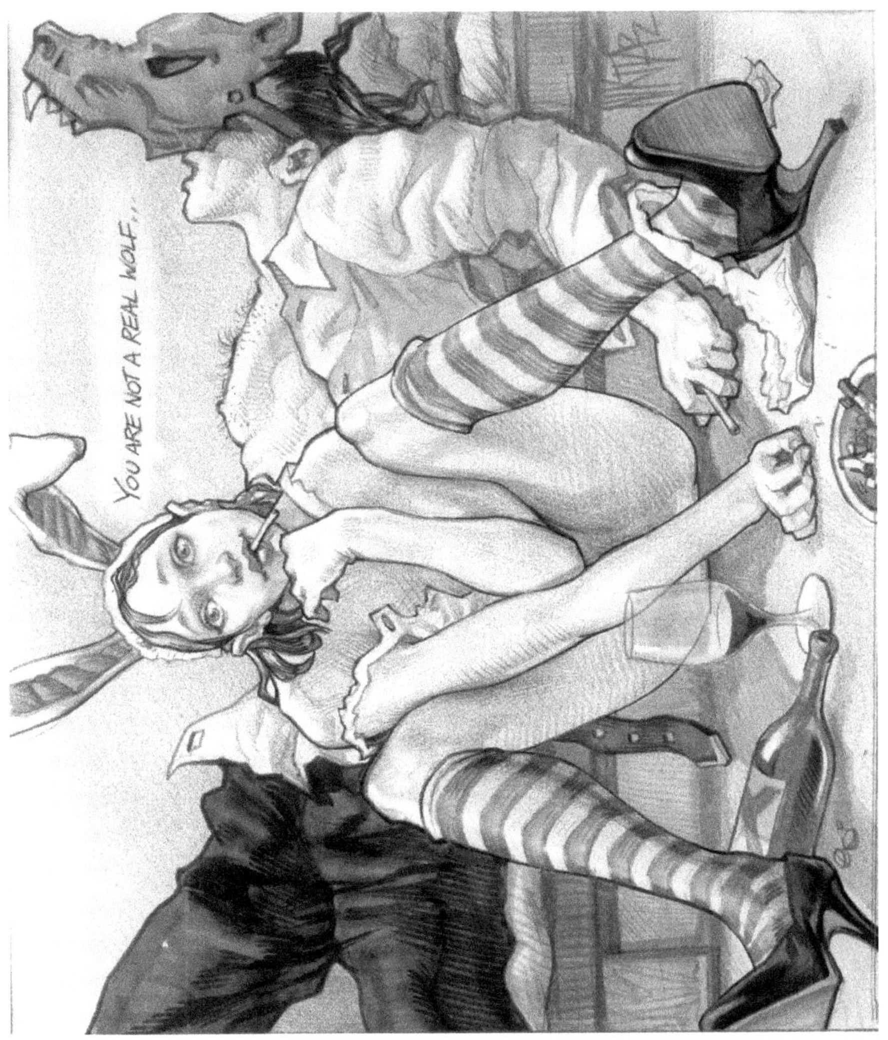
YOU ARE NOT A REAL WOLF...

INVISIBLE LOVERS

Servicing three men
Depicted without substance
Only in the mind?

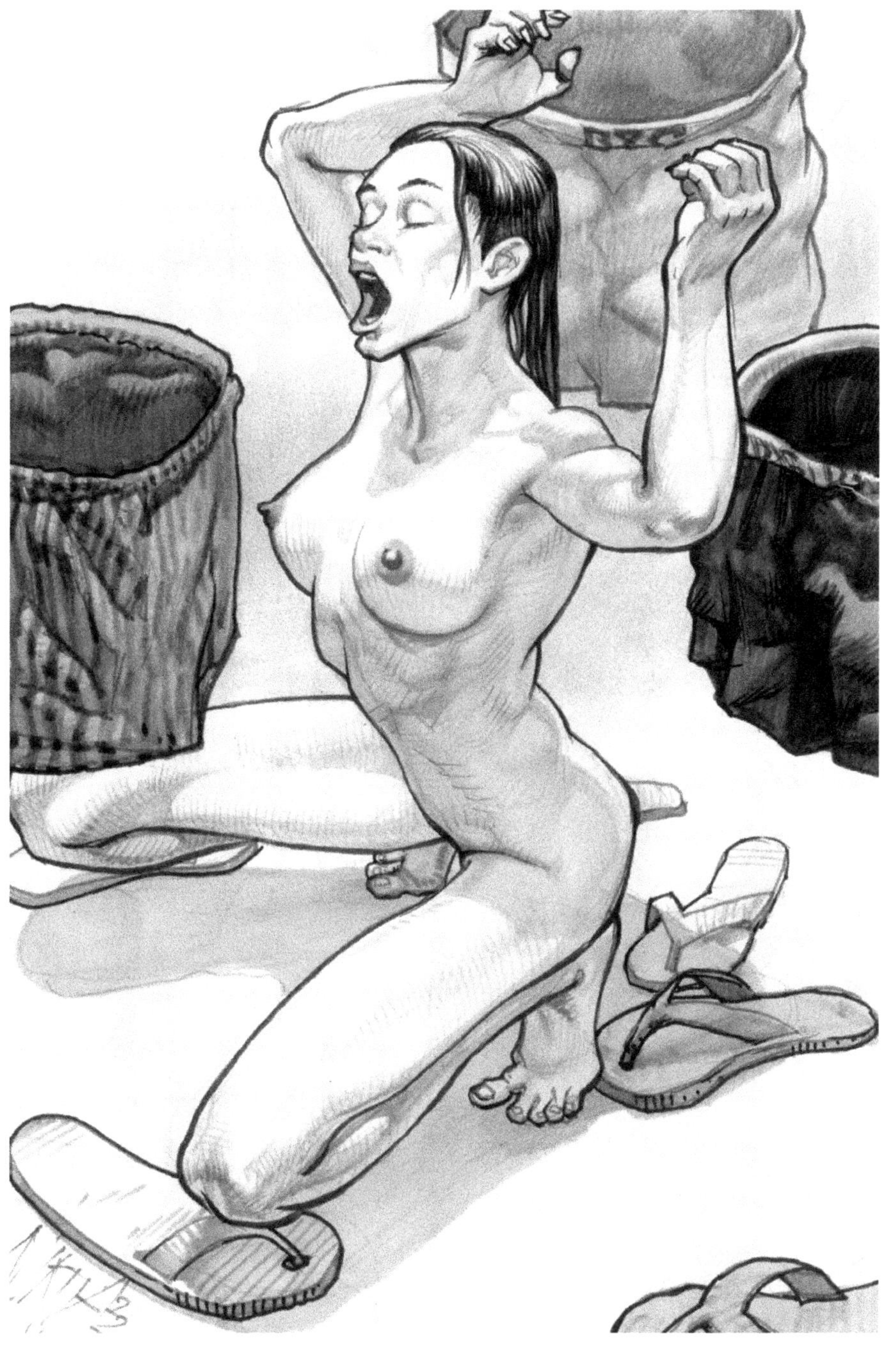
BYC

TRIAL

There was a young lady called Bess
Who was happy to quickly confess
To a few misdemeanours
Because, strictly between us,
She liked those whips on her flesh

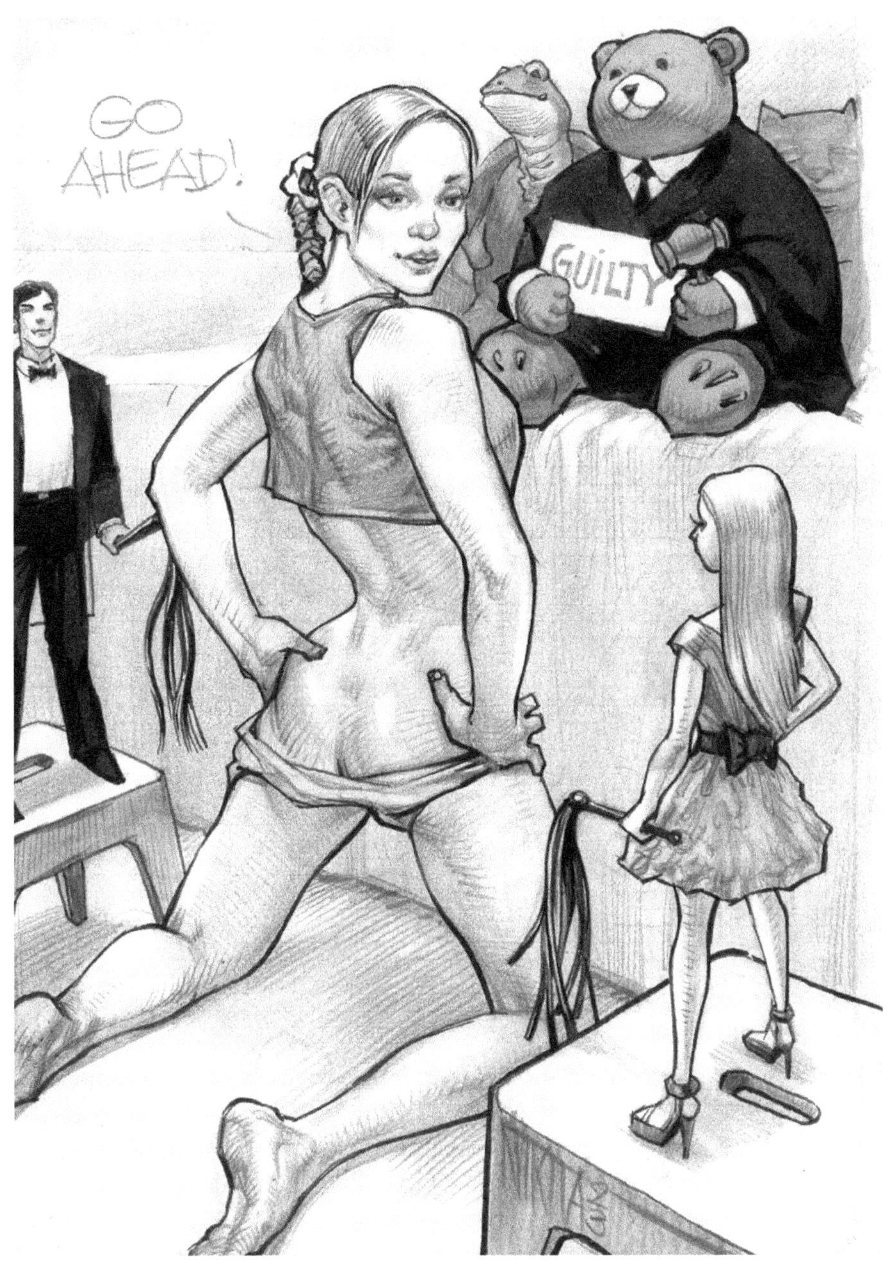
GO AHEAD!
GUILTY

3

WAR

It is not our intent to glorify war,
indeed rather the opposite.
Into the chaos and despair we have brought
hope and love and humour.
Mind you we have also discovered
certain young ladies with a
predilection for war-like actions.
Some of these are angels, but viewed
from the opposing side they
more likely seem to be devils!

SHOOTER

There was a young girl they called Cher
Who was ace with her gun in the air
She aimed and she shot
And she killed quite a lot
But it filled her with grief and despair.

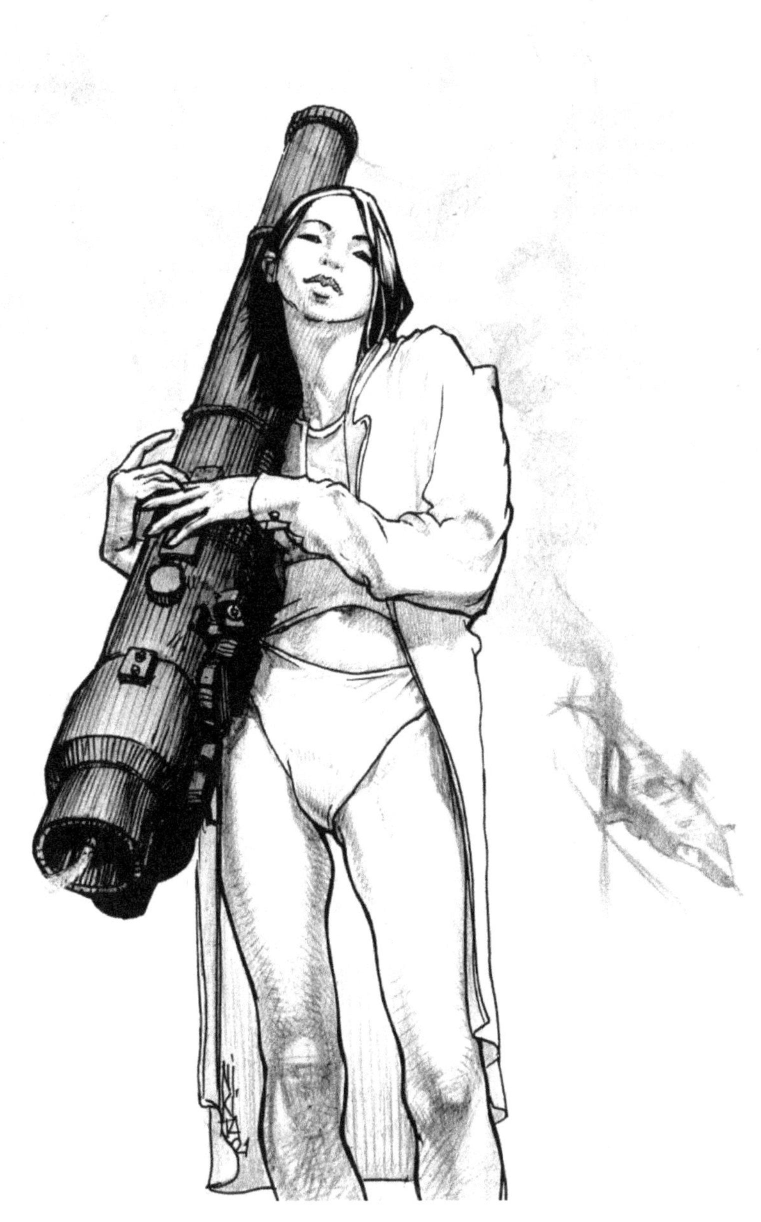

GUARDIAN ANGEL

Amidst the battle
Hang on very tight to your
Guardian Angel

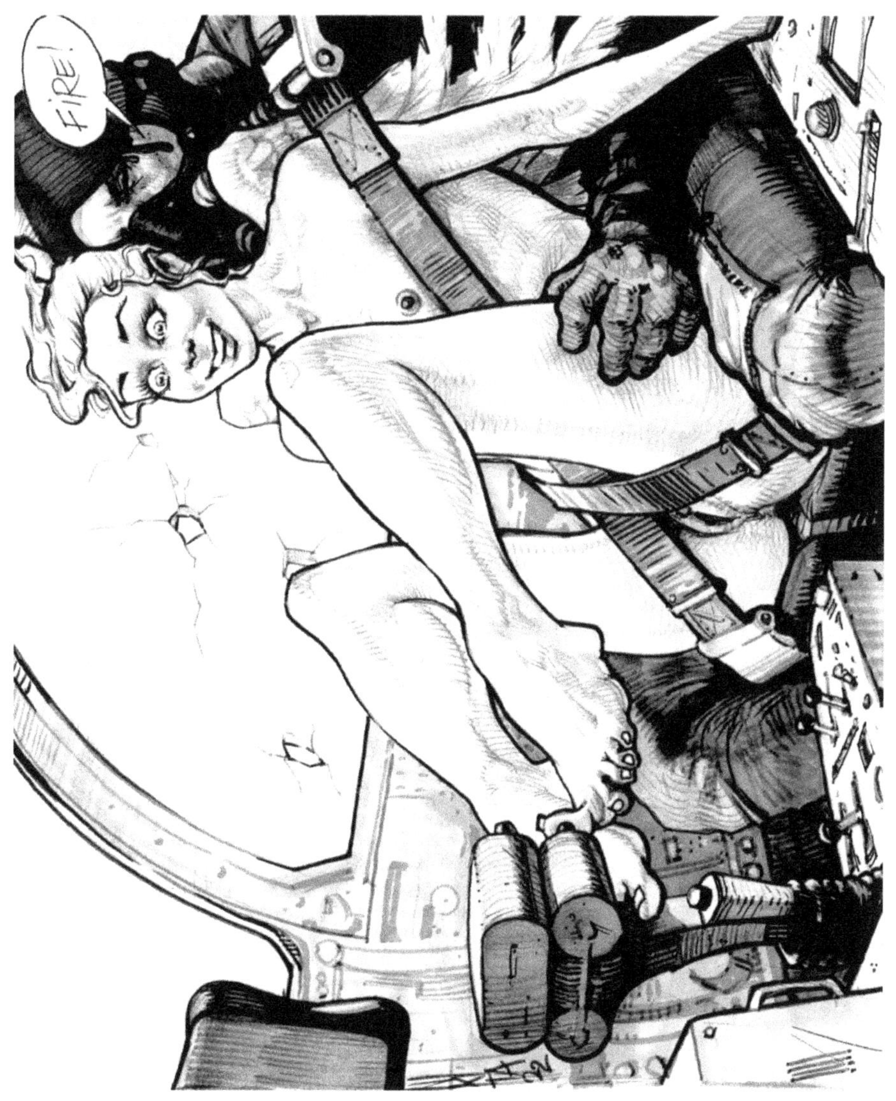
FIRE!

BEACH

The beach is yours, just sand and sea
Where you build sand-castles for fun
You read and drink and play silly games
To relax for a time in the sun

To relax for a time in the sun
But a tank now threatens your day
An aggressive intrusion crossing the sand
Crawling quite quickly your way

Crawling quite quickly your way
Disturbing your quiet and your peace
It seems you must stand and resist
To ensure that this tank attack cease

To ensure that this tank attack cease
You must shoulder your launcher to fight
Them when it comes into range,
Blast the damn thing out of sight

Blast the damn thing out of sight
So once again you will be free
To relax for a time in the sun
For the beach is yours, sand the sea

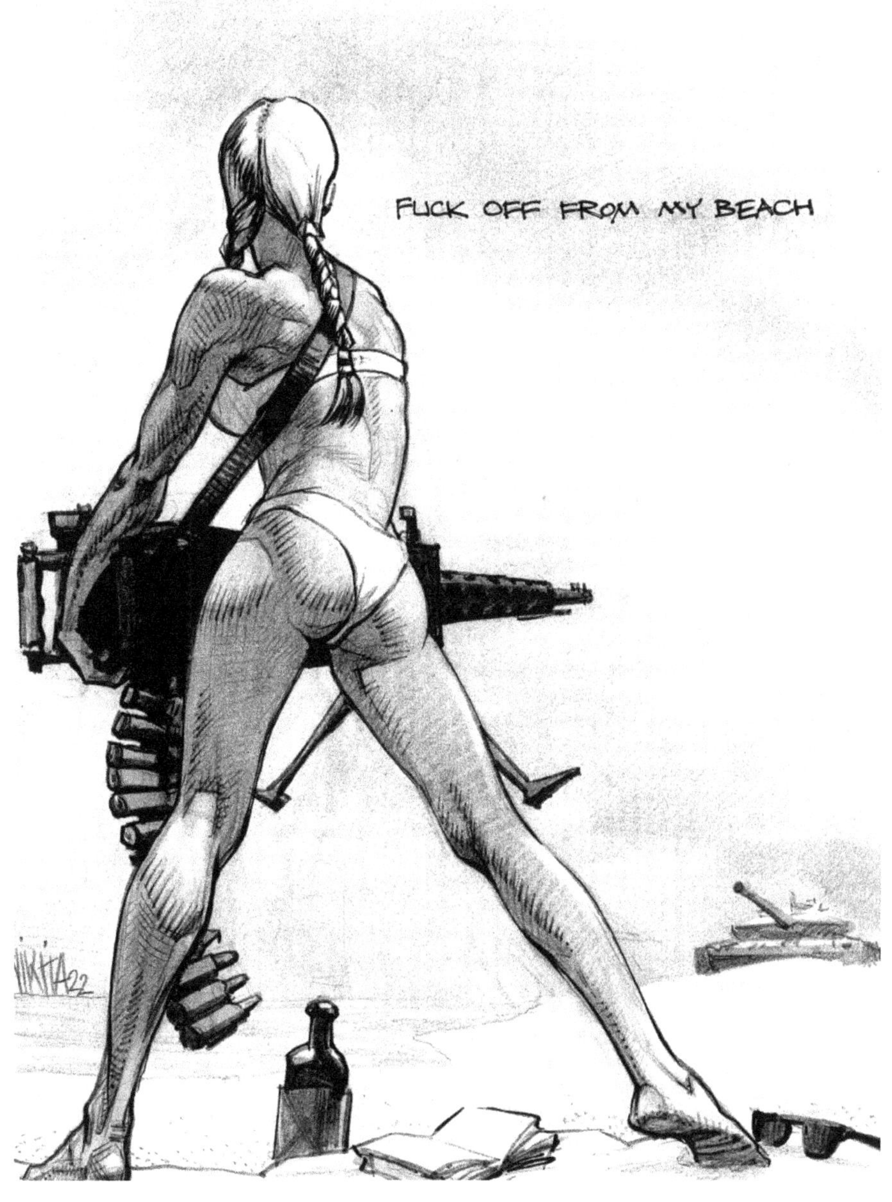
FUCK OFF FROM MY BEACH

COFFEE TIME

Coffee time is when we all relax
Relax from our worries and woes
Woes that beset us unbidden
Unbidden except by our foes
Foes that we might expect
Expect on a calm, perfect day
Day that posed some worry
Worry this tank just might stay
Stay, treating our town like this
This is not what we want to see
See our poor houses crumble
Crumble as tanks make free
Free is what you must fight for
For you hide a bomb in the flower
Flower will destroy that damned tank
Tank at last without power

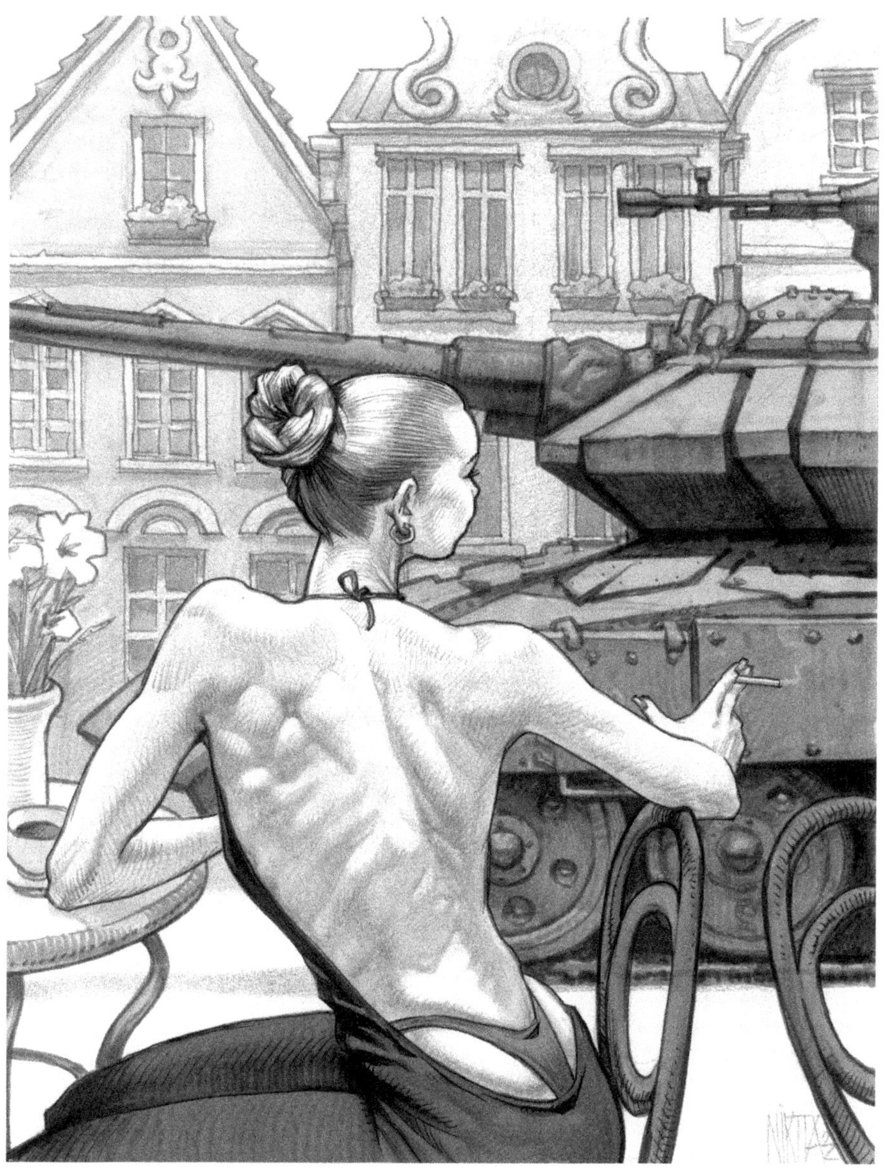

APE ESCAPE

There was a young lady I knew
Whose name was Liperty Lou
She made her escape
Upon a Great Ape
That she stole from the neighbouring zoo.

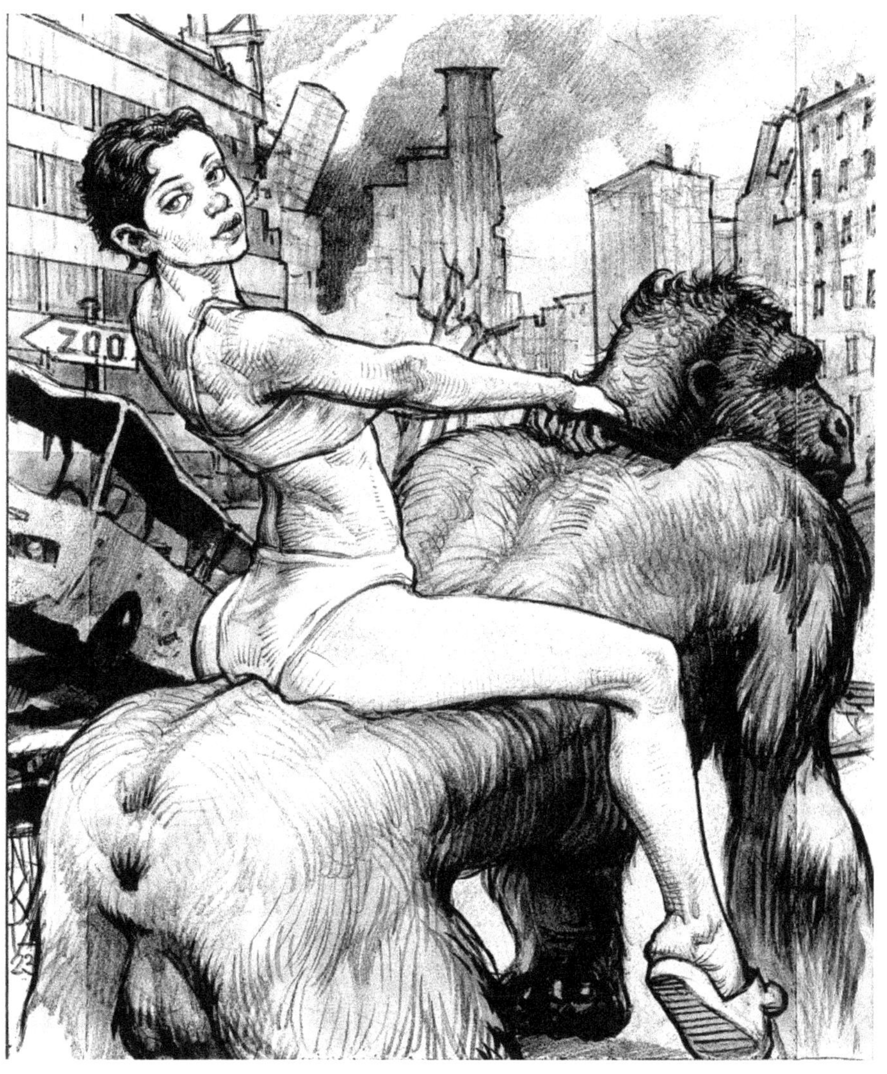
ZOO

SNIPER

They are misguided
For they think
That I am that stupid!
“We need a sniper”
They told me
“Here is a machine gun,
Grab a quick fag
Enjoy the company
Of your mate with his accordion”
So the enemy already has me
In his sights
Just waiting
To squeeze
The trigger.
Out in Kenya
When they wanted
To shoot a lion
They would tie a goat
To a tree
By its balls.
The goat would bleat
The lion would pounce
The hunter would shoot
But the goat would die.
Makes you think
Doesn’t it?

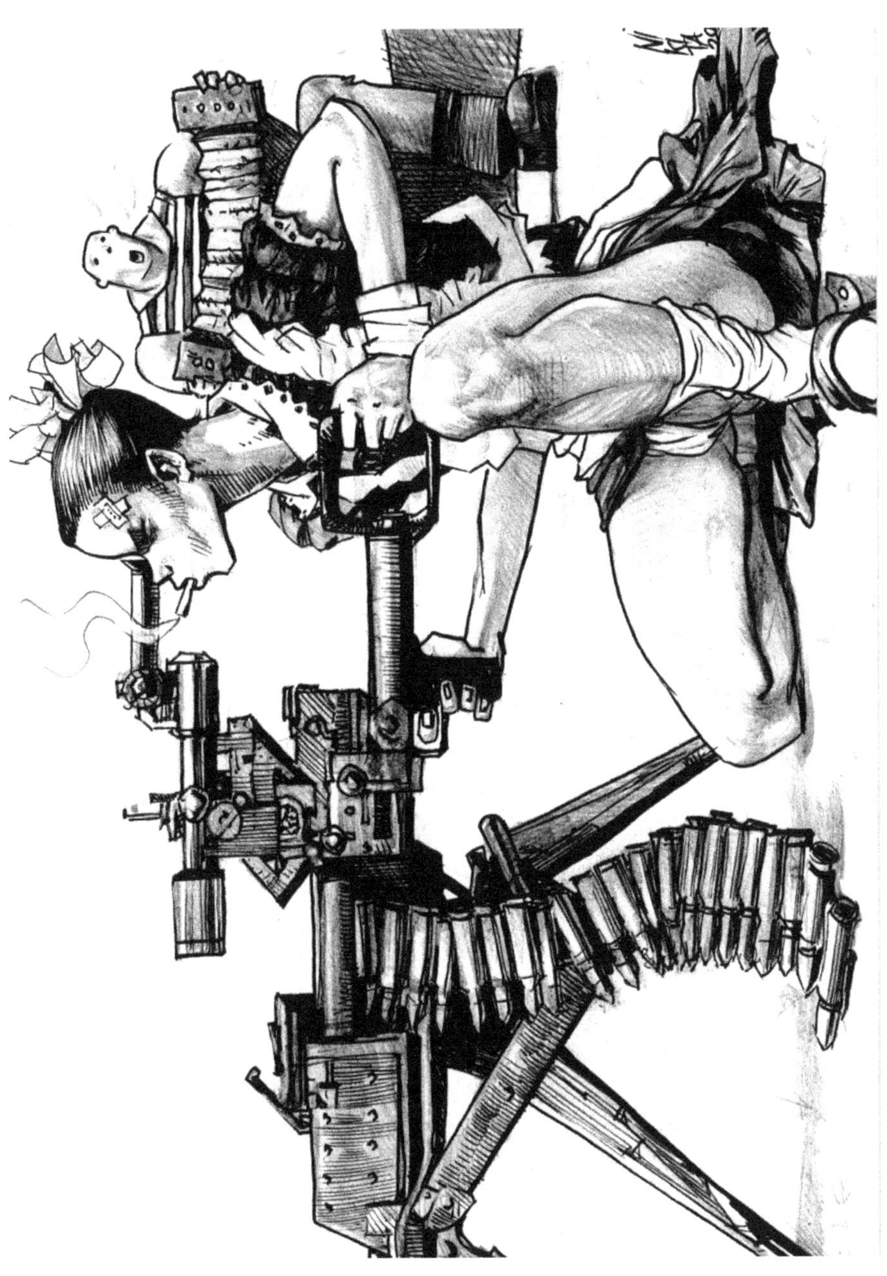

HITCHHIKER

Your city lies in ruins,
It is time for you to go
To leave familiar streets
And the places that you know
There is no public transport
Buses torn to shreds
Apartment blocks dismembered
No fuel, no food, no beds
You hope to bum a lift
On a tank or armoured car
But you will travel back again
This is only *au revoir*
Slung tightly on your shoulder
Your Kalashnikov must show
That your route is one of danger
As you go to fight the foe
The luggage that you carry
Is an innocuous disguise
Your spirit won't be broken
And the long-term's looking bright
For that teddy bear upon your back
Is not The Bear you fight

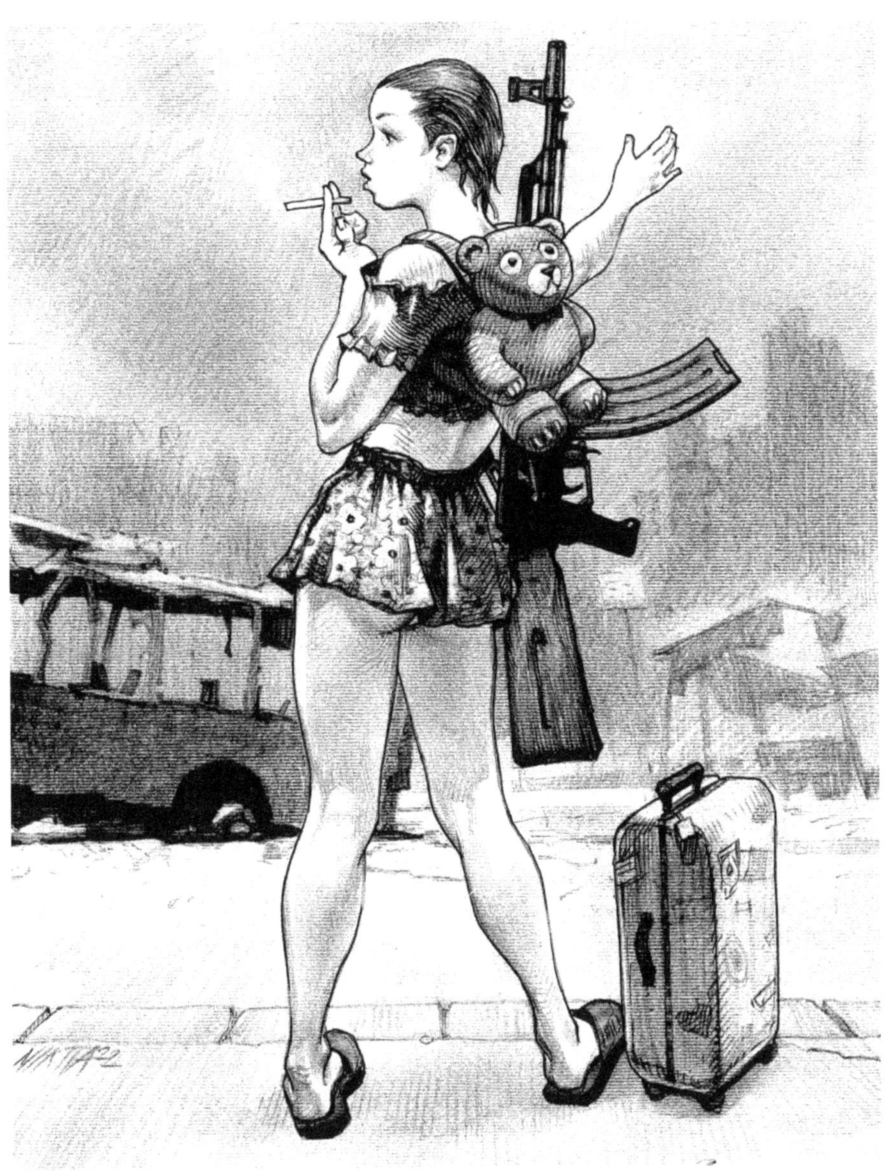

BAIT

As with all sirens
The danger that she poses
Lies undetected

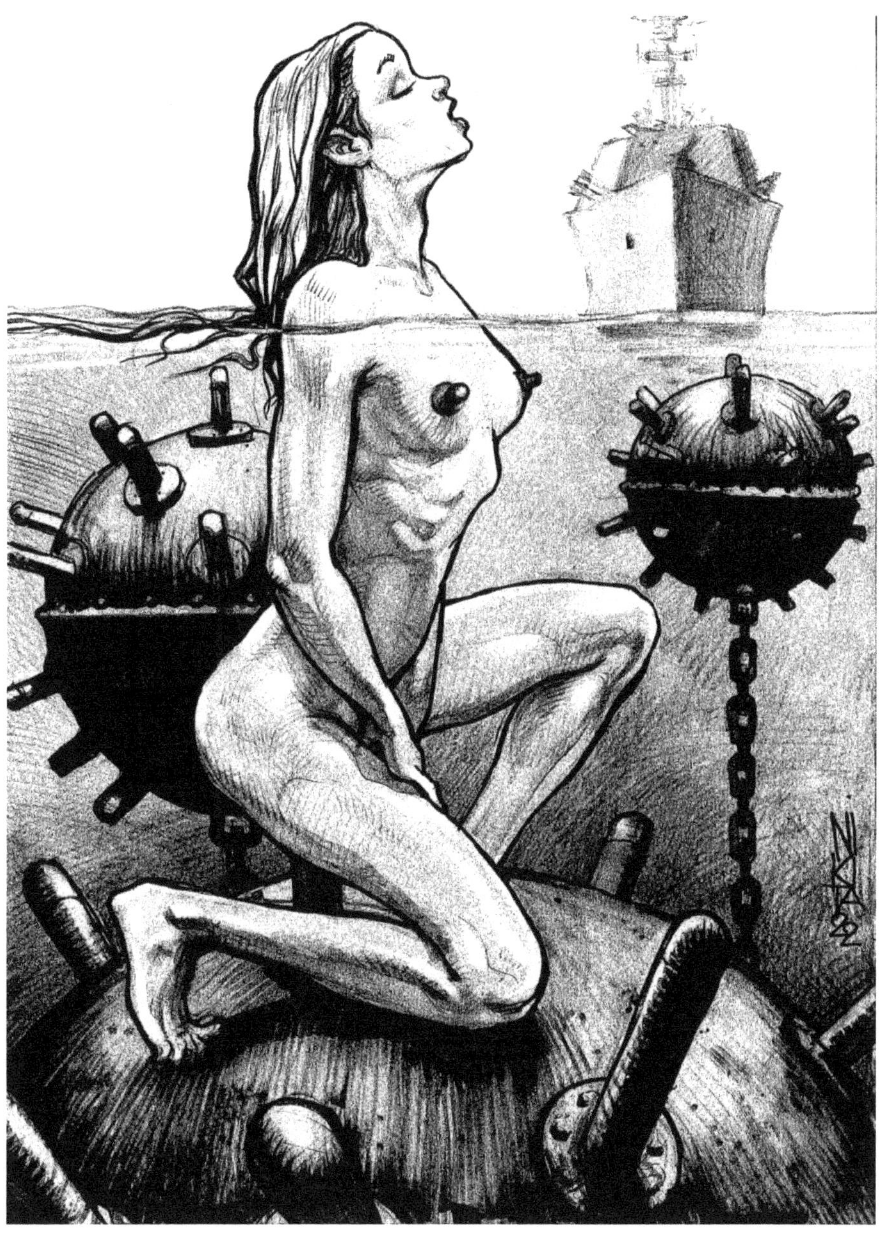

SNIPER & BEAR

There was a young girl called Louise
Who could shoot her gun with such ease
That her war-weary bear
Took to booze in despair
And drunkenly stared at her knees

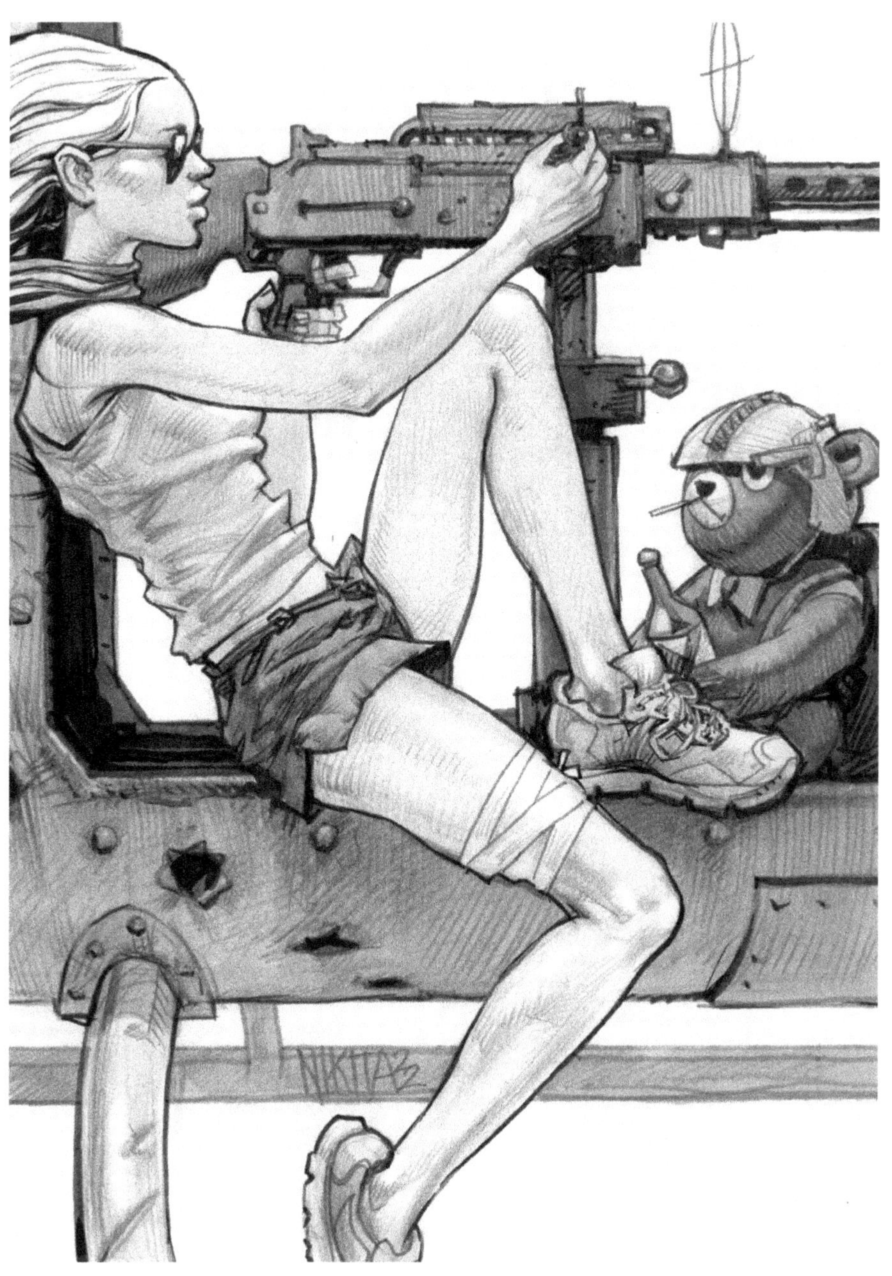

DANCER RECOVERY

There was a young girl Isabella
Who danced with a rum sort of feller
He was prone to collapse
But she dowsed him with Schnapps
So he danced to a fast tarantella

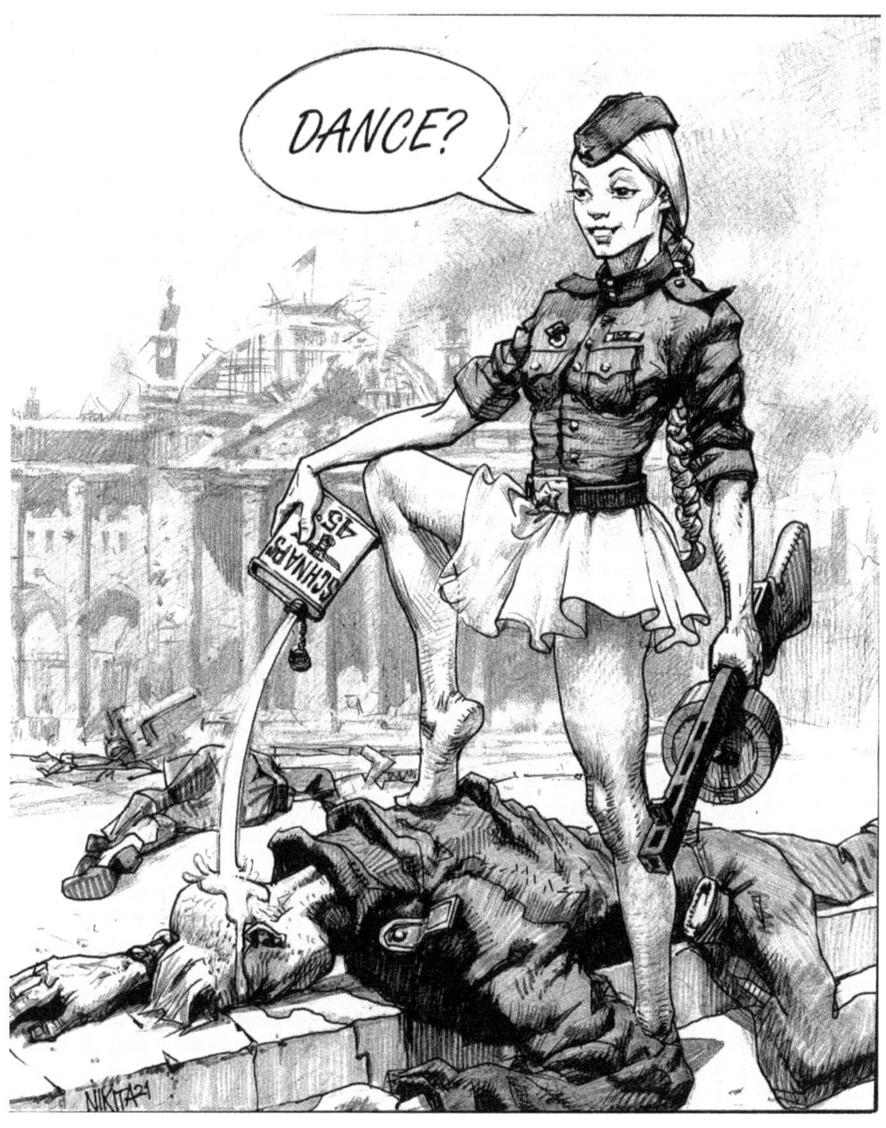
DANCE?
SCHNAPS
45

NEW YEAR 2023

Now the year is over
Let's cast a quick glance back
Not at that gruesome February
'Special Ops' attack
But rather at the highlights
Of our efforts to amuse
The dedicated followers
Of Nikita/Gwymbach news
With a multitude of angels
Falling from above
All wearing next to nothing
Because that's what Angels love
We followed Thumbelina
Along a rocky road
As this dismal doomed damsel
Was married to a toad
Beauty and her Beast
Were there to entertain
Whilst the artist and his model
Were with us yet again
Displayed for titillation
Were boobs and bums and beavers
Although Facebook took the latter
As reason to exclude us
And so with drawings stylish
With Limerick, Haiku, and Free
The team (Nikita and Gwymbach)
Will be with you, just wait and see!

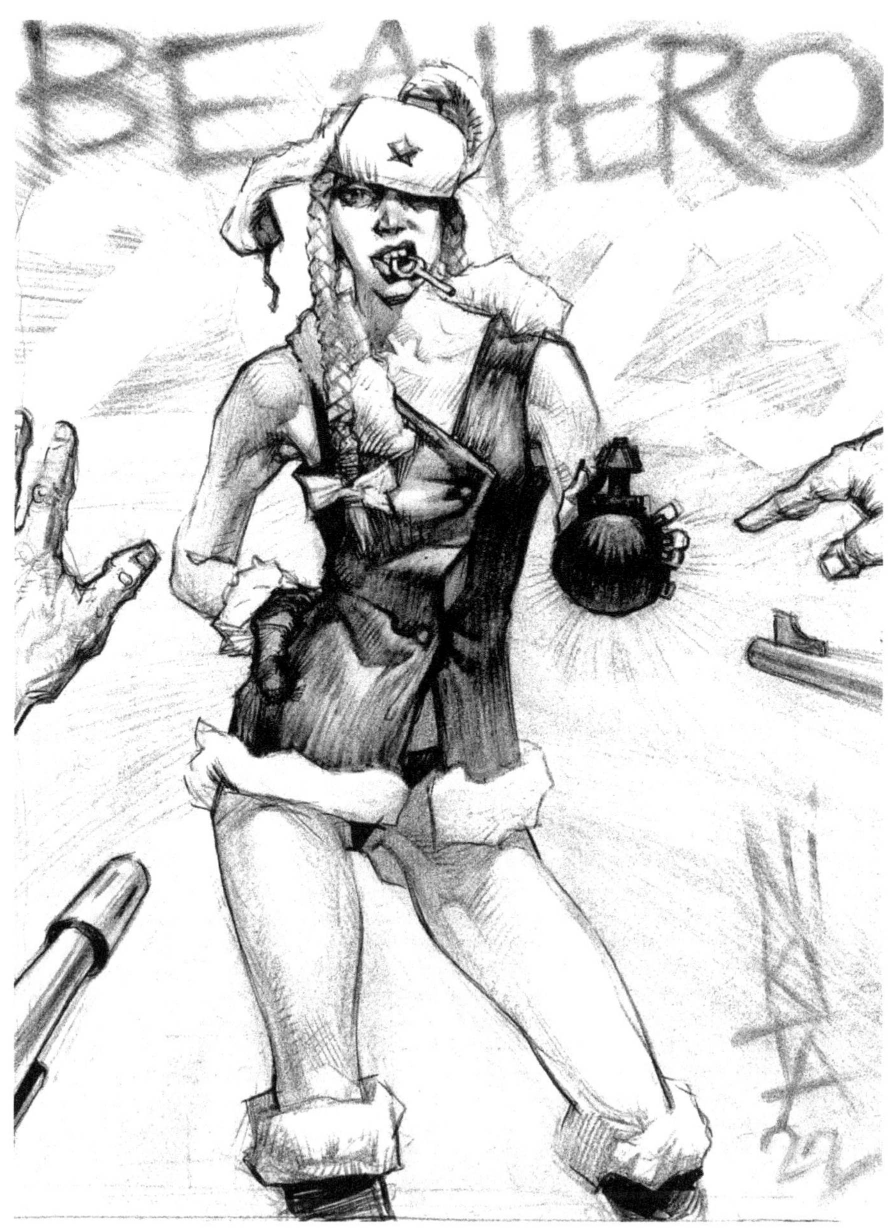
BE A HERO

4

SCHOOL

School is supposedly a calm place,
a place where you get all the right
opportunities that will set you out well-
equipped to face your journey through life.
We are not so sure about the calmness
and whilst education may help you to
get on in life - there are all sorts of
different types of education . . .

BACK TO SCHOOL

Back to school today
Today is the end of summer
Summer was when I was free
Free to do my own thing
Things have changed this morning
This morning it's satchel and books
Books that hide my intentions
My intention of living my dream
Dreaming of finding a tool
A tool that will stand and deliver
Deliver my message of pain
Pain that is hard to bear
Bear is worried no doubt
No doubt it is all imaginary
Imaginary revenge for my loss
The loss of summer

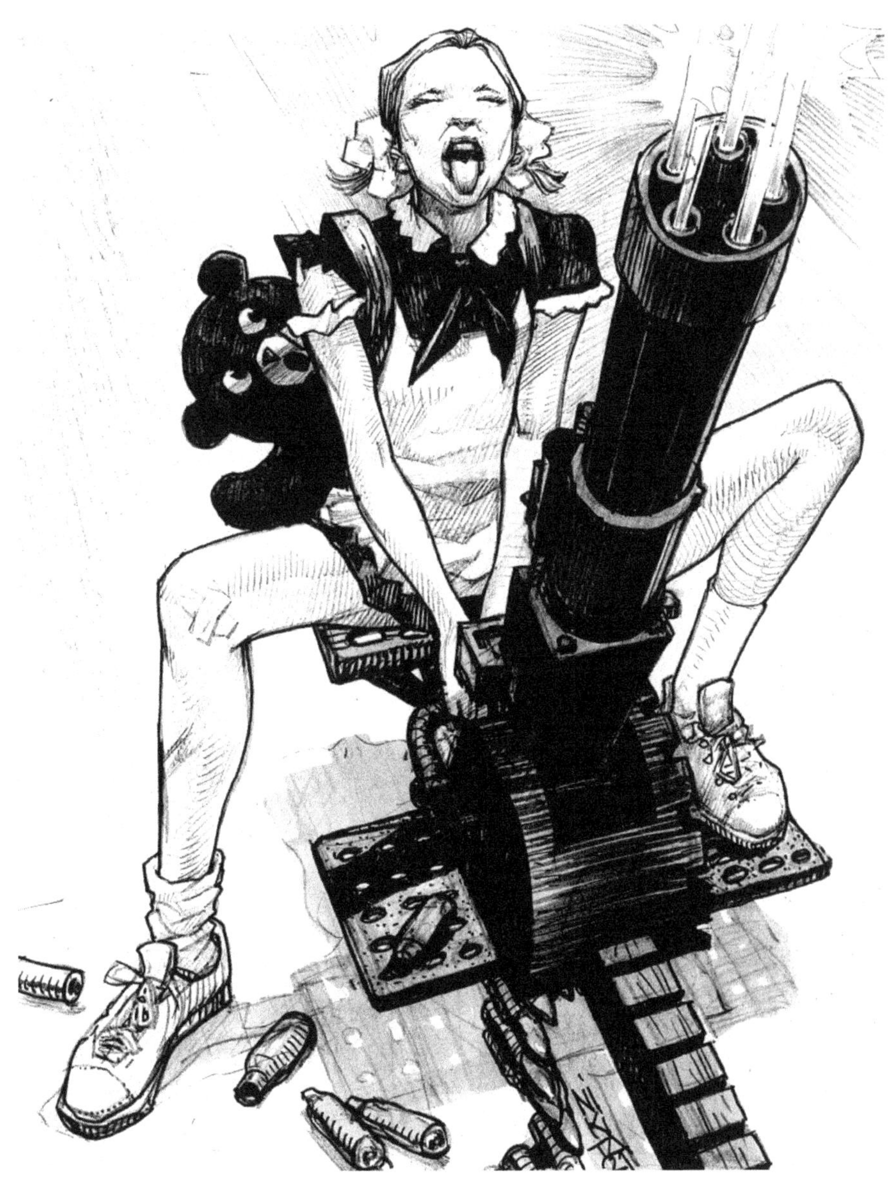

BEST STUDENT

Experiments prove
Synthesizing solutions
Produces rich rewards

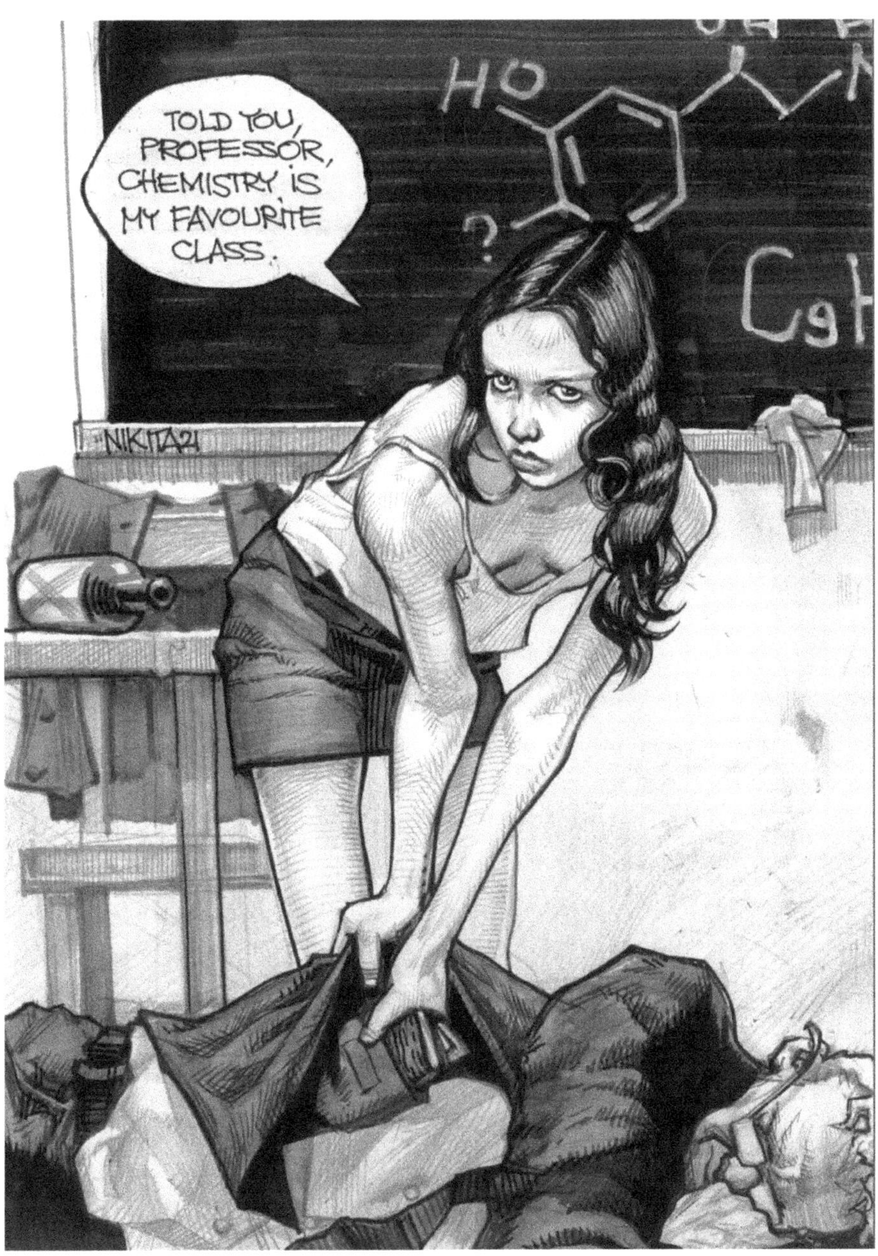
TOLD YOU, PROFESSOR, CHEMISTRY IS MY FAVOURITE CLASS.
HO

MEDICINE CLASS

The first thing to do
Is to carefully inspect
The whole of the site
You intend to inject
To do this you must
With infinite care
Remove her knickers
So the bum is quite bare
Now tell the lady
"Bend over please,
For penetration
At forty degrees"
For ninety degrees
Is not correct
In this round fleshy site
Where I will inject.
Now it's really important
That you take good care
Of the firm exposed buttock
That presents to you - bare
And tell the young lady
"I won't be a tick,
And in just a short while
You will feel a small prick!"

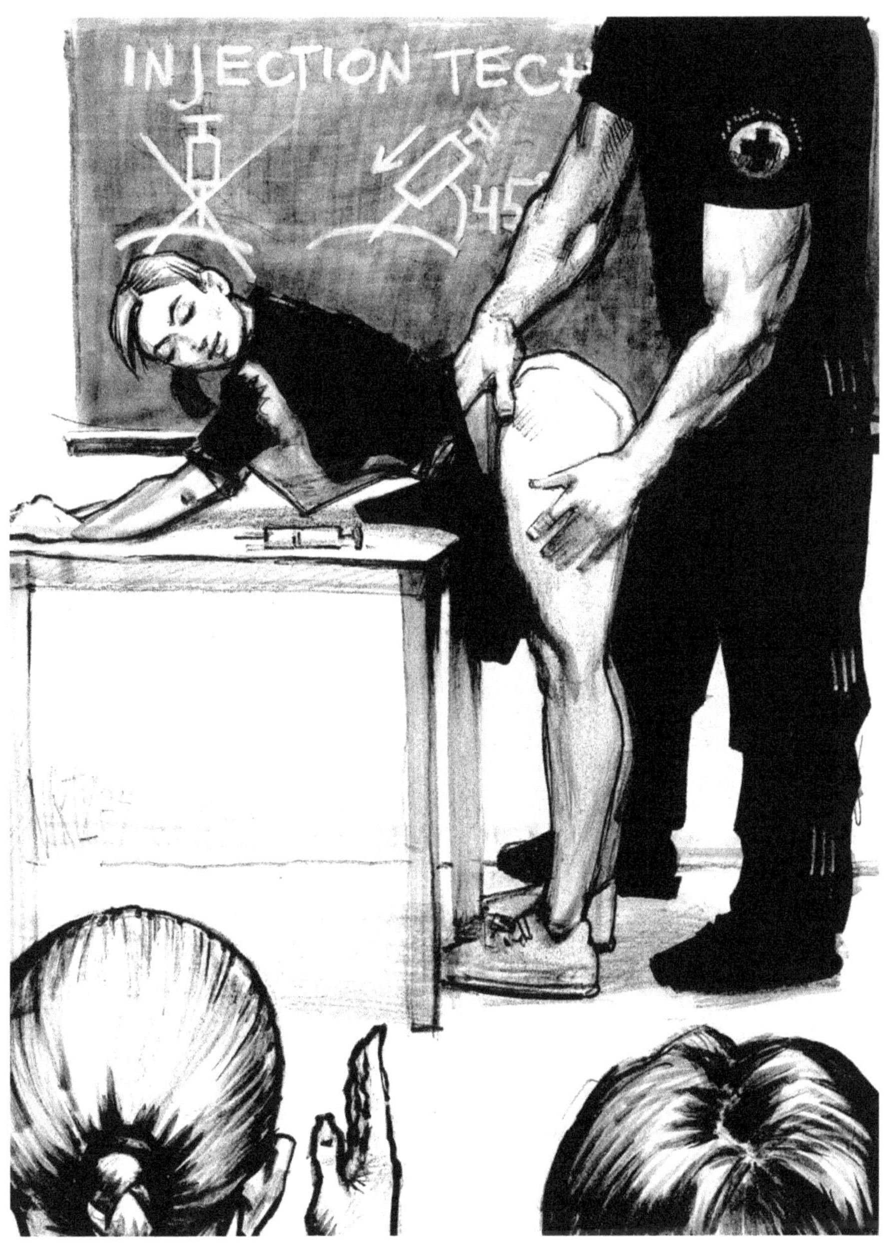
INJECTION TECH
45

REHEARSAL

There is a young lady called Joyce
Who rehearses in front of her toys
The resulting stares
As she displayed her wares
Shows that which her fan-cub enjoys

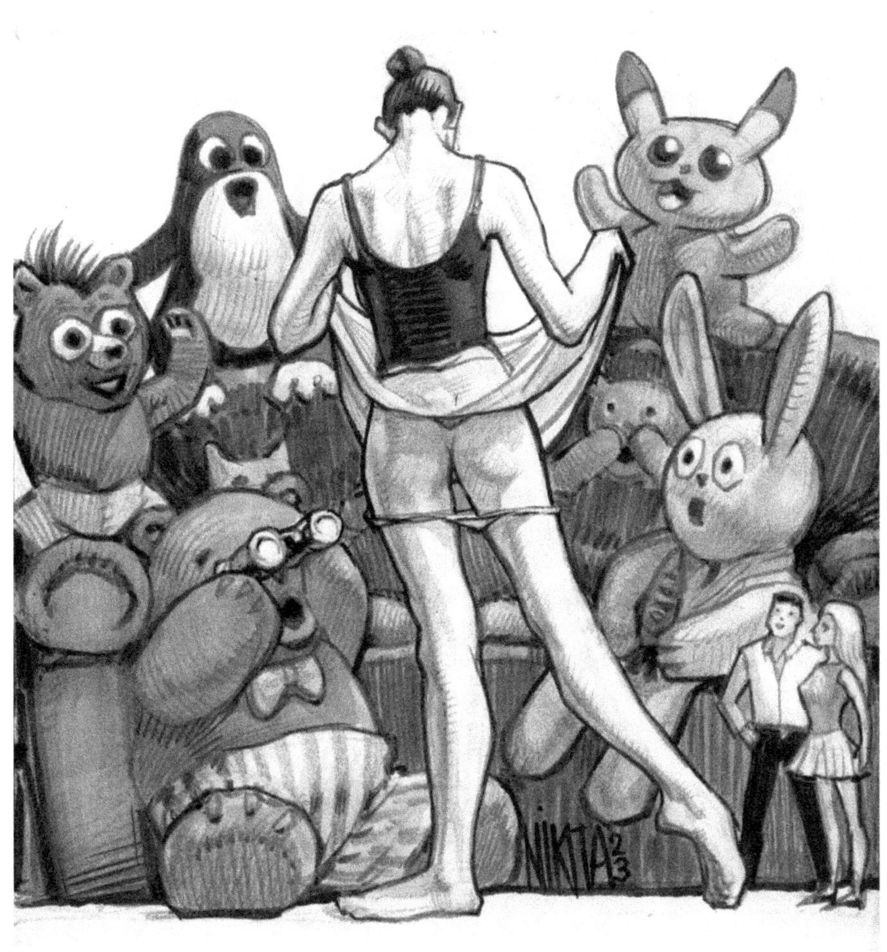

STUDENT'S WILES

There was a young girl they called Sam
Who came first in every exam
When asked why this was
She said "it's because
Of the exams that I have from that man"

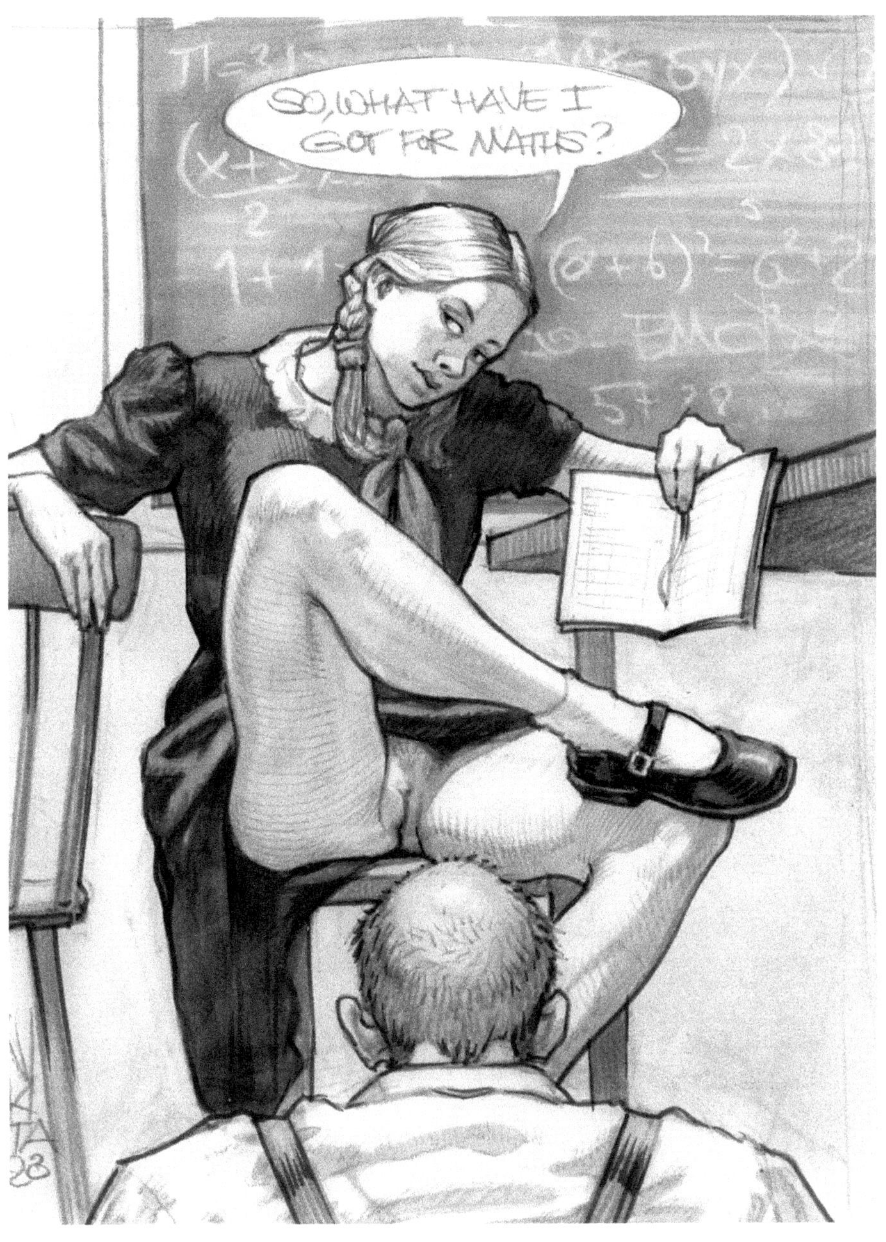
SO, WHAT HAVE I GOT FOR MATHS?

KISS

All too often men fail
To meet the expectations
Or hopes of women

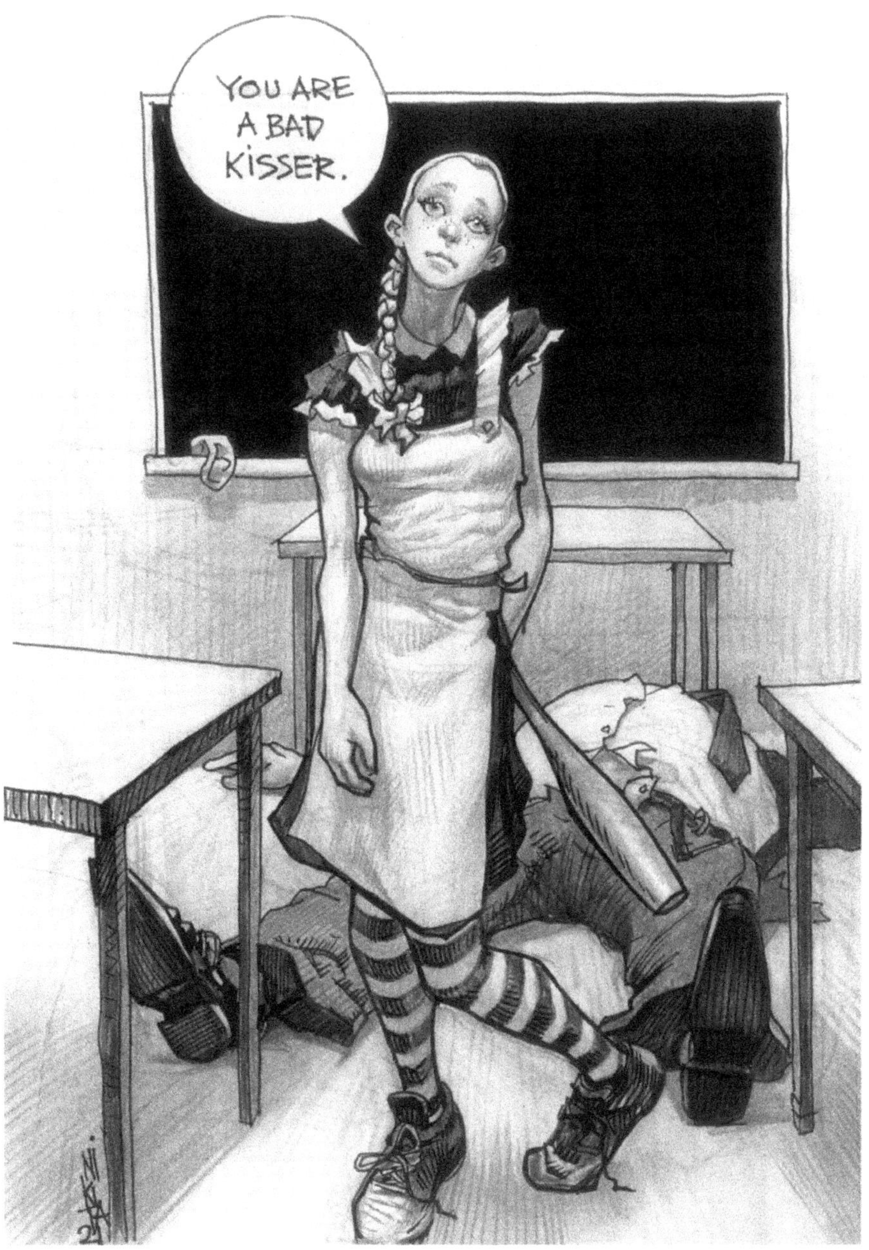
YOU ARE
A BAD
KISSER.

SHAMELESS

If you pick on me
I will certainly shoot you
And not be ashamed

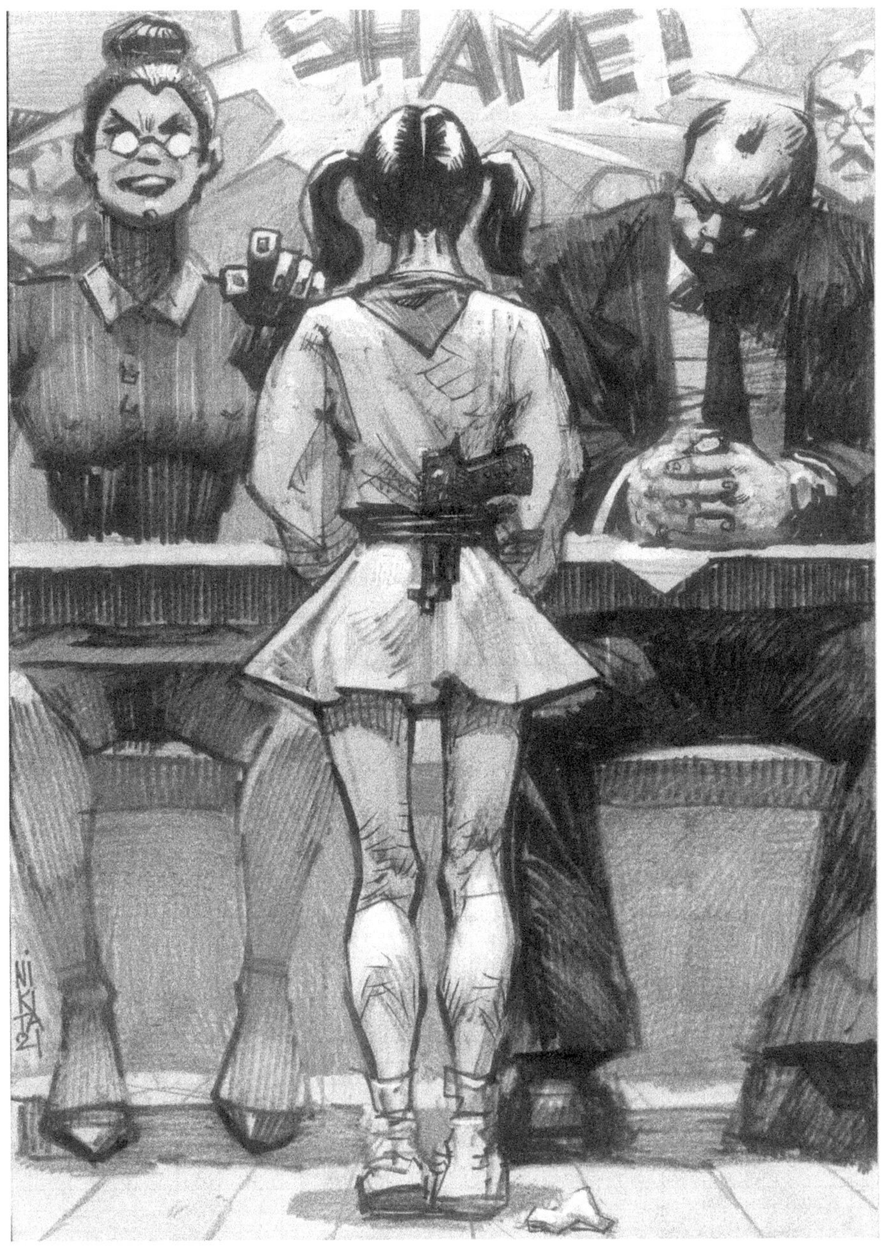
SHAME!

5

MUSIC

We understand that music powerfully
affects our thinking and our moods.
In this chapter we find a myriad
of young ladies who are also intent
upon changing our mood, many employing
musical instruments to do so.
As the Bard would have it
'. . . if music be the food of love, play on . . .'

DUET

There was a young lady called June
Whose music made everyone swoon
But her pianist, poor chap,
When she sat on his lap
Found he played to a quite different tune.

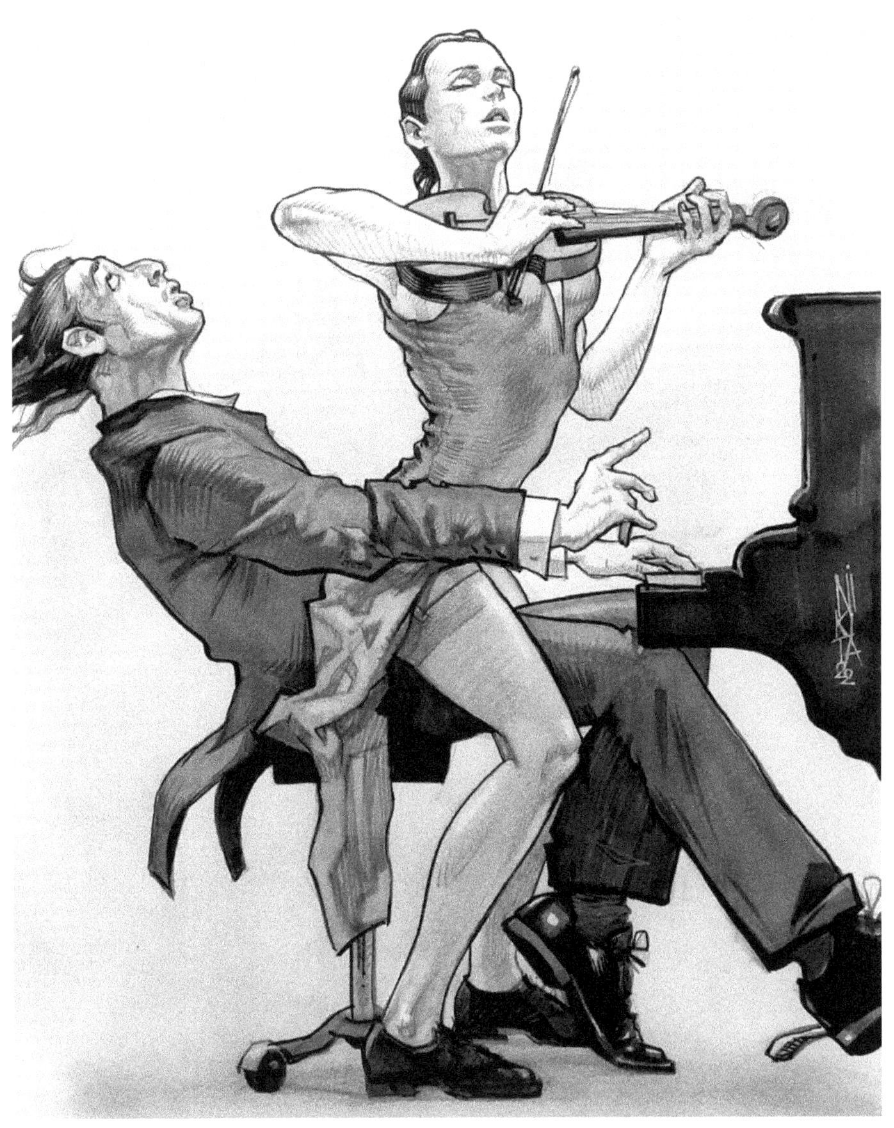

NOTES

Hitting the right notes
Can be a key distraction
Finding middle C

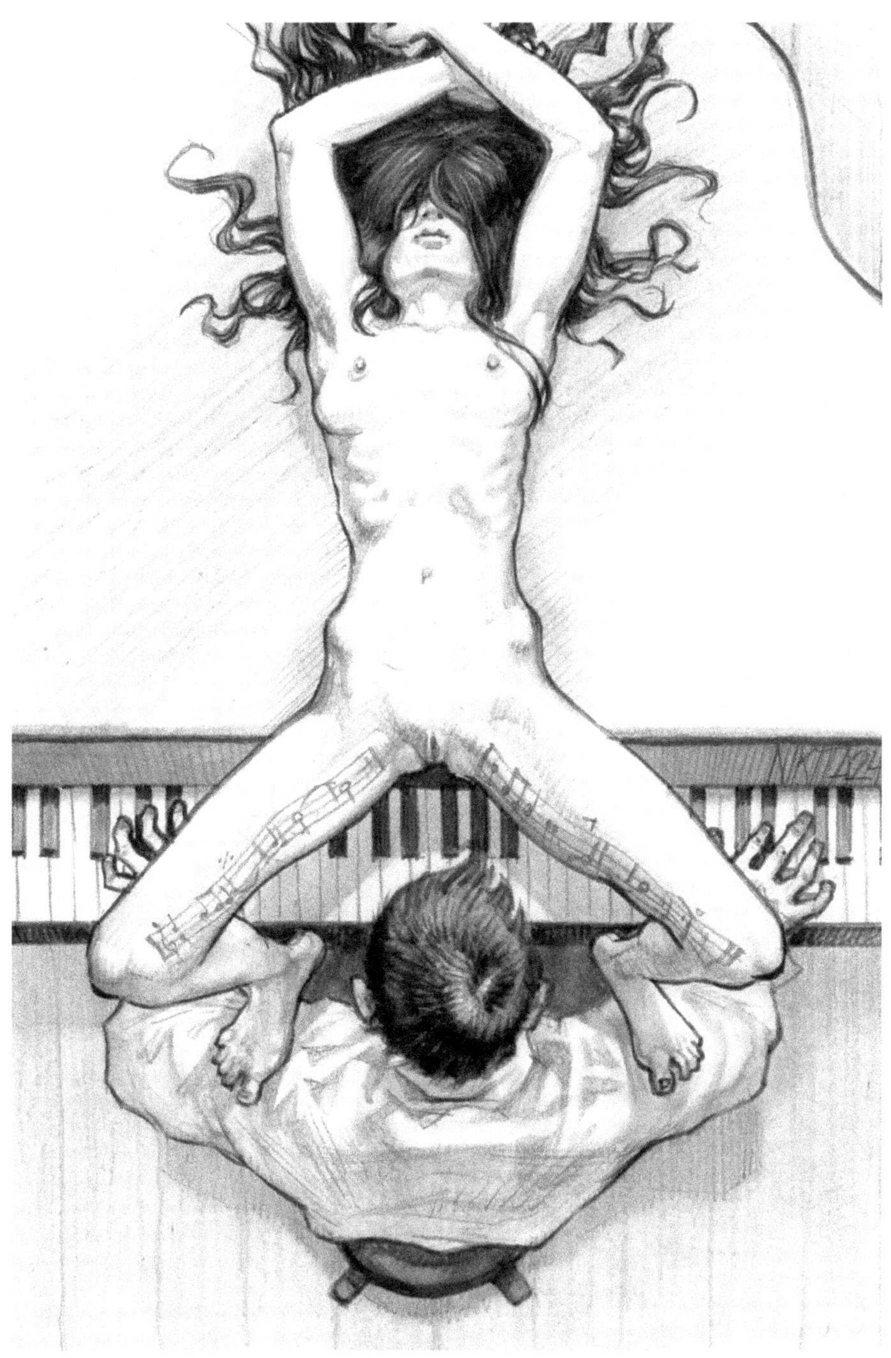

BALALAIKA

If you really like her
Play your balalaika
As you romp in the hay

The voyeurs may be horses
Which really just endorses
The songs you want to play

But to play without your clothes
Every living beastie knows
Is a way to amuse yourself all day

With a game that I am told
Is millennia old
So enjoy yourselves romping in the hay.

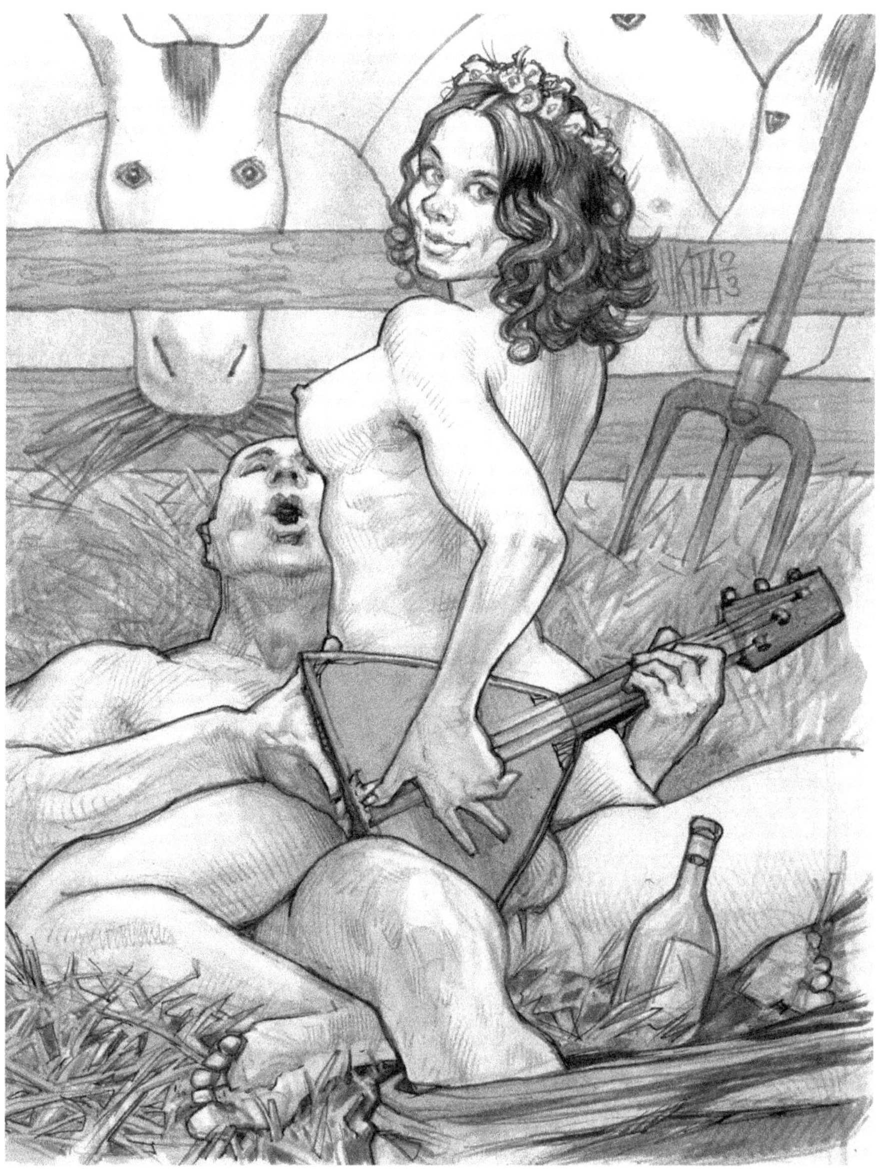

METRO

There is a young girl they call Flo
Who takes up her fiddle and bow
For she dreams that one day
She'll be able to play
On the Thessaloniki Metro*!

*Although it is up and (mostly) running, the Thessaloniki Metro had a gestation of many decades, during which it became the butt of numerous sarcastic jokes.

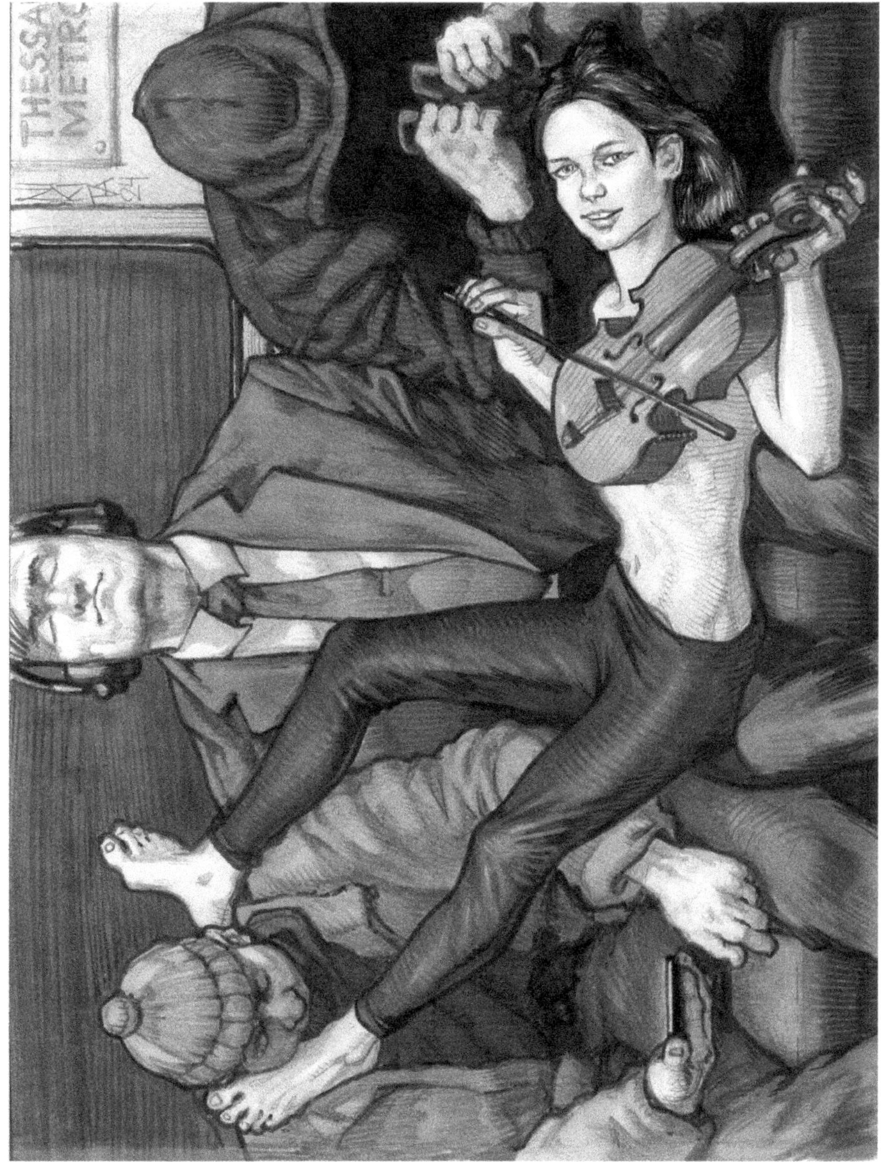

1

SNAKE CHARMER

There was a young girl from Beirut
Why used to charm snakes with her flute
And because now and then
She also charmed men
The snake was half snake and half boot.

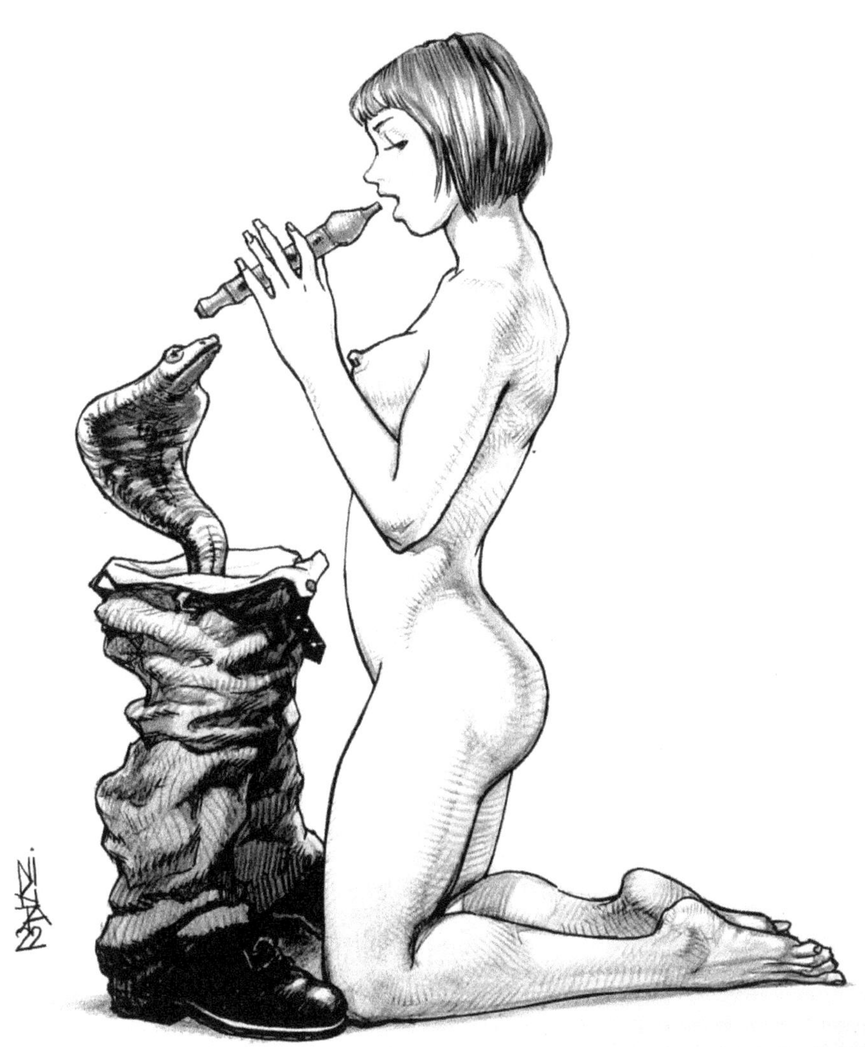

ACCORDIONIST'S LOVE

Hey you! Yes you!
Accordion man
Play for me, play with me
As fiercely as you can
Squeeze it, squeeze me
Accordion man
Let me feel your rhythm
Let me be your fan
Push in, pull out
Accordion man
Hit the keys that matter
And I'll be your tympan

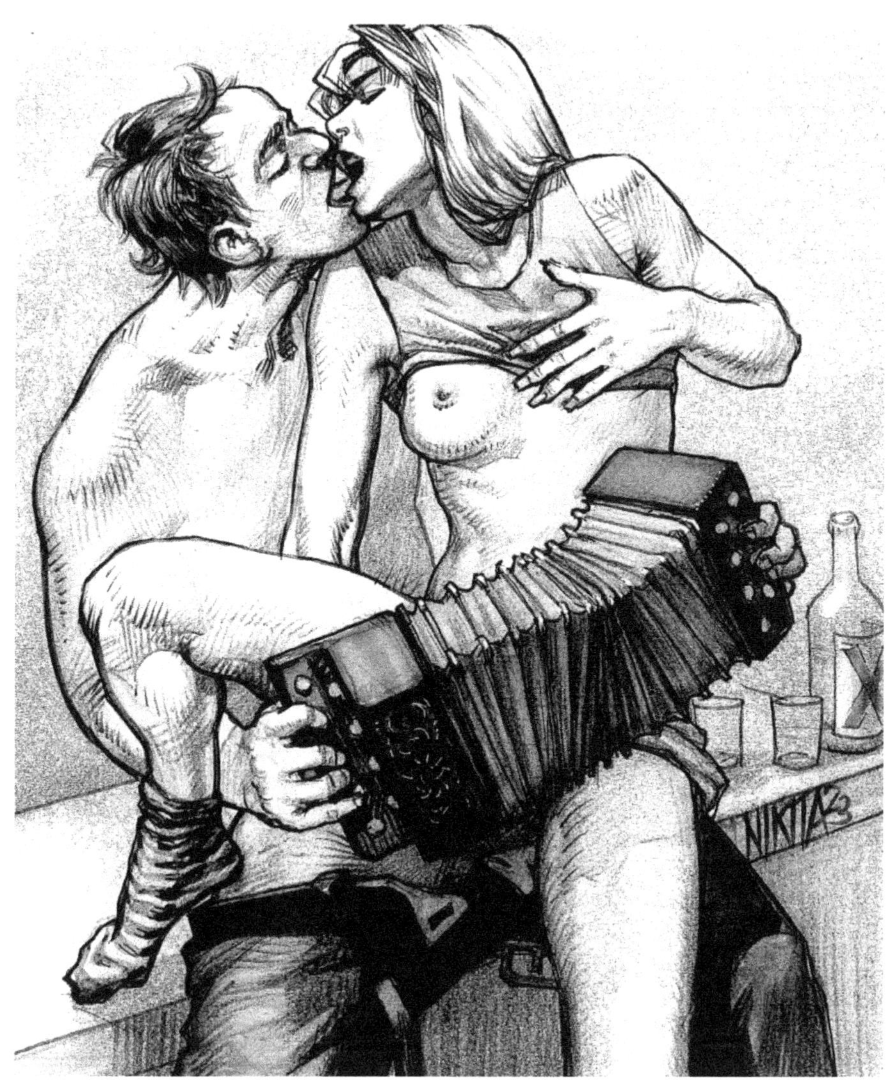
NIKITA

6

ROBOTS

With the advent of AI the world is
suddenly faced with a new type of robotic.
However we are a bit old-fashioned
when it comes to our robots,
but whilst they clank about the place
as all old-fashioned robots should
they are surprisingly human
in both looks and attitude

DELIVERY

There was a young lady called Bess
Who called Delivery Express
But the robot that came
Put her to shame
By trying to tear off her dress

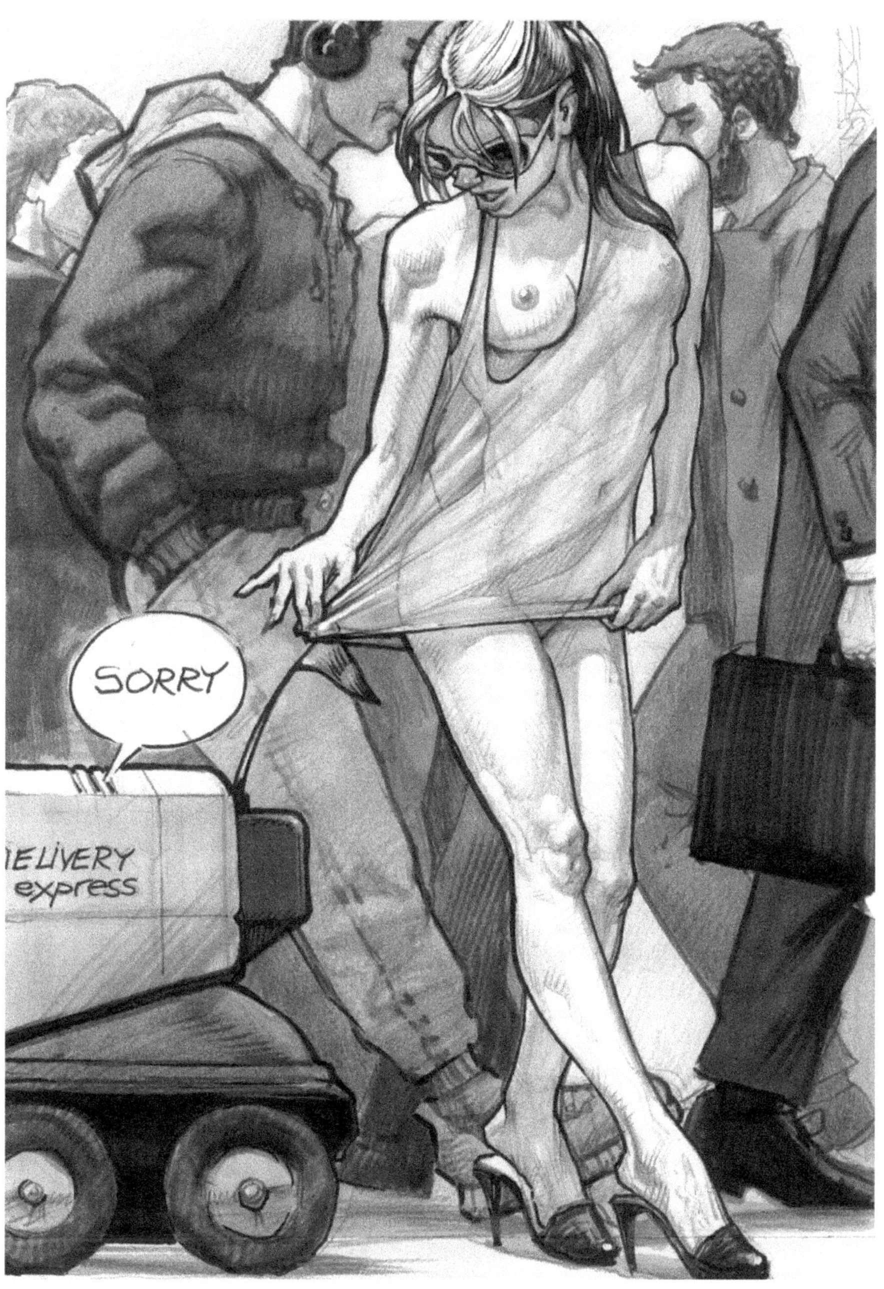
SORRY
express

LEASH

If you have discovered
Someone who is wonderful
Be she an Angel or a human
Then there will be within you
A natural desire
To keep hold of this delight.
If she is human you can
Bribe her with gifts
Such as flowers or chocolates
Or you can impress her with
Your strength or your intellect
As a last resort
You can even marry her.
However no such schemes
Will work with an Angel
Such beings are notoriously
Uninterested in chocolates
Immune to muscular display
And averse to matrimony
So, you, being a Control Freak
Will no doubt resort to
Shackling her in an
Iron collar and chains.
Thereby destroying
The whole concept
Of Angelic Visitation

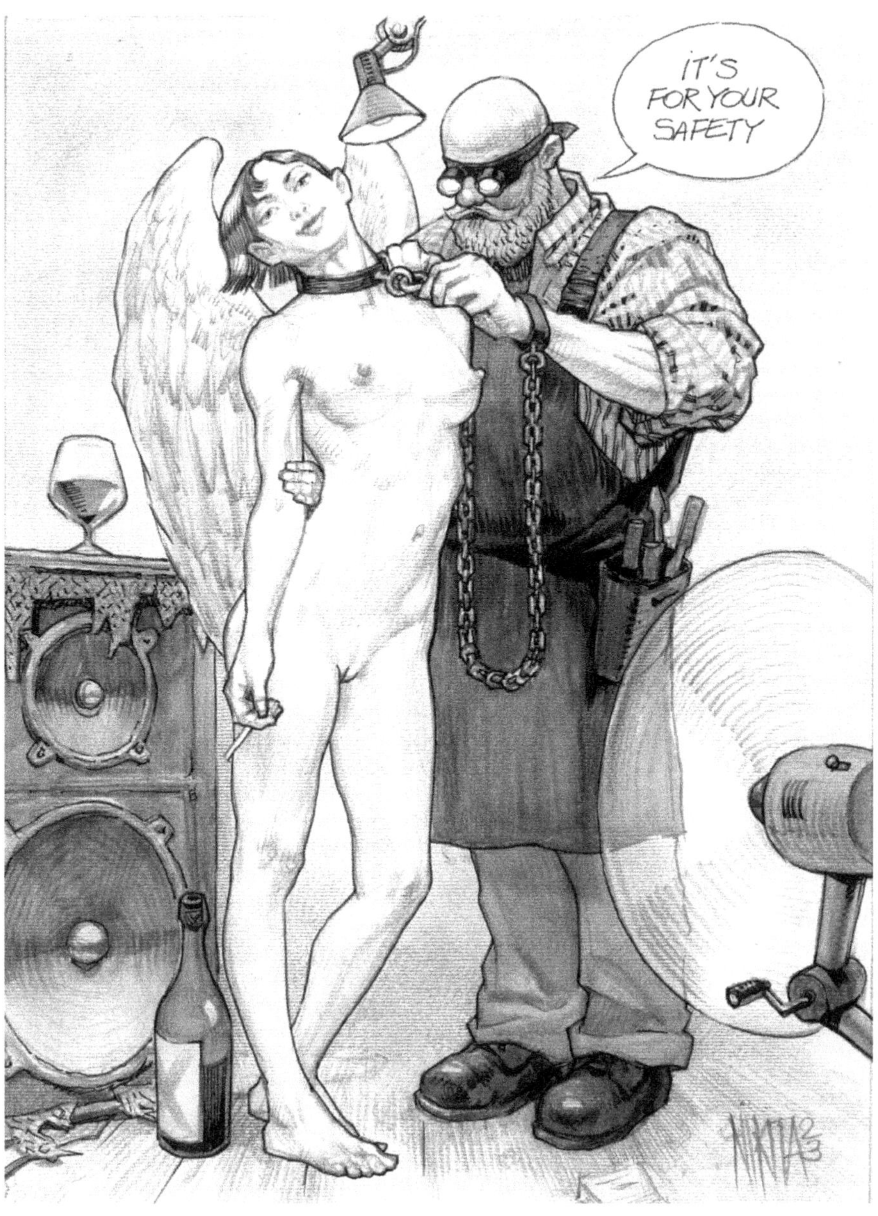
IT'S
FOR YOUR
SAFETY

BATTERIES

A girl that they used to call Flower
Would rent herself out by the hour
And when her batteries ran low
She knew just where to go
To charge herself up with more power

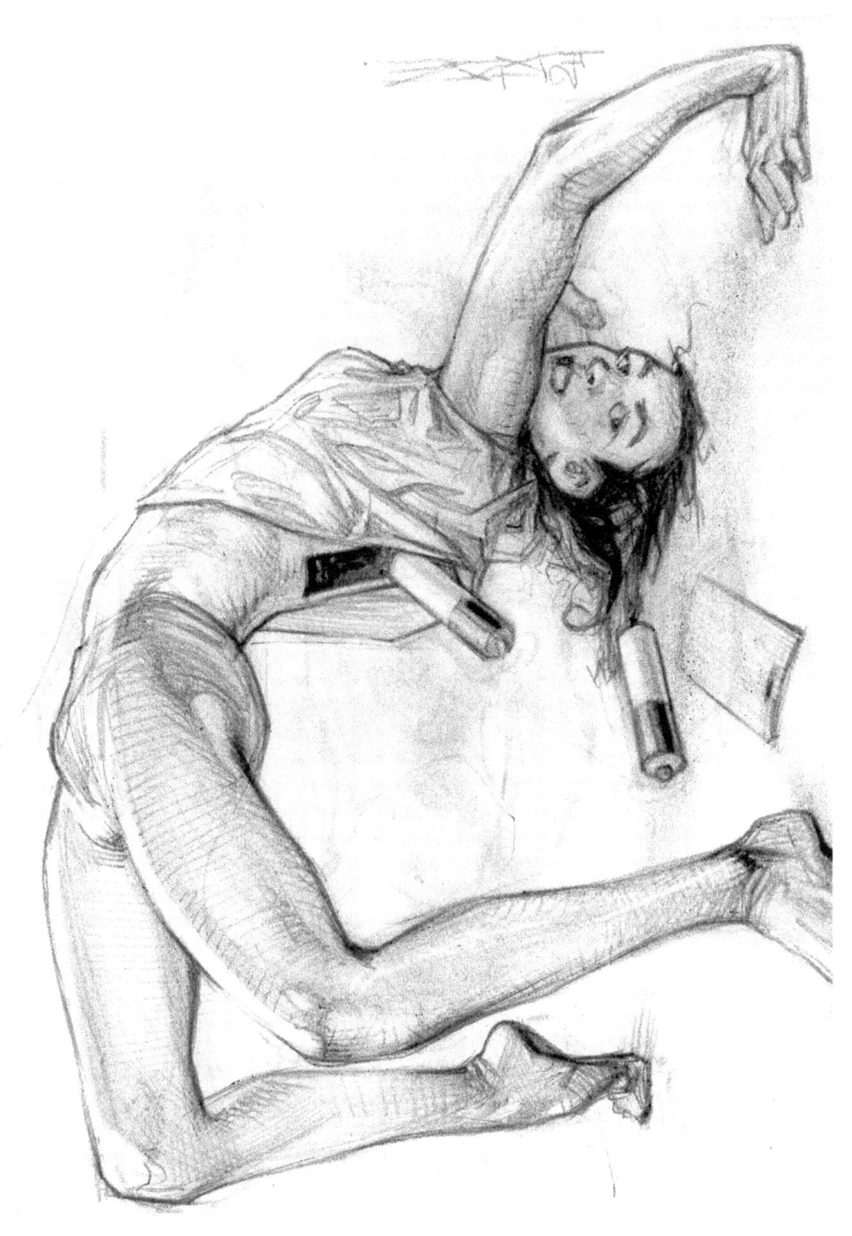

LAMP

There was a girl they called Flo
Who decided she wanted to glow
She attached to her tits
Some electrical bits
That lit up her world from below

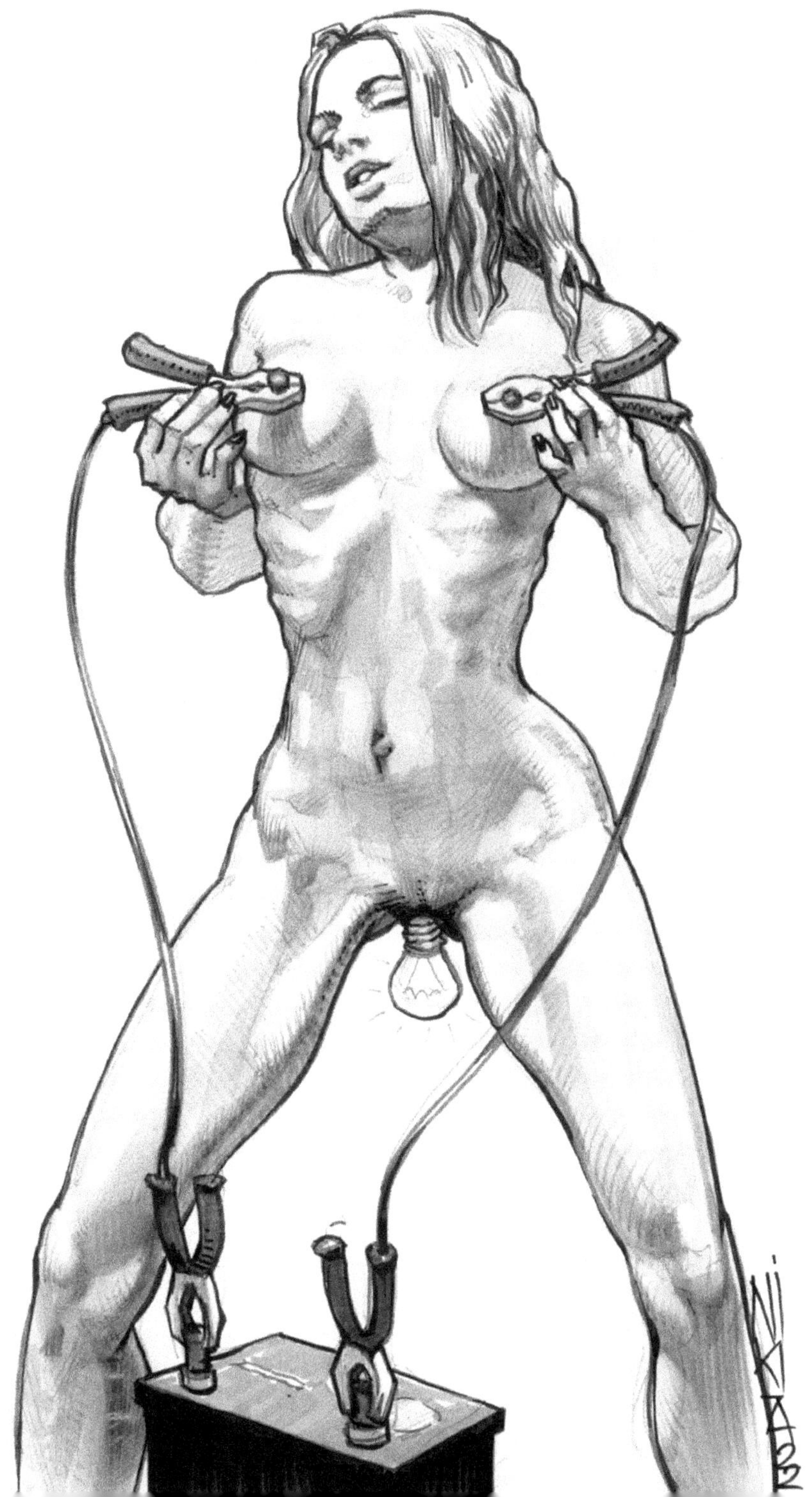

POWER

They come
One by one
And they're done
One by one
I have fun
One by one
'Cos I flaunt it

Flaunt and screw
Two by two
Yes, I do
Two by two
Join the queue
Two by two
If you want it

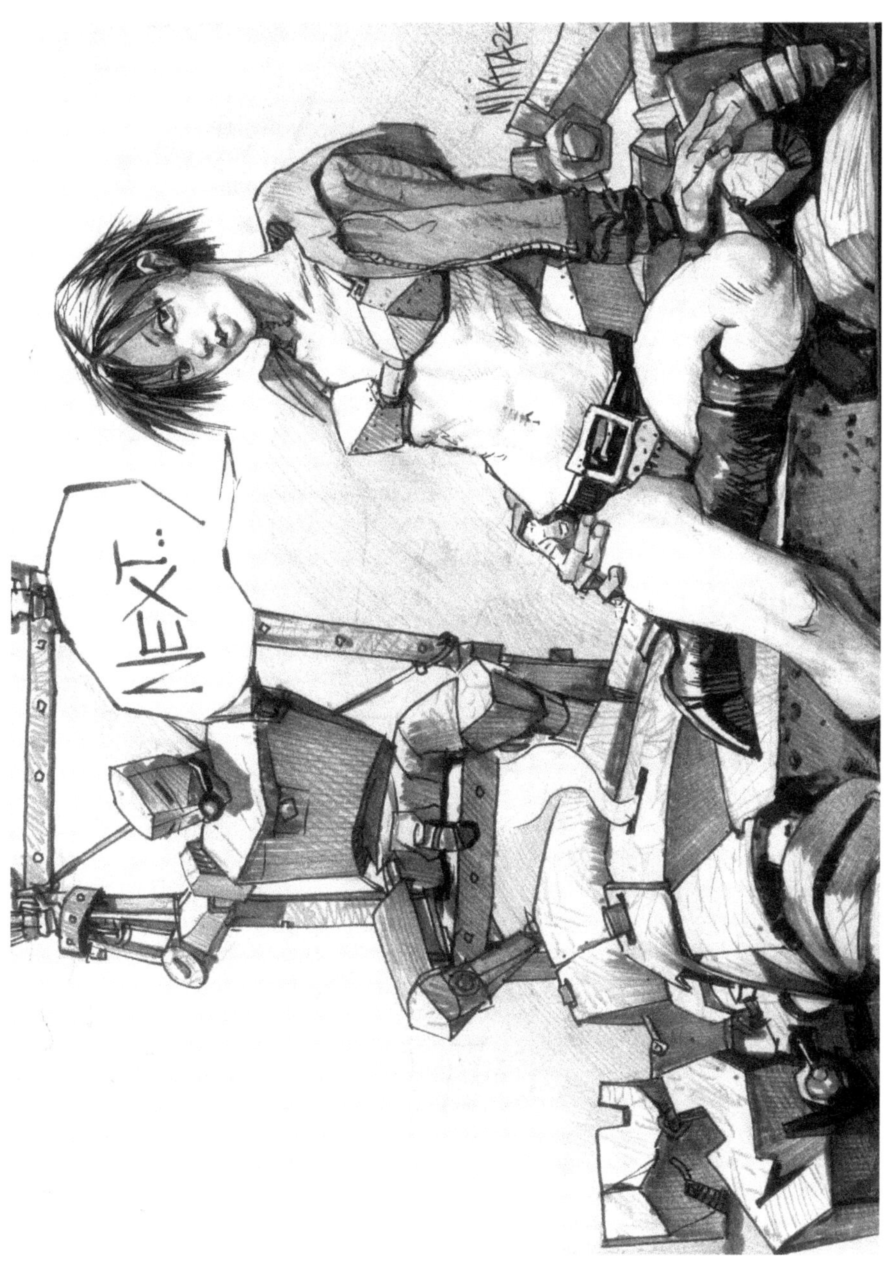
NEXT..

DIY

When building a robot, business or life
It would be really best to comply
With the intricate set of instructions
In a manual of DIY

Robots are fairly simple
When bought as a basic flat pack.
You just bolt the bits together
Plug in the power and step back!

Business is rather more trouble
With cash flow and spreadsheets and things
And what's now called 'Human Resources'
With all the trouble that brings

But we are all Do It Yourself-ers
When building a life for ourselves
There's no manual for sorting our problems
And no spare parts on the shelves

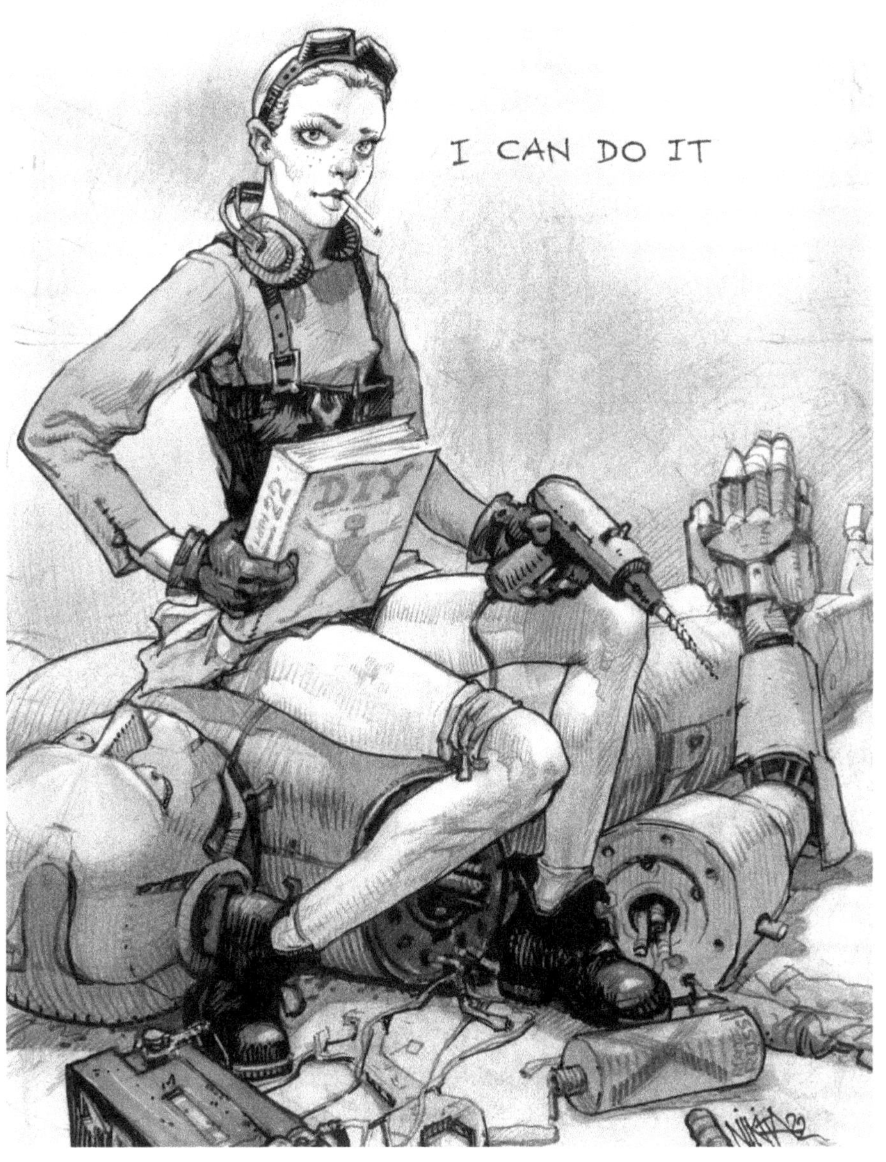
I CAN DO IT
DIY

PARTY SET

Along with the crisps and beer
You have picked a delicious woman
There were plenty stacked on the shelves
But you really fancied this one

It is best to buy them naked
So you can see any physical flaws
The ones that have any blemishes
You really don't want for yours

So off you go to the party
Enjoy the drink and the food
Enjoy the delights of this woman
For the cash she cost you should

And now the party is over
It was one hell of a bash
You can chuck out all of your empties,
Including the girl, in the trash.

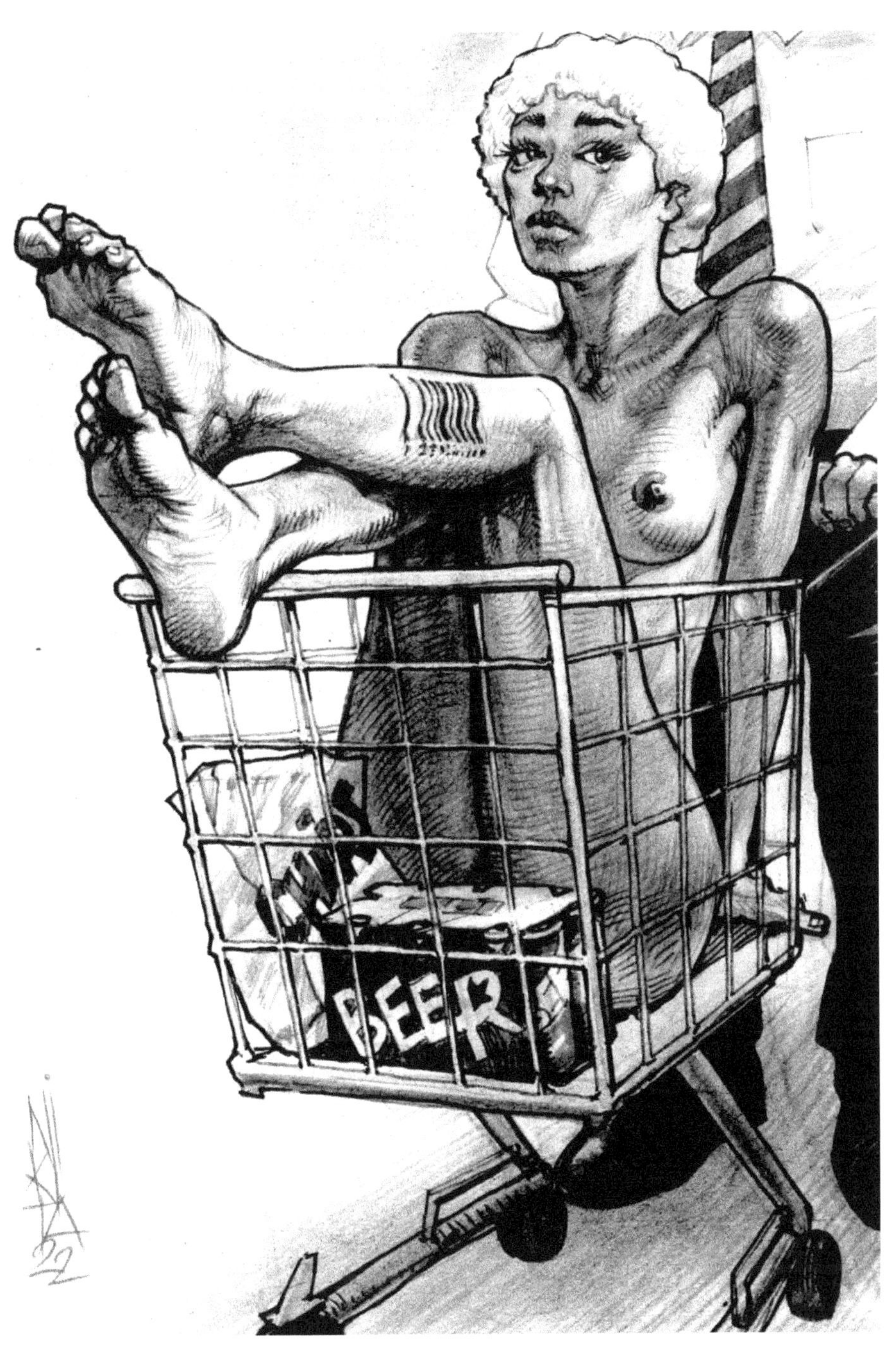
BEER

RECHARGE

A challenging pose
Shows artistic playfulness
And something darker
Female empowerment but
Exploited women

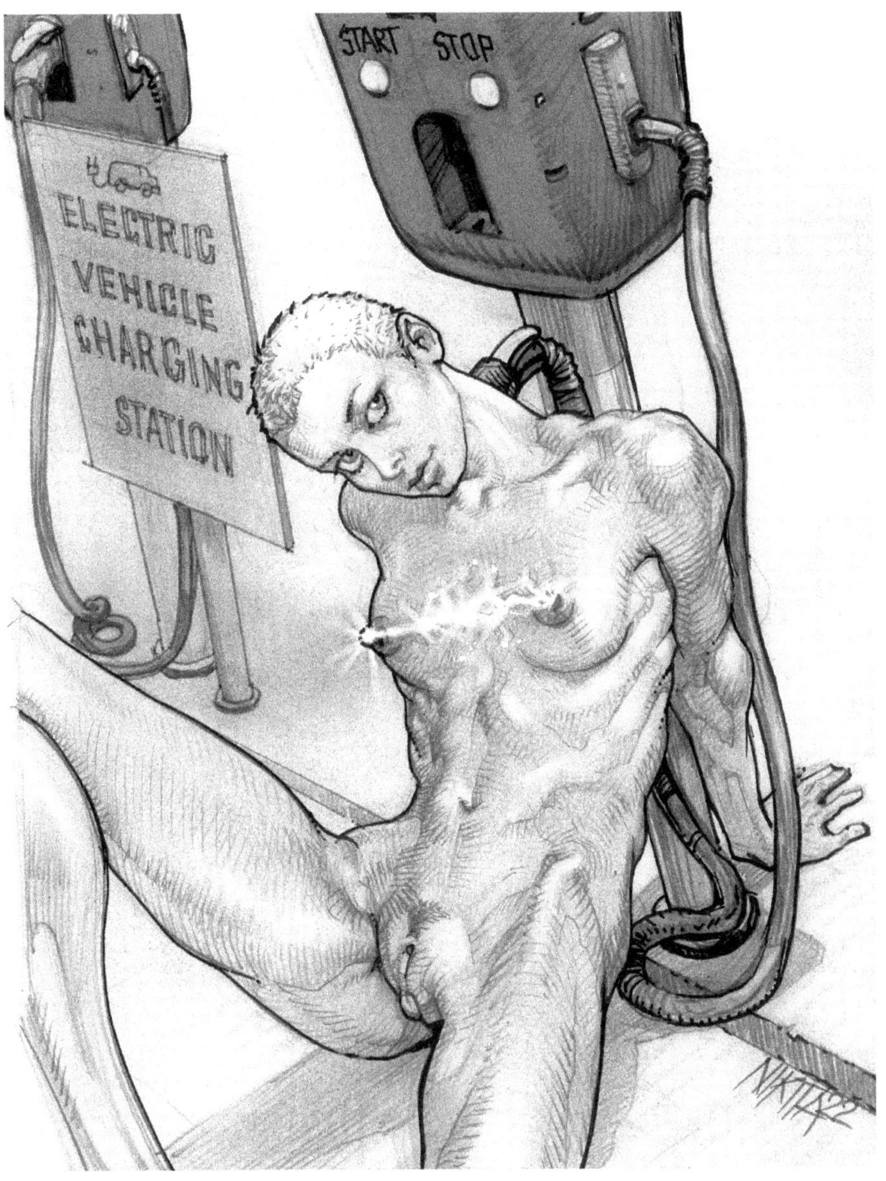
START
STOP
ELECTRIC
VEHICLE
CHARGING
STATION

DELIVERY

Whatever you want
Delivered to you by drone
Increases desire

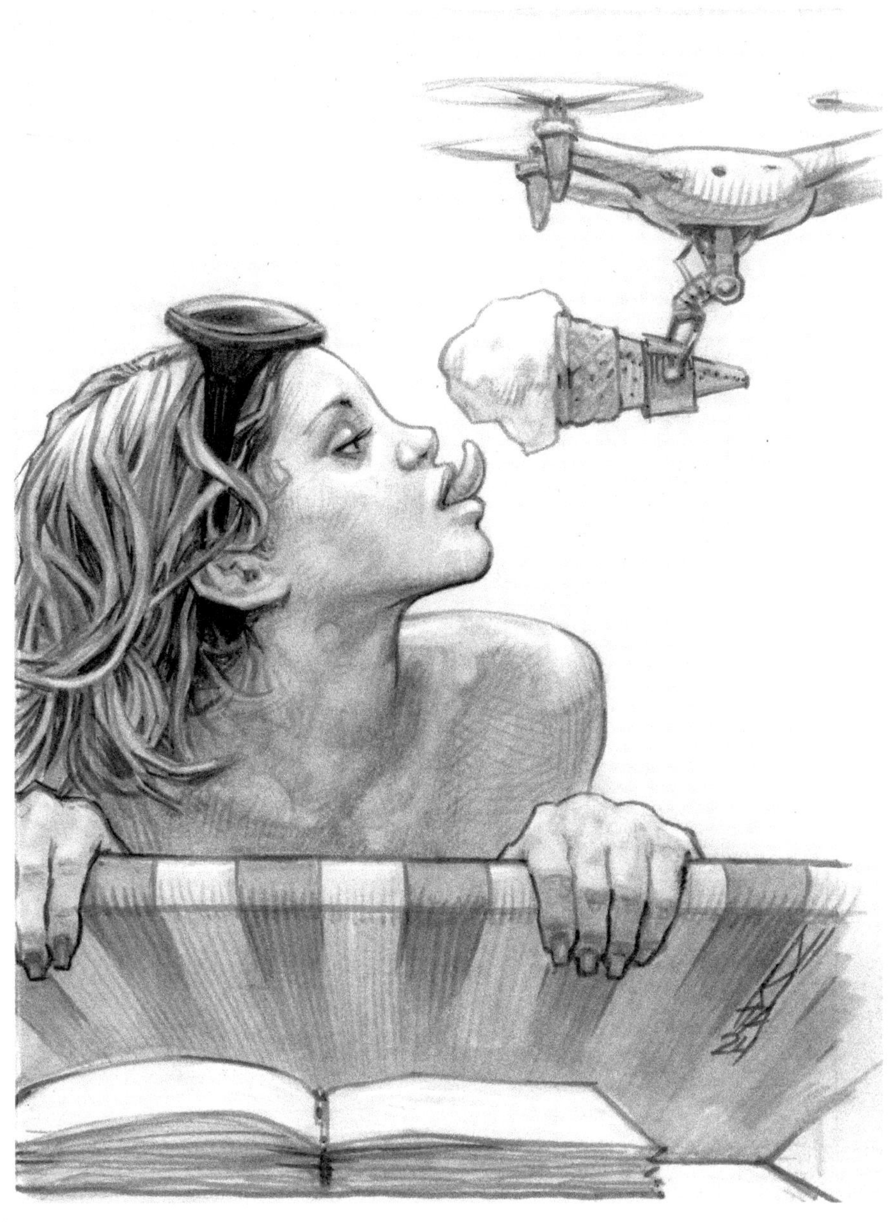

DRUMMER

Sometimes in her wildest dreams
She is titillated, so it seems,
By rabbits - one a drummer
The other rather more a bummer

Such is her heightened quest for kicks
That the drummer-boy needs no sticks
Whilst the other bunny's tongue just flickers
As he rids her of her knickers

Sadly we are now voyeurs
Excited by these playboy furs
Whereas we should dismiss and scorn
This leporine venture into porn.

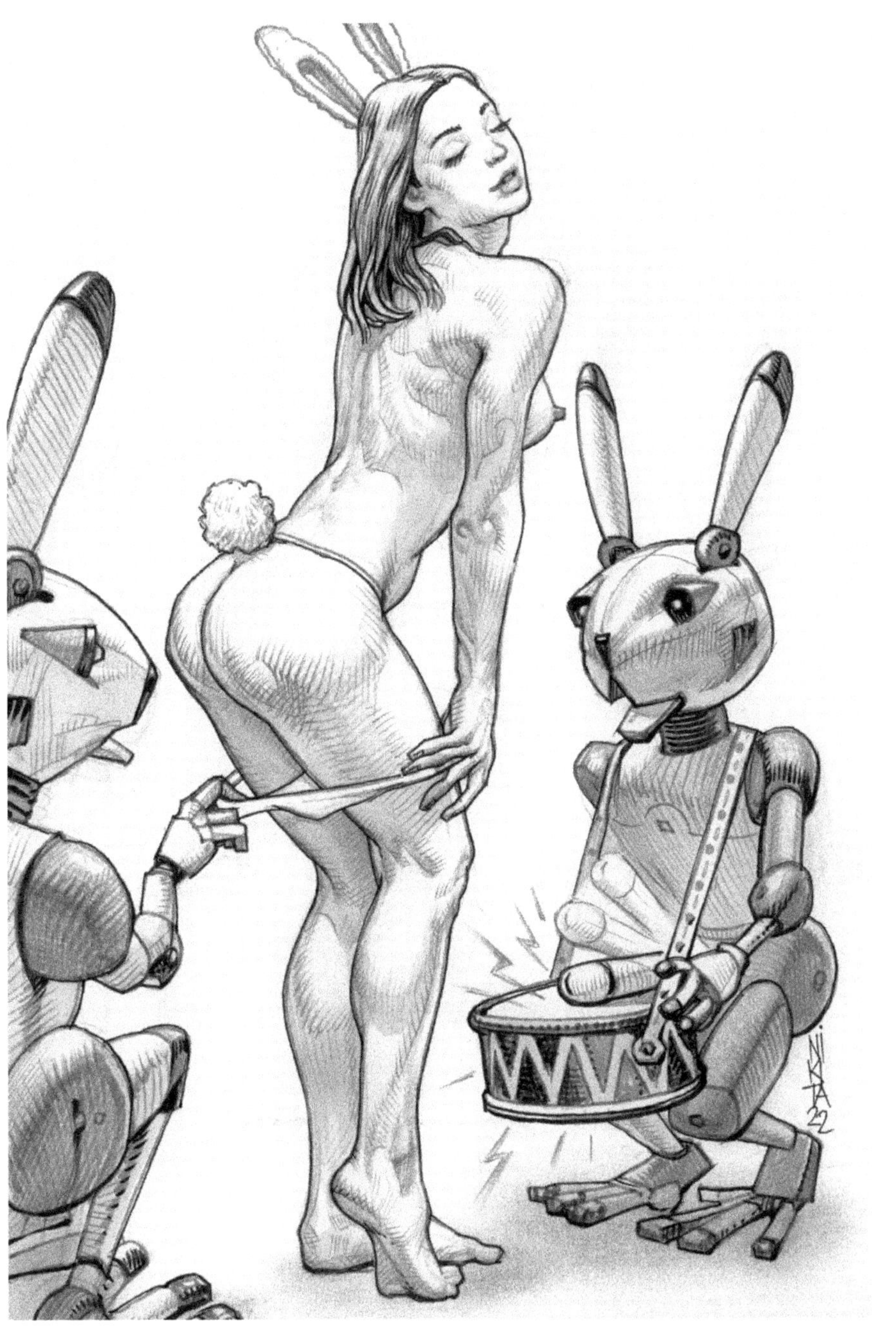

FAN CLUB

Fantasy fan club
Providing stimulus for
Robotic urges

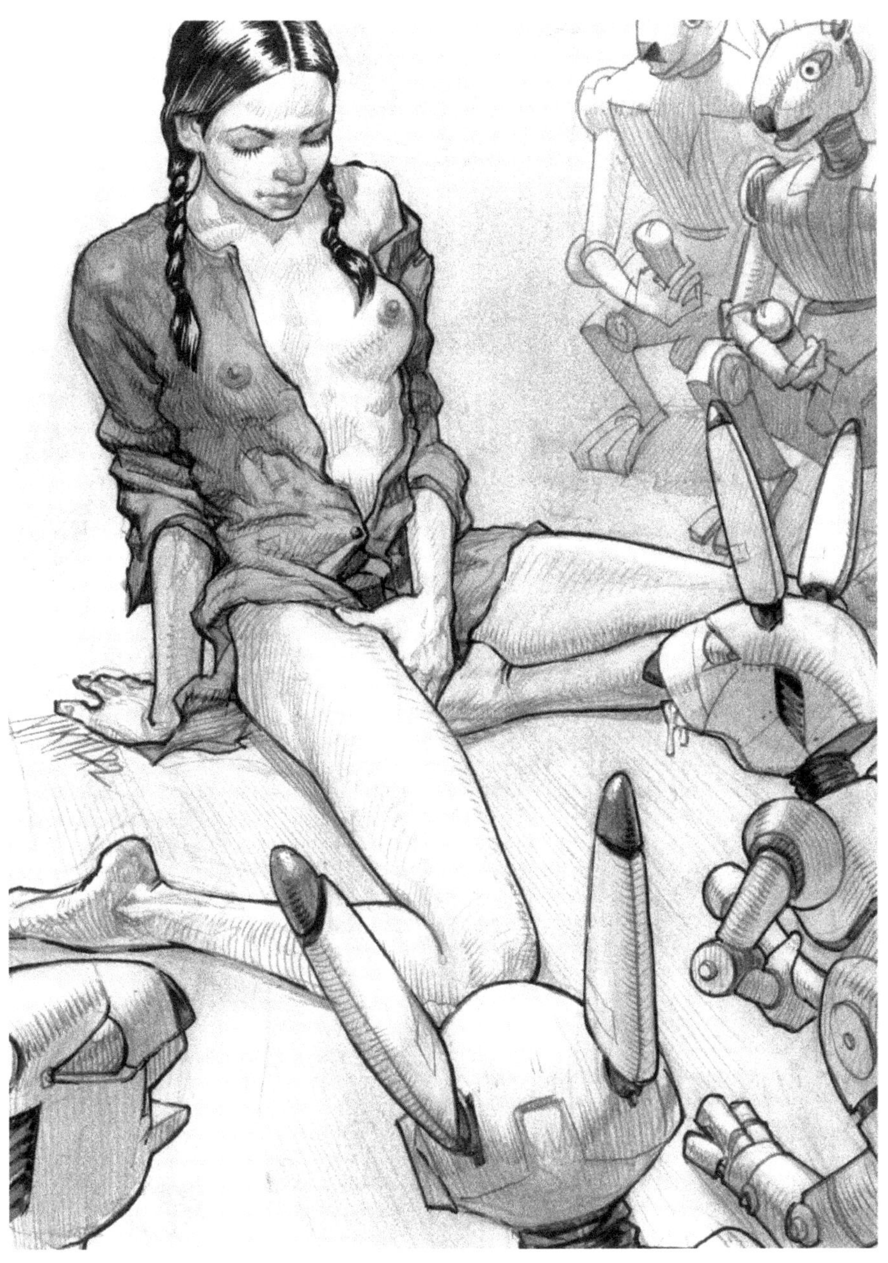

TECHNICAL SERVICE

A pretty robot, Felice,
Very much needed some grease
‘cos things would get stuck
When she ran amok
But now greased she can do it with ease.

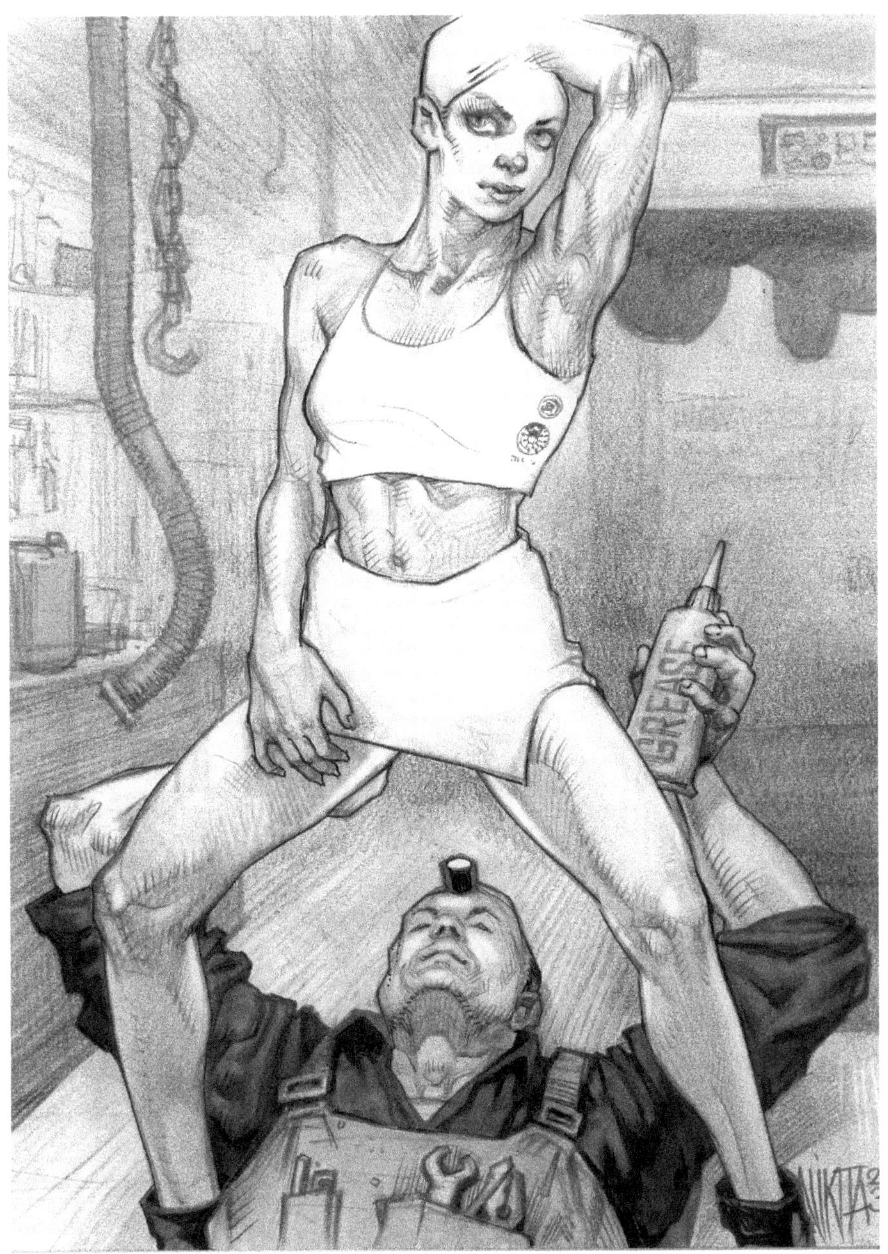
GREASE

7

SPORT

A great many of us enjoy
or indulge in sport.
Most people have a favourite sport that
they follow. Our "take' on the subject
is wide and perhaps just a tad bizarre,
but nonetheless we trust that
you will be entertained by it

TRAINING

To train the common frog or toad to leap
Does not present a task that is too hard
This is because they like to jump, not creep
And travel not one inch, but yard by yard

So jumping is just a natural thing
From leaf to leaf they cross their native pond
Tongues unfurled as the flies they try to catch
Buzz safely out of reach and far beyond

But try to coach this leaping to your will
Is far from the easiest thing to do
For their arms and legs just will not stay still
As if co-ordination was taboo

But perseverance might just save the day
With toads and frogs well trained to jump your way

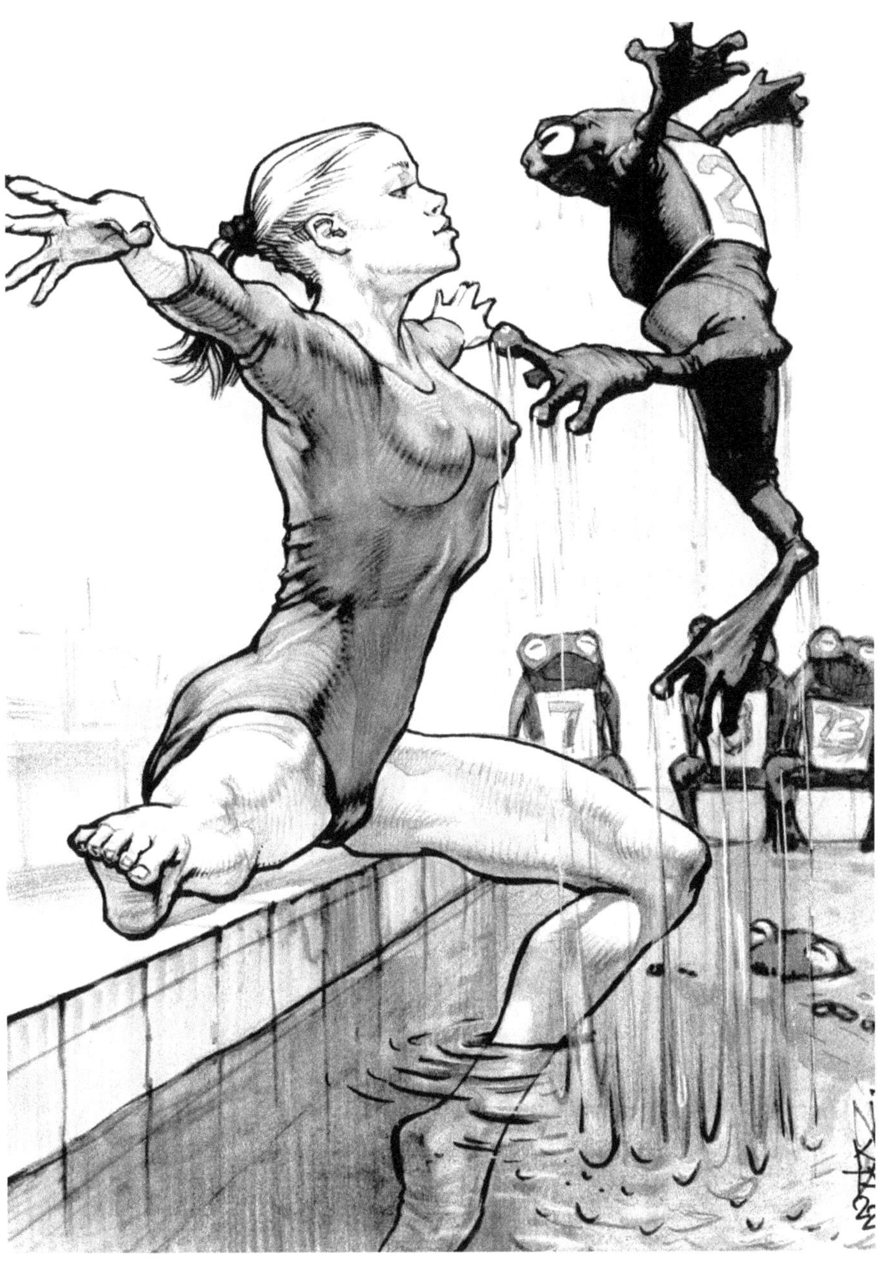
2
7
23

JEALOUSY

There was a young lady called Myrtle
Who fell in love with a turtle
But his jealous young friends
said however this ends
Their offspring will all be infertile

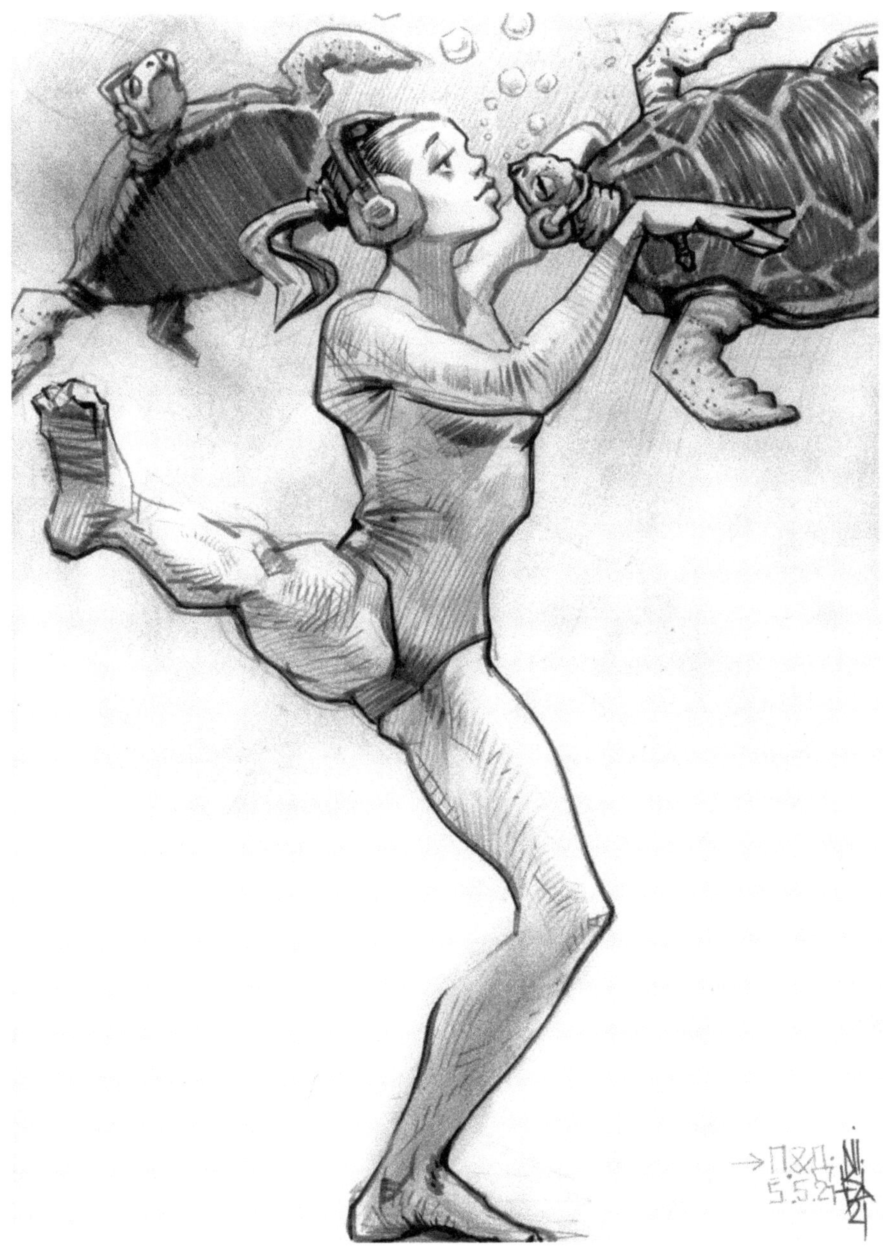

DOLPHIN

When you ride dolphins
They take you to strange places
Just imagine it!

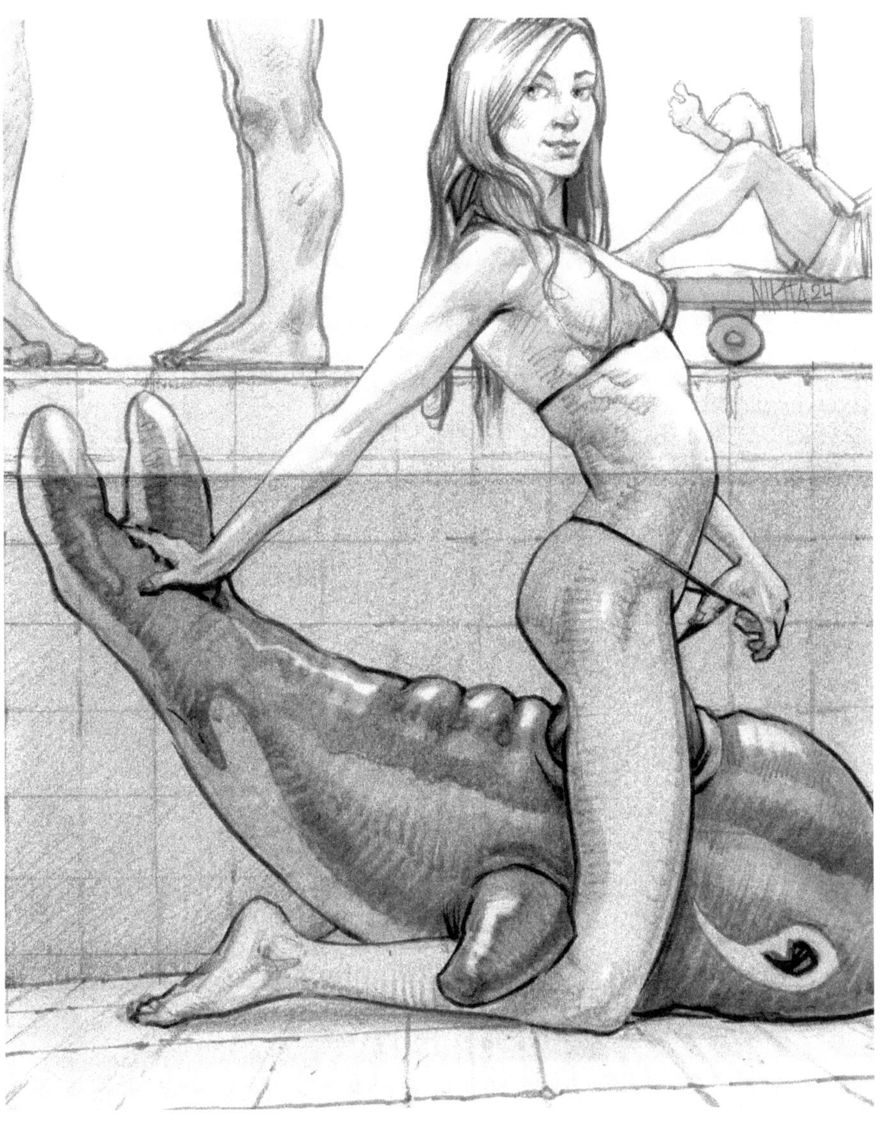

LADY RACER

Lady car racer
Laid bare by a lust for speed
The crunch is coming.

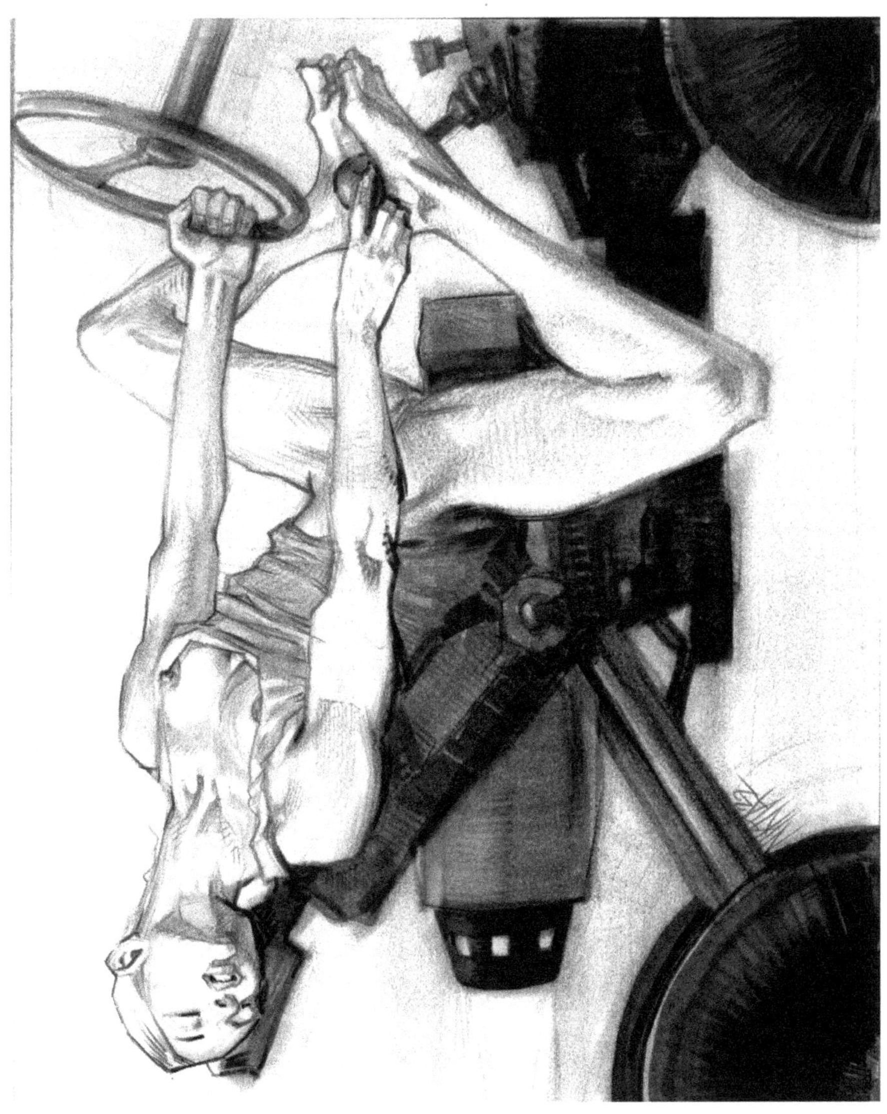

SHOWER

There was a young girl they called Flower
Who would stand upside down in the shower
But of course she forgot
That the Cold would be Hot
Which caused pain when turned to full power

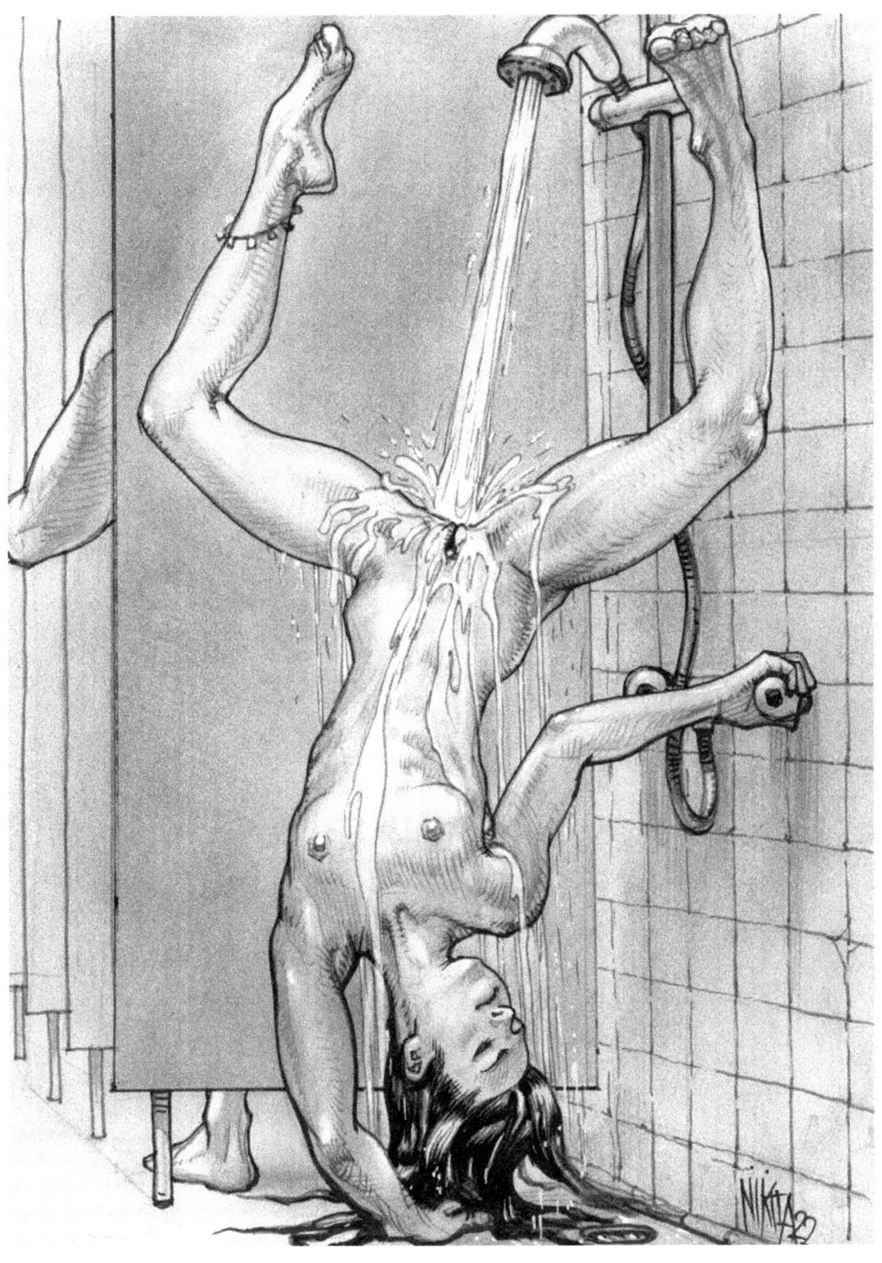
NIKITA

HAIR DRYER

There was a young lady called Cher
Who had really beautiful hair
And she could not care less
At the chaos and mess
As she blasted herself with hot air

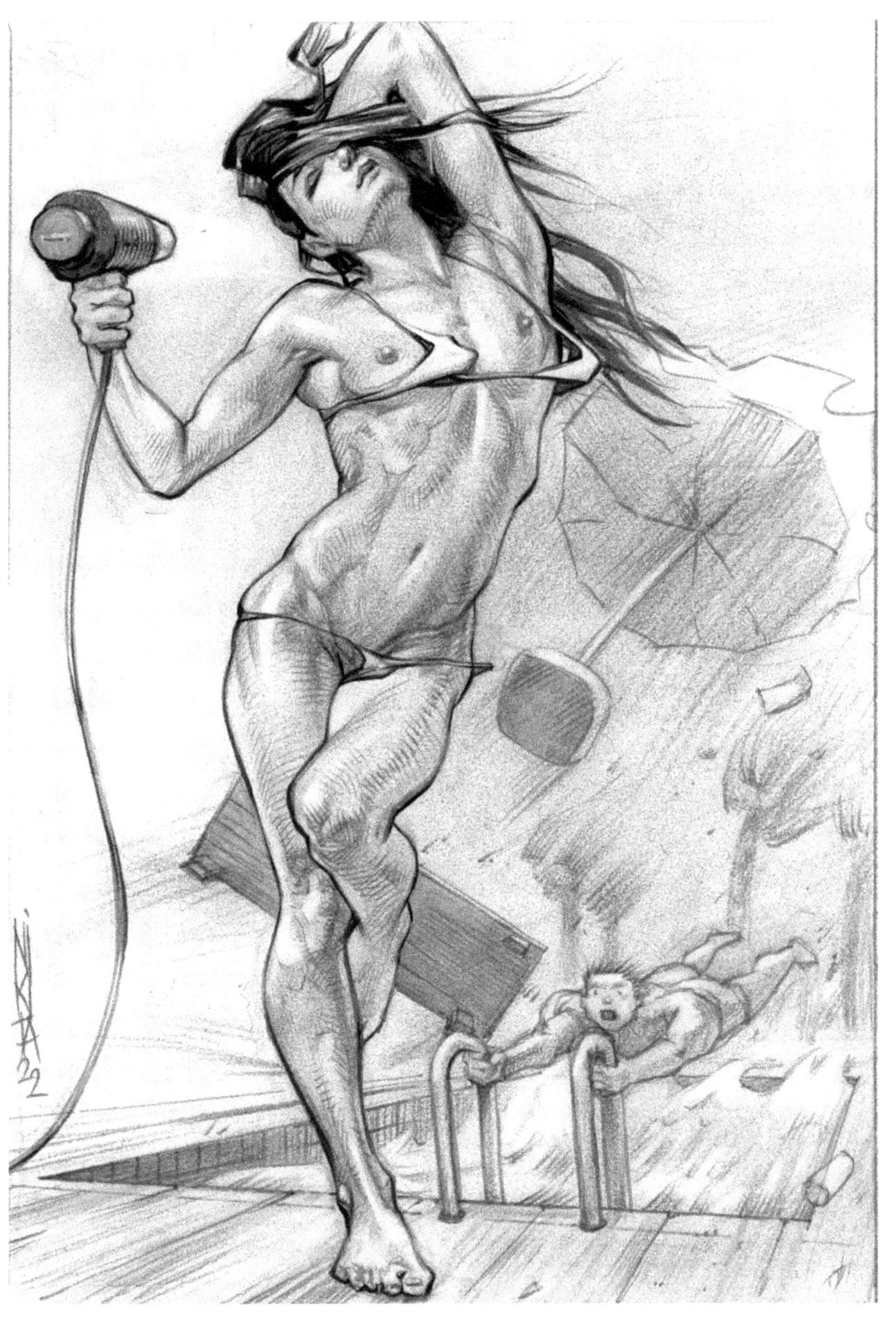

RACER

A young racer from the Oblast
Was quite incredibly fast
As she was no prude
She raced in the nude
So competitors never came past!

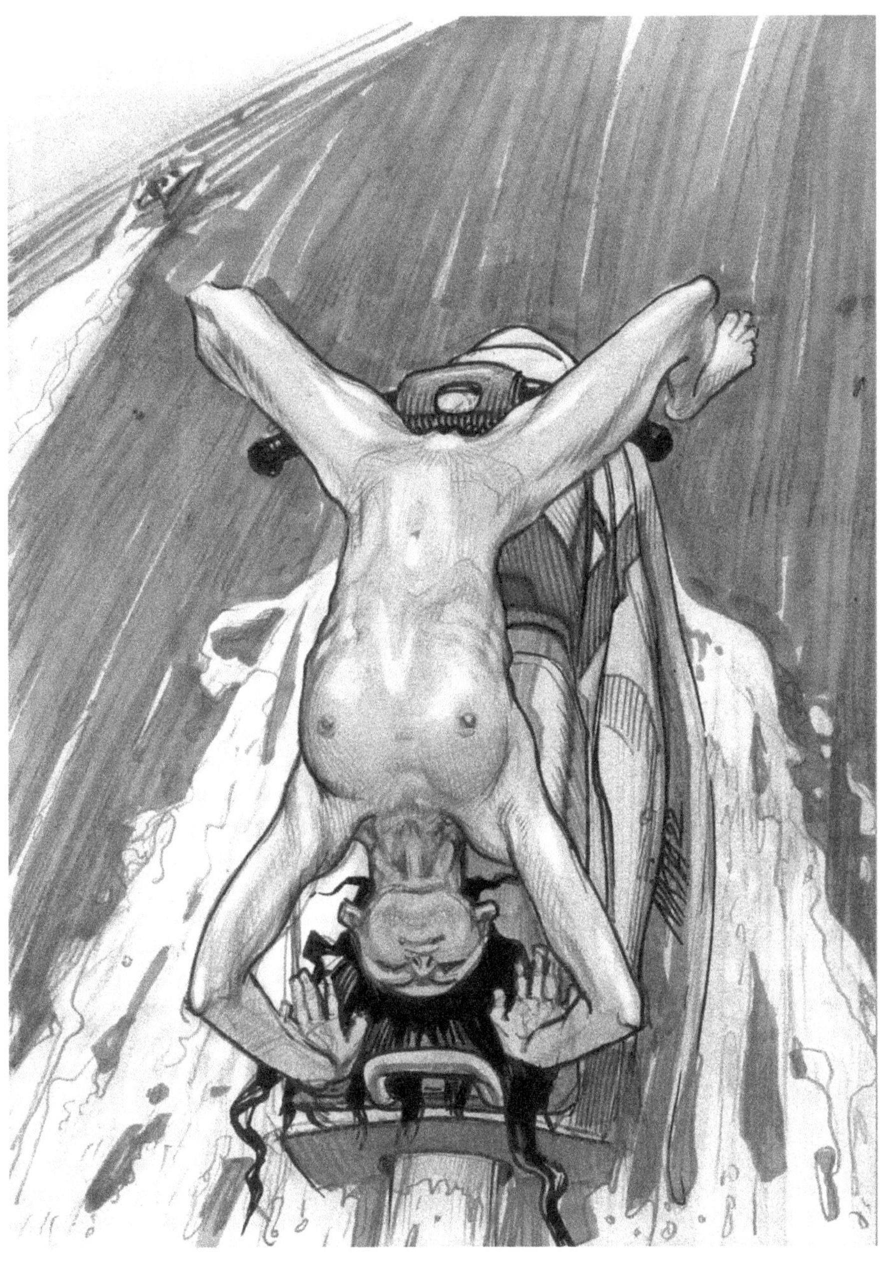

PROVOCATEUR

A young acrobat they called Jill
Always sought a new thrill
She cured her frustration
With twin masturbation
Knowing over-excitement could kill.

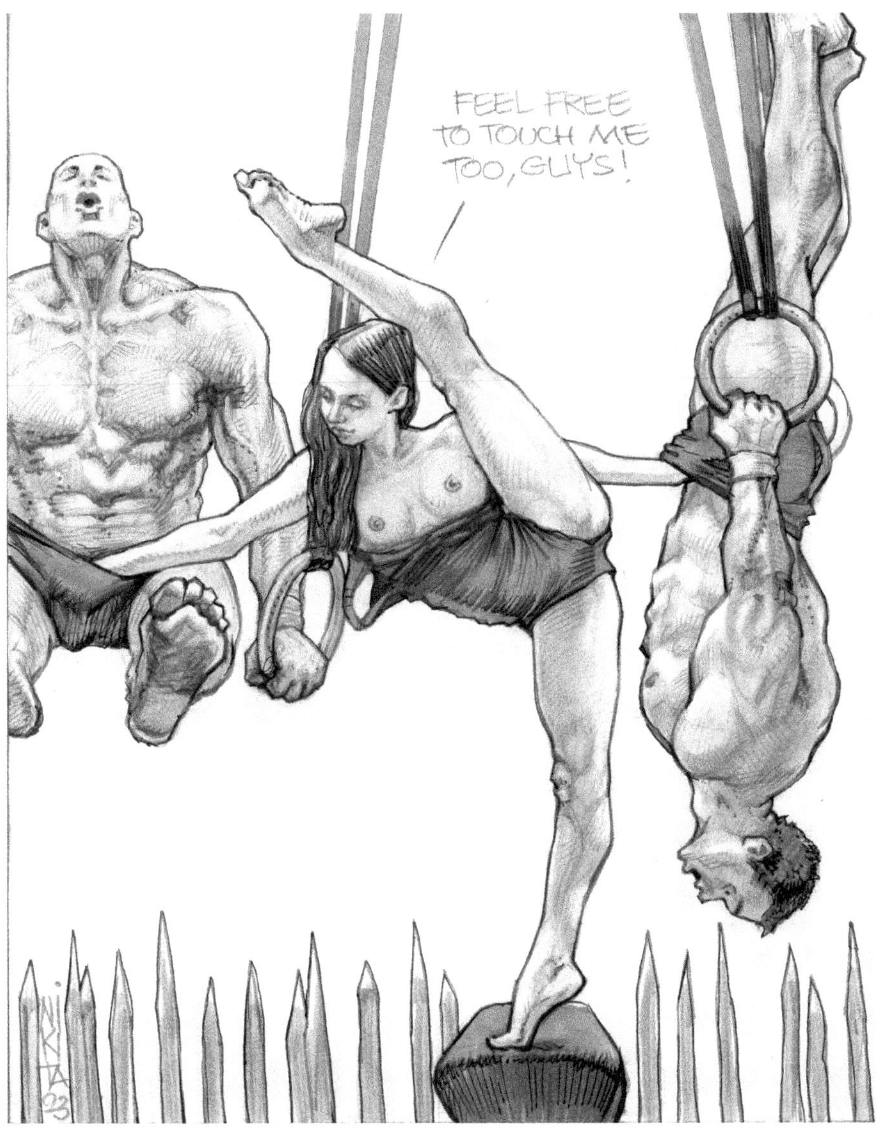
FEEL FREE
TO TOUCH ME
TOO, GUYS!
NIKITA
03

TICKETLESS

There was a young lady called Fi
Who really wanted to ski
But the ski-lift price
Was not very nice
So she daringly travelled for free.

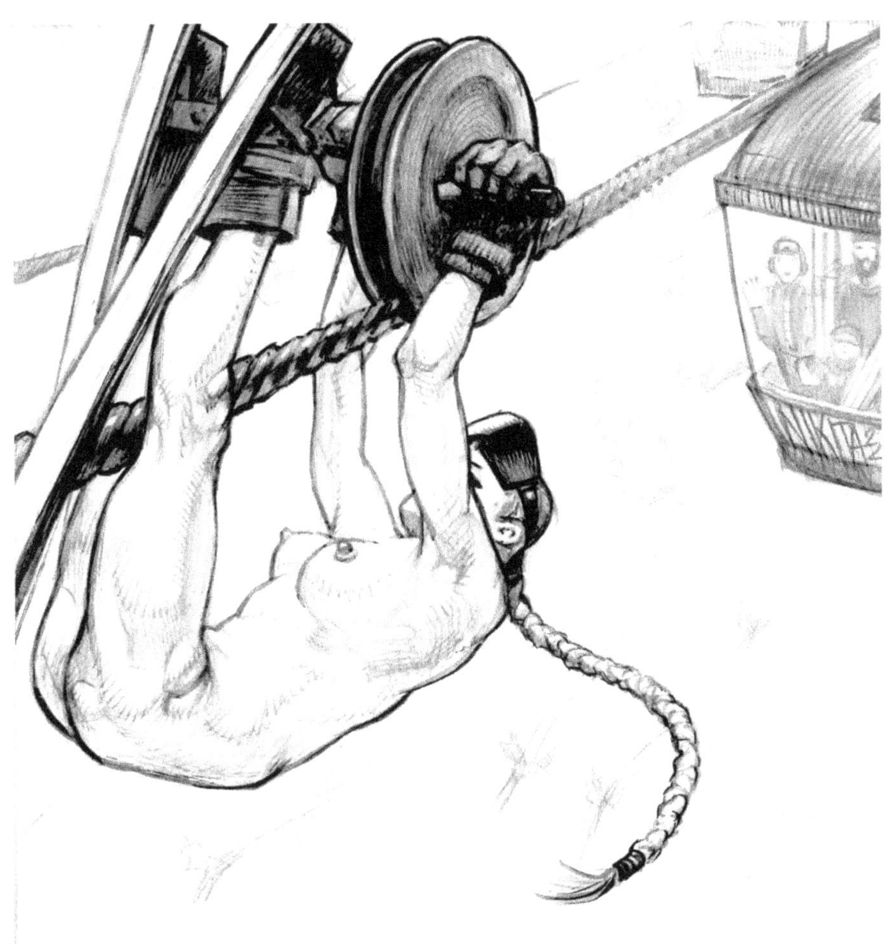

CHAMPION

Body thrusting
Bladder busting
Never missing
Bulls-eye hitting
Score-cards topping
Not for stopping
Not for kissing
Urine pissing
Panties downing
Champion crowning

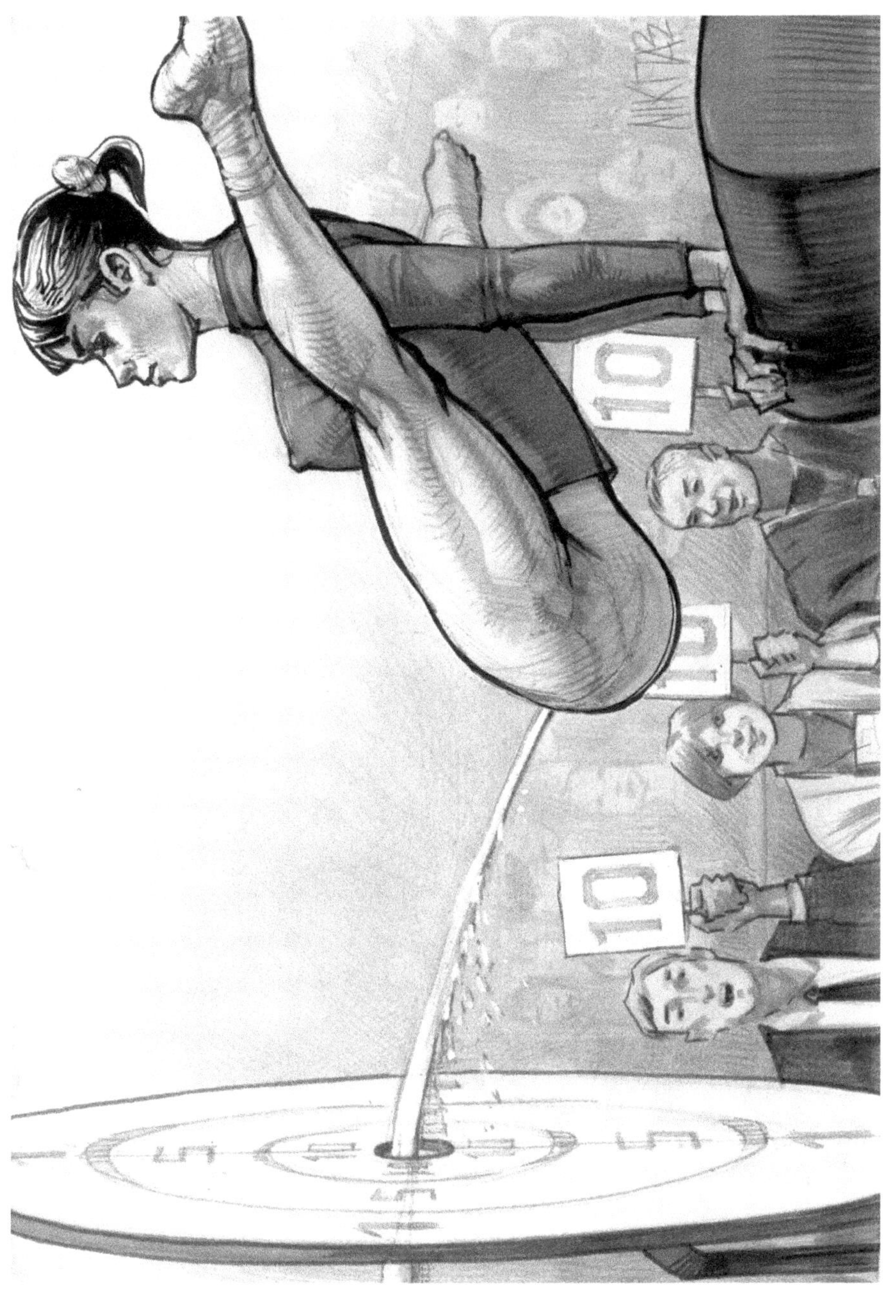
10
10
10

REFEREE

Declaring winners
Is done by raising an arm
Or another part

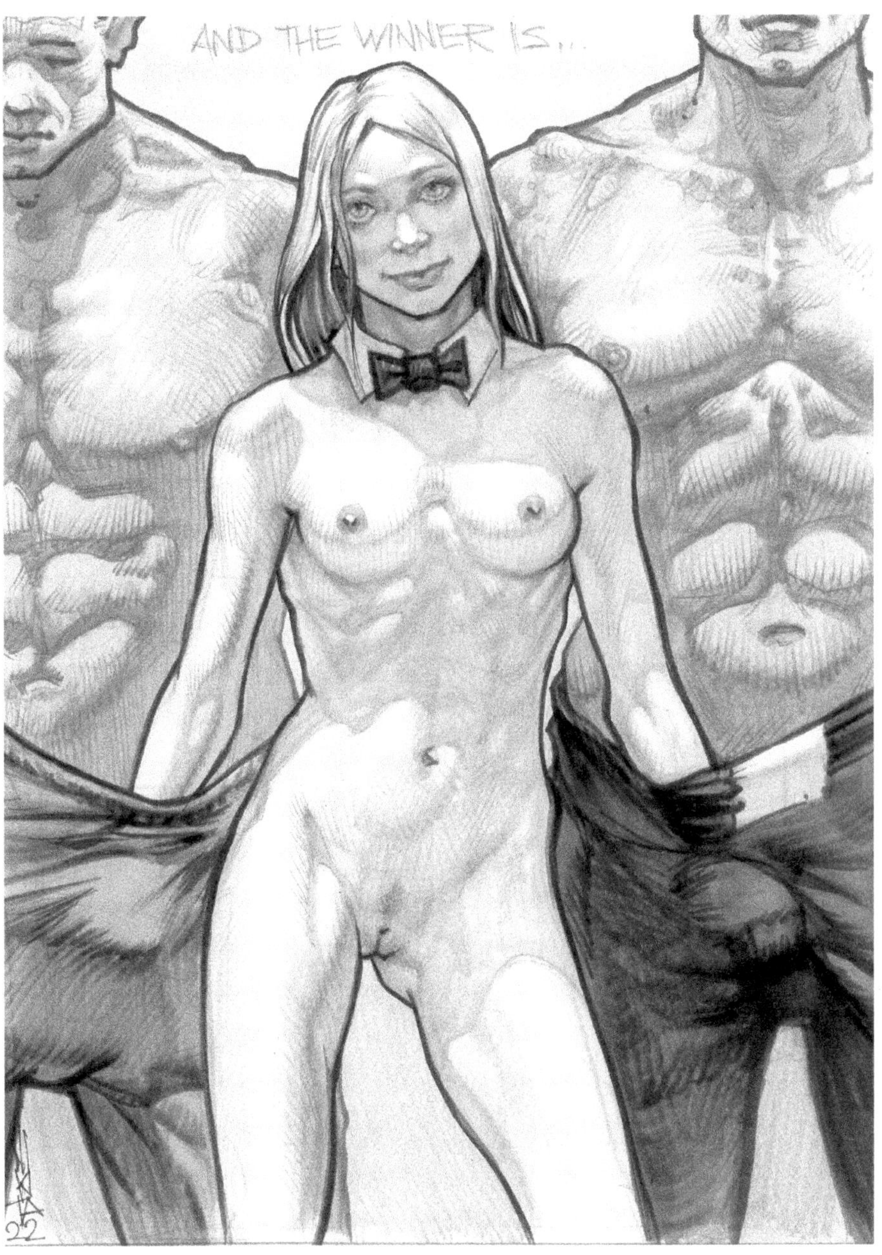
AND THE WINNER IS...

STREET BATHING

There was a young girl, most petite
Who suffered in summer from heat
So she took off her clothes
And turned on the hose
Then lay down with her bear in the street

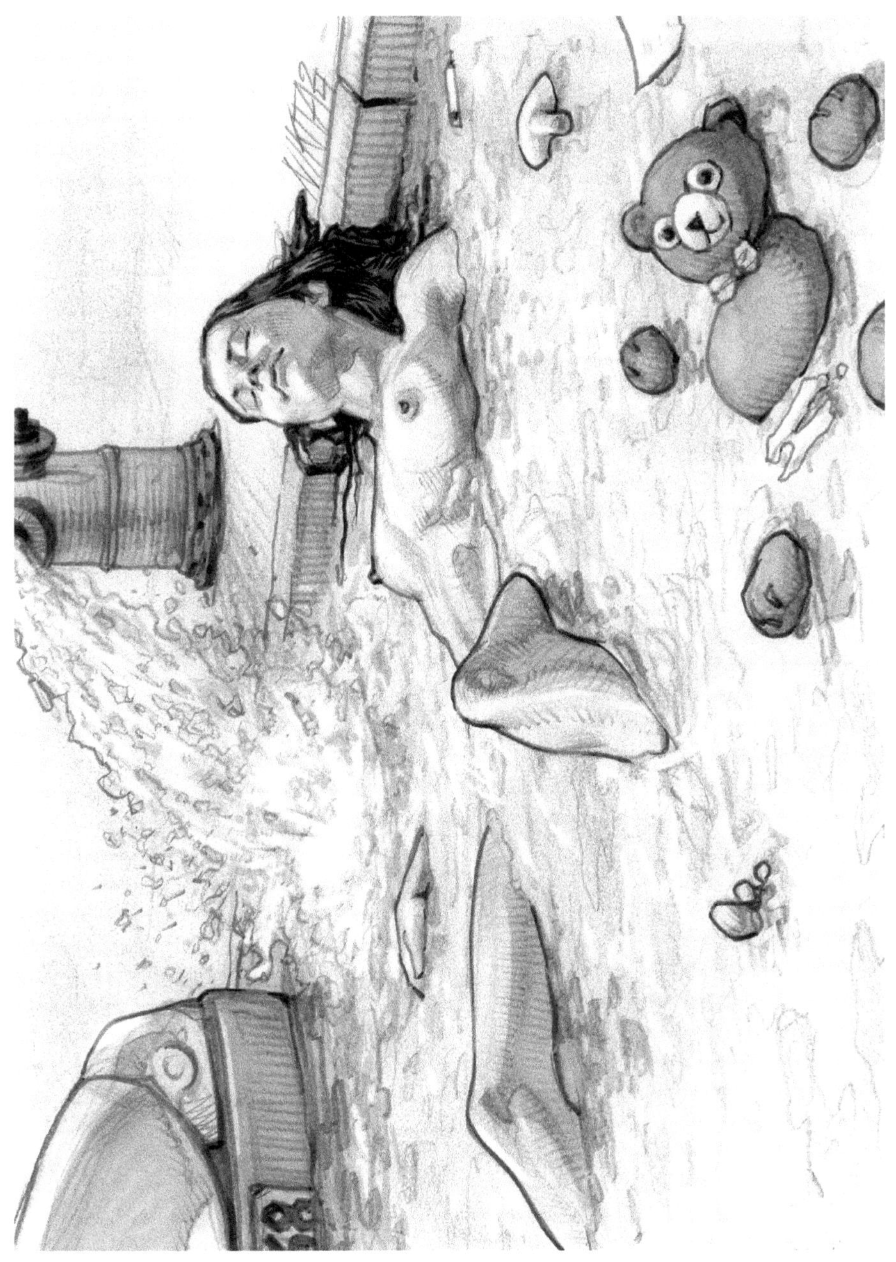

FUNAMBULIST

There was a young girl called Louise
Who tight-roped and worked the trapeze
When she showed off her tits
Her fans loved it to bits
So she went for a total striptease

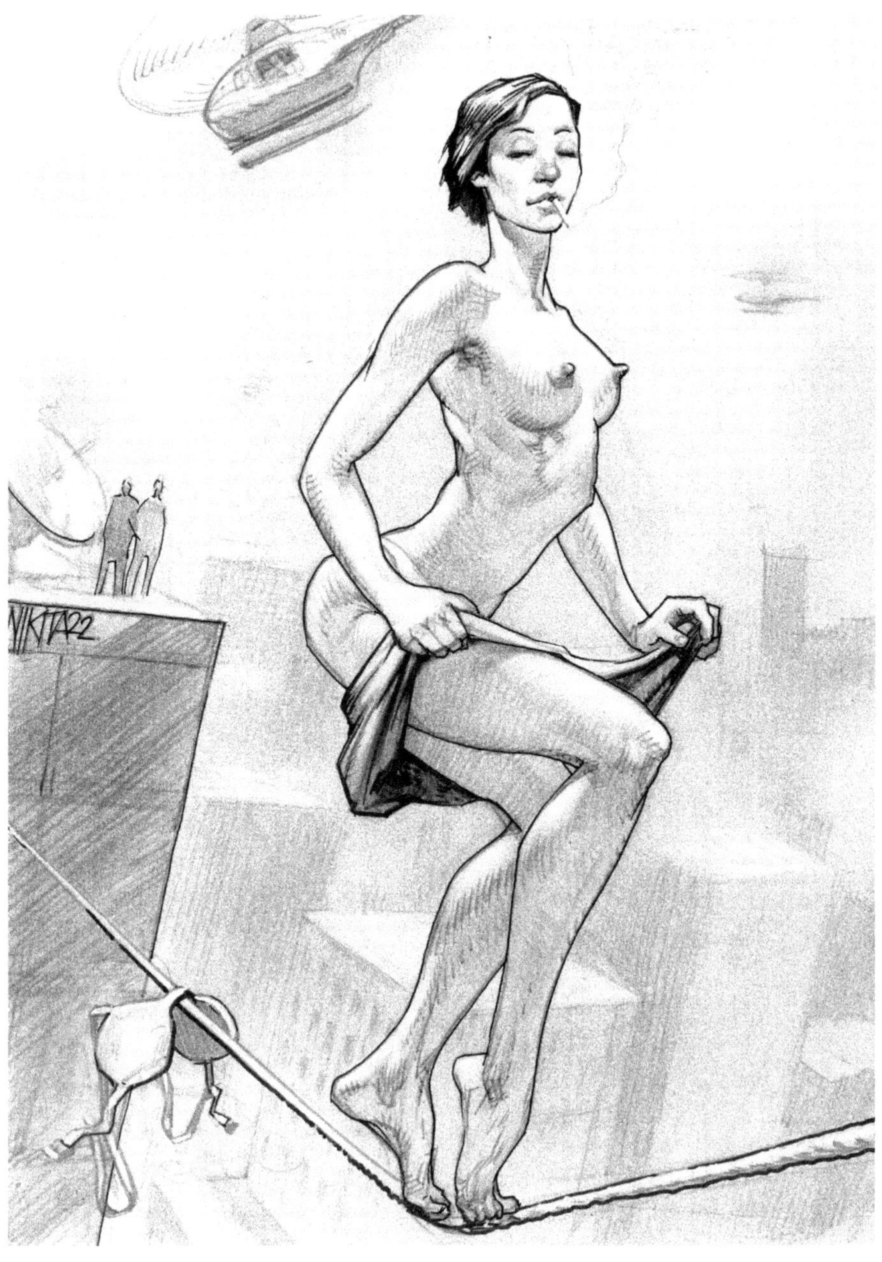

SKY DIVERS

Chute is entangled
Enticing bare bum exposed
His hand will sort both.

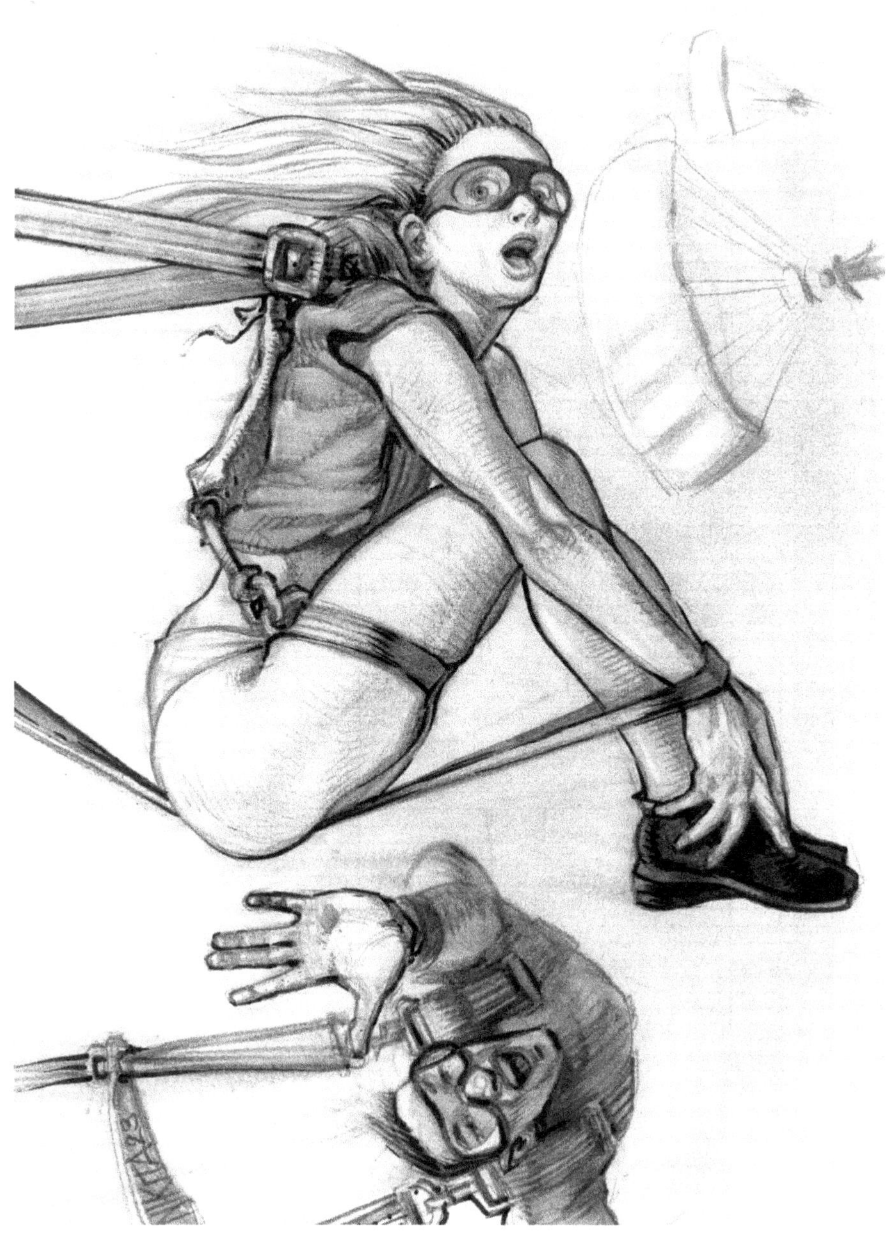

GOALKEEPER

It is not just balls
Although to properly
Keep to your task
Of attaining your goals
You will need some.
Goals should be kept
Not so much in public
For that leads to
Self-aggrandisement
But quietly and without fuss
As befits a goalkeeper
With or without balls.

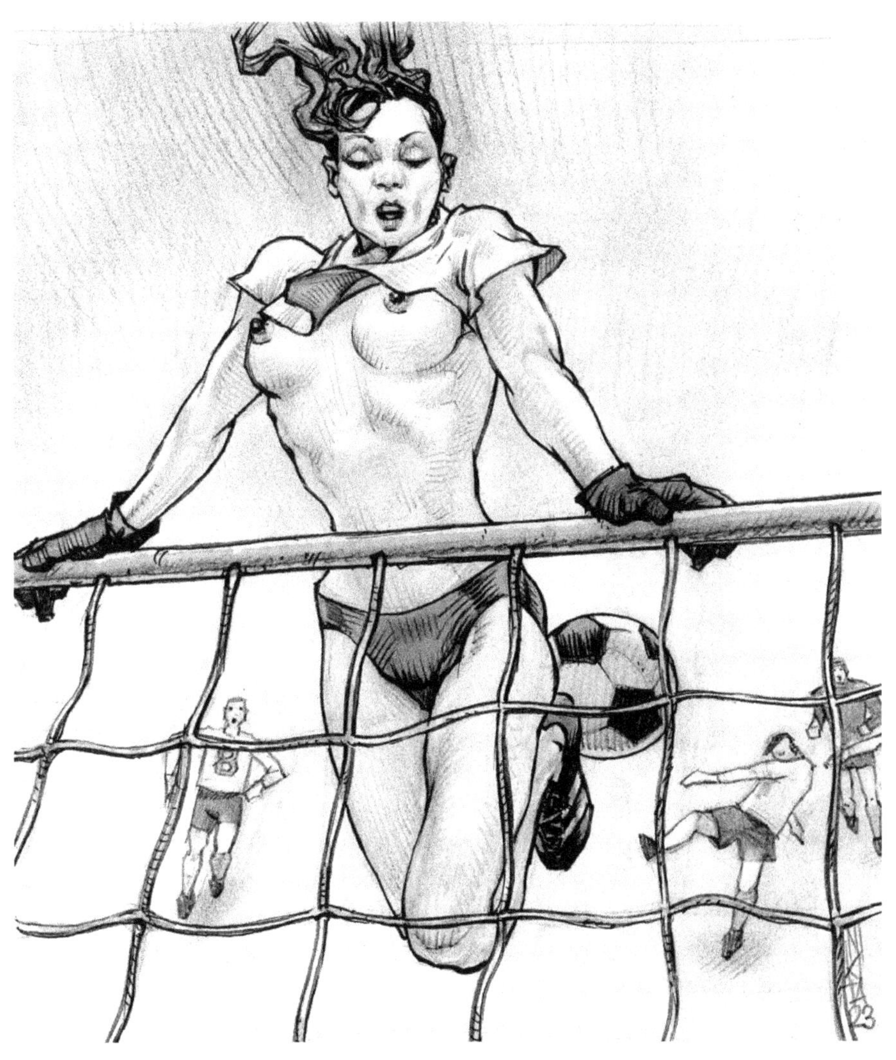

8

FAIRIES

There are people who say, very convincingly,
That because they have never seen a fairy,
It's obvious that they don't exit
Well, to them fairies don't exist,
because to see them you must believe in them
That is not so stupid really
It is a matter of having faith
Most of the world's religions are built on faith!

FAIRY

There is a small part of me
That has always believed in fairies.
Well not so much believe,
From which you might infer
A degree of faith,
But rather just wholeheartedly
Acknowledge existence of.
Not to do so
Would be to close off
A large part of
That elusive area of the mind
That lies between
Dreaming and imagining.
There are tales about bad fairies,
Hobgoblins, gremlins and the like
But my fairies
That is the fairies that come to me,
Are good
And beautiful
And. kind.
If you come outside with me
On a summer's evening
And sit beside me
On a grassy bank
And watch the fireflies
Flitting amongst the cumquat
Then, in the corner of your eye,
You might catch a glimpse
Of something ethereal.
See! I told you so!

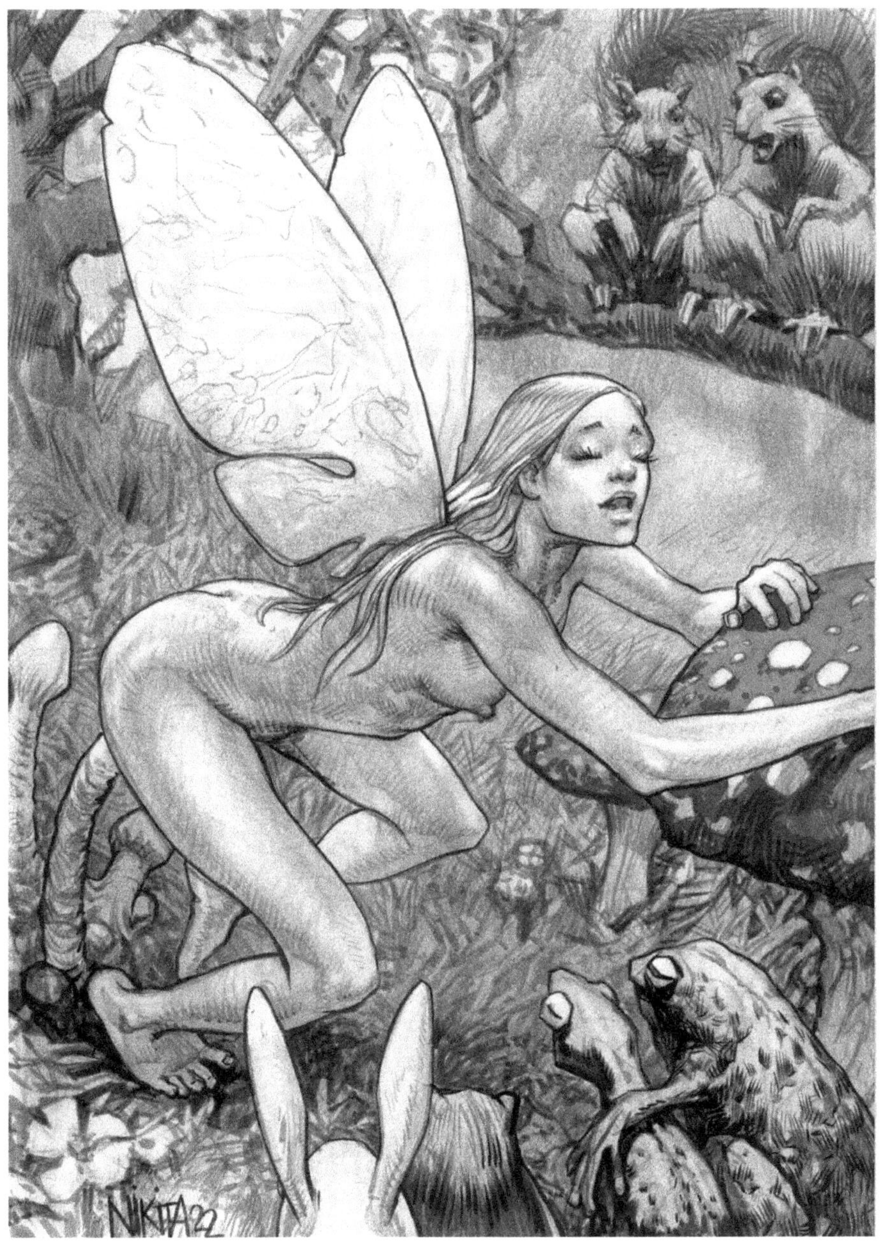
NIKITA22

GARDEN FAIRY

Of all the fairy's that I've met
(And I have met quite a few)
None are fairer fairies than
The fairest fairy, that's you!

You are the sort of fairy,
The Common or Garden kind,
That attracts all men like circling moths
And sends them out of their mind

You use sprinklers a lot for cooling
When bits of you get too hot
But first you take all your clothes off
Which tends to help a lot

So princess, fairy, temptress,
Whosoever you are
You really are quite gorgeous
So please don't fly too far

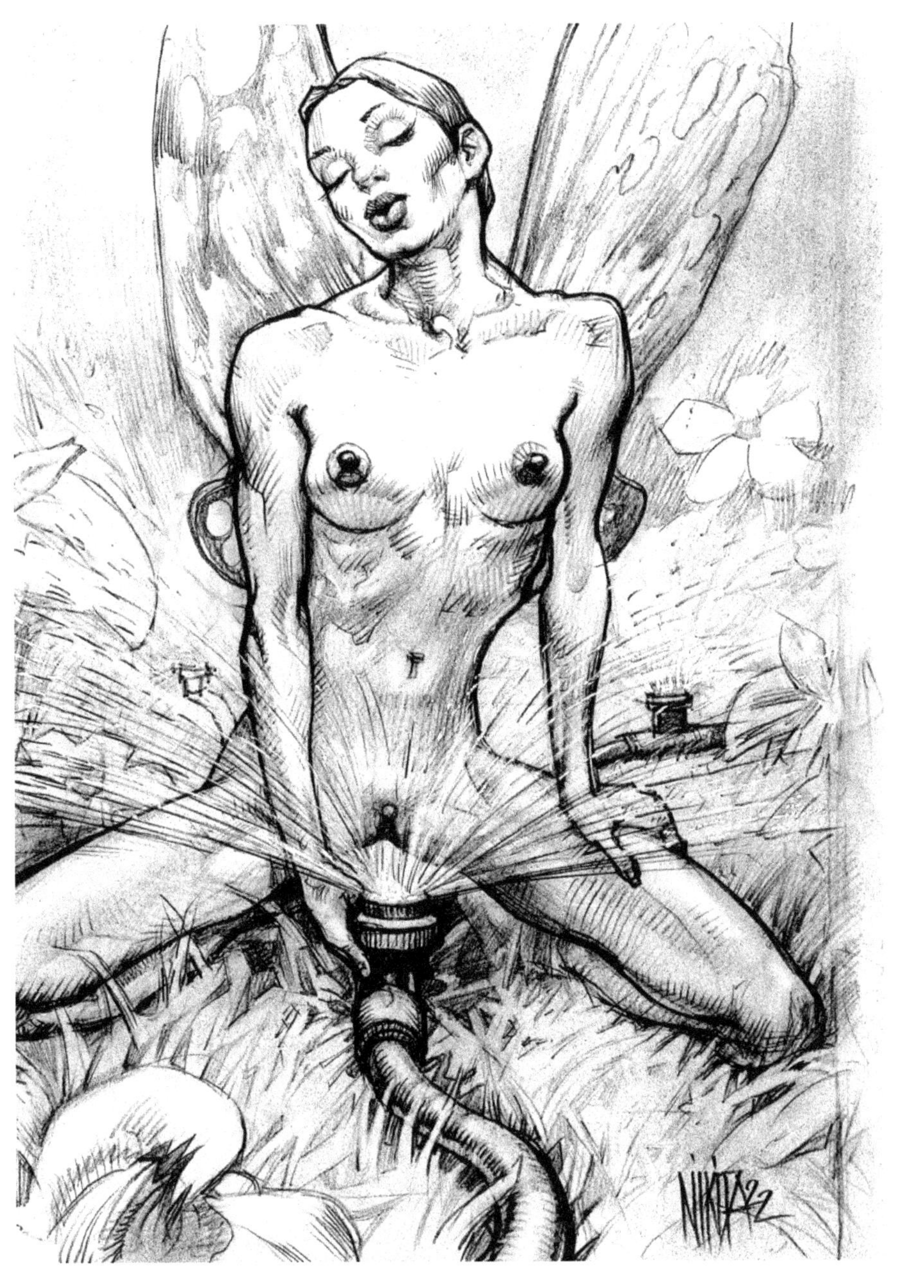

HOLLOW

This is a warning to those who might stray
Down to the woods on a lovely day
For whilst you are taking a gentle stroll
Those pesky squirrels will look for a hole
This means that to you they could pose quite a threat
For likely as not a trap will be set
And you'll find yourself hanging upside down
With your toes in the air and your head on the ground

But the squirrels' interest lies in between:
In a part of your body that rarely is seen.
Their singular interest is to explore
Your body cavities to make a store

So don't despair, you'll be quite all right
As long as your orifice stays small and tight.

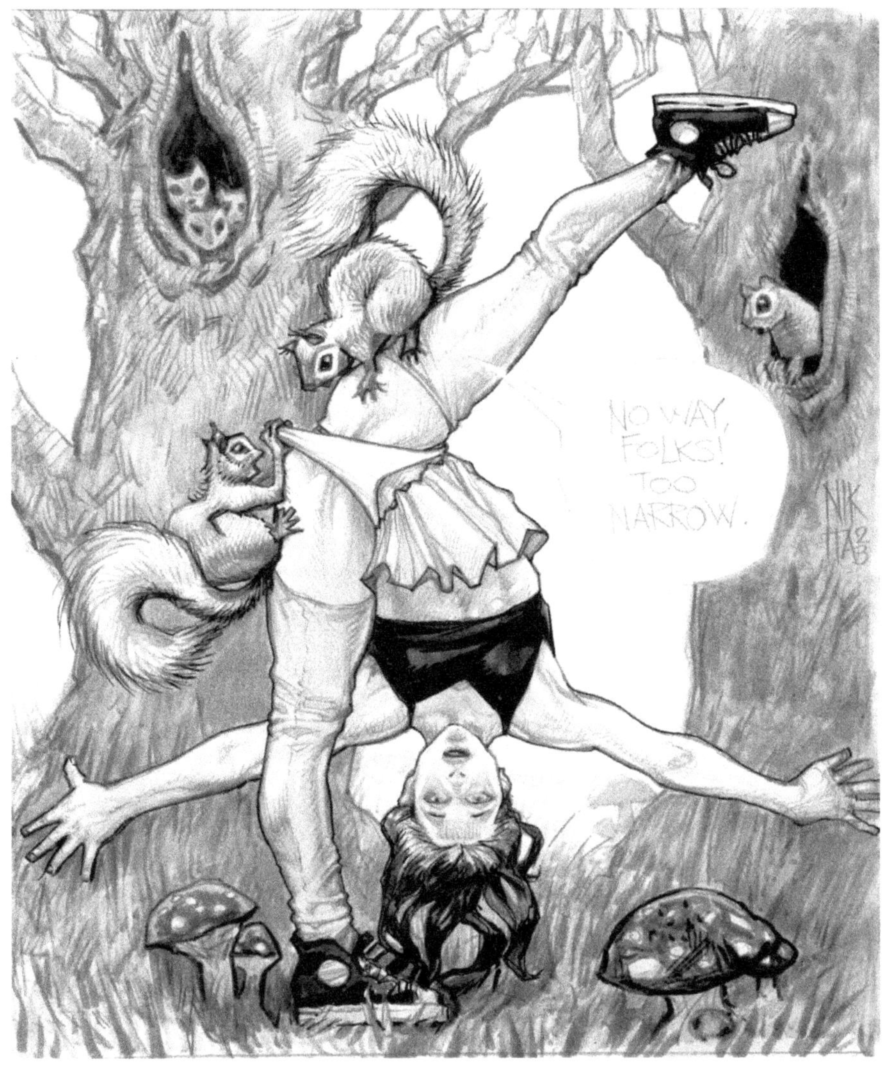
NO WAY, FOLKS! TOO NARROW.
NIK TA

INK BEE

She lives
In the pen of every writer
In the brush of every artist
Like the very smallest
Of gremlins, and
Very nearly as mischievous.
When words tumble out
In the wrong order
When shading is applied
To the opposite side
You can be sure that
She has clapped
Her hands to
Summon such peccadilloes
And that even now she is
Performing somersaults
In celebration of her
Naughtiness.
To appease the Ink Bee
Writers pen sweet words
And artists employ
Paint containing honey.
For although she is
Gorgeous and amusing
Be warned that
Just occasionally
Her sting can prove
Fatal

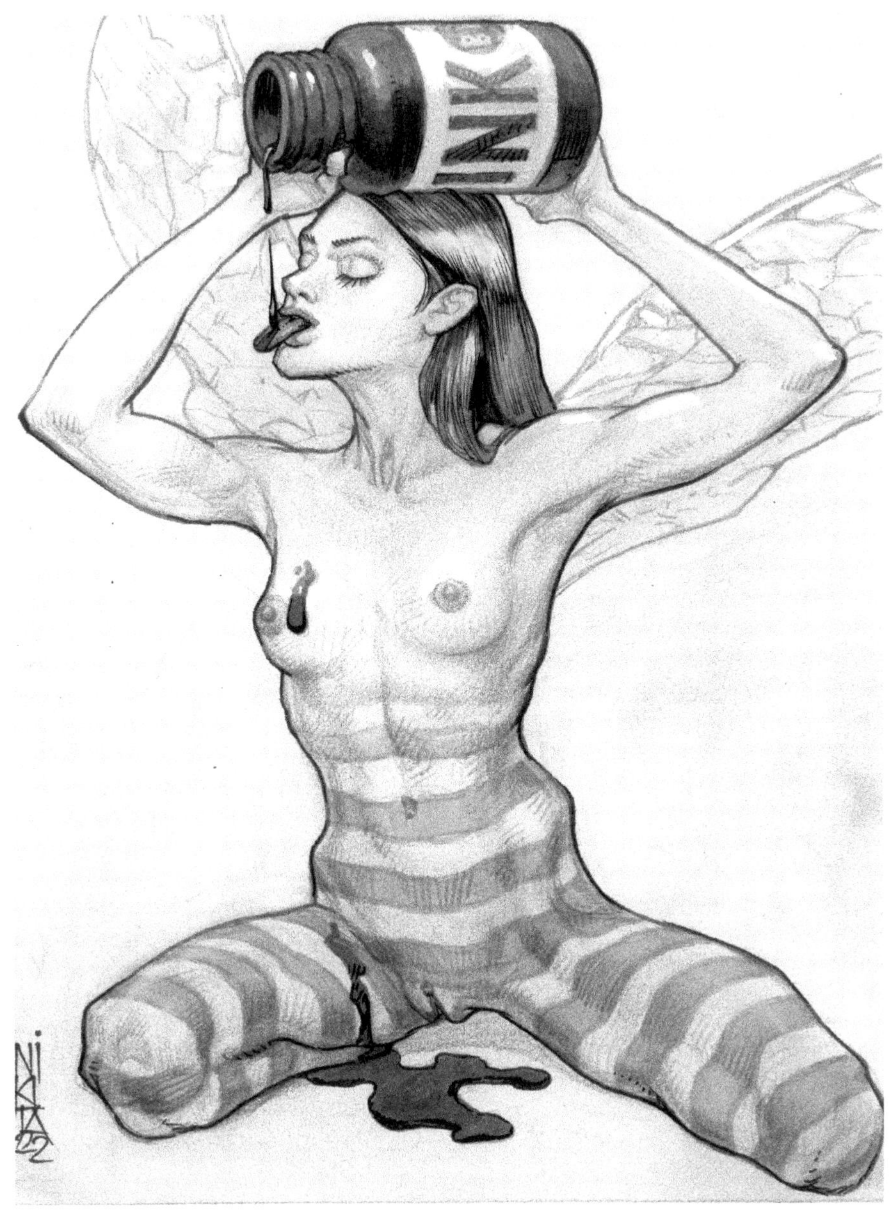
INK

9

PINOCCHIO

Since his inception Pinocchio has been copied
and reinvented countless times in books and in films
There are all sorts of stories about him, the only certain
elements are that he is made of wood
and has a nose that gets longer whenever he tells a lie.
Our interpretation of this international symbol
may seem a bit far-fetched - but for goodness sake
so is the concept of an animated puppet!

PINOCCHIO

"Oh My God".
That could mean "No"
Or it could mean
"Wow Pinocchio!"
It's her instant reaction
to his wooden erection
But can he assume
It's a happy expression?
Will she say she's been assaulted,
Raped, exposed and attacked
Or is she frightened of the splinters
If a certain member cracked.
The situation is confusing
For our poor Pinocchio
Does OMG mean she wants him
Or will she say that she meant No
And for many a man
It is confusing too
When the signals are mixed
What on earth should you do?
The only advice
I can give for certain
Is 'consult your lawyer
Before insertion'.

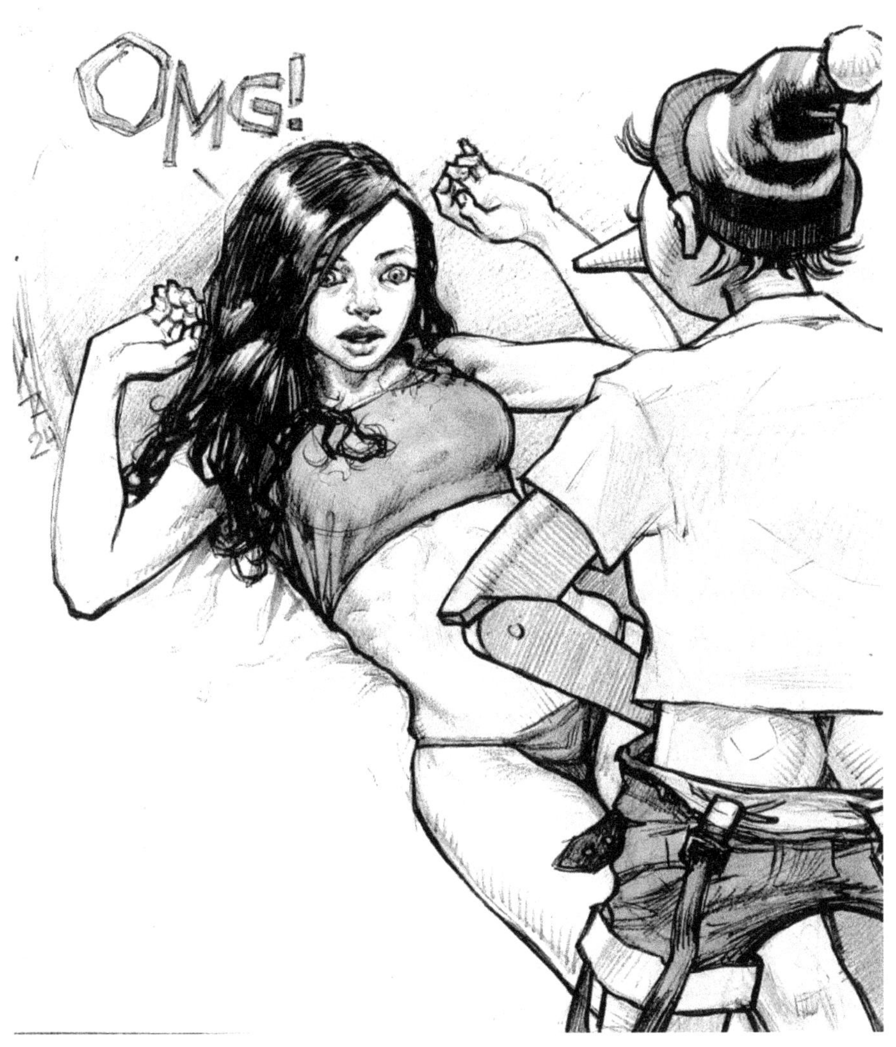
OMG!

PINOCCHIO'S NOSE

There was a young girl called Kate
For whom cunnilingus was great
 But Geppetto was alarmed
That she might be harmed
As Pinocchio's nose tempted fate

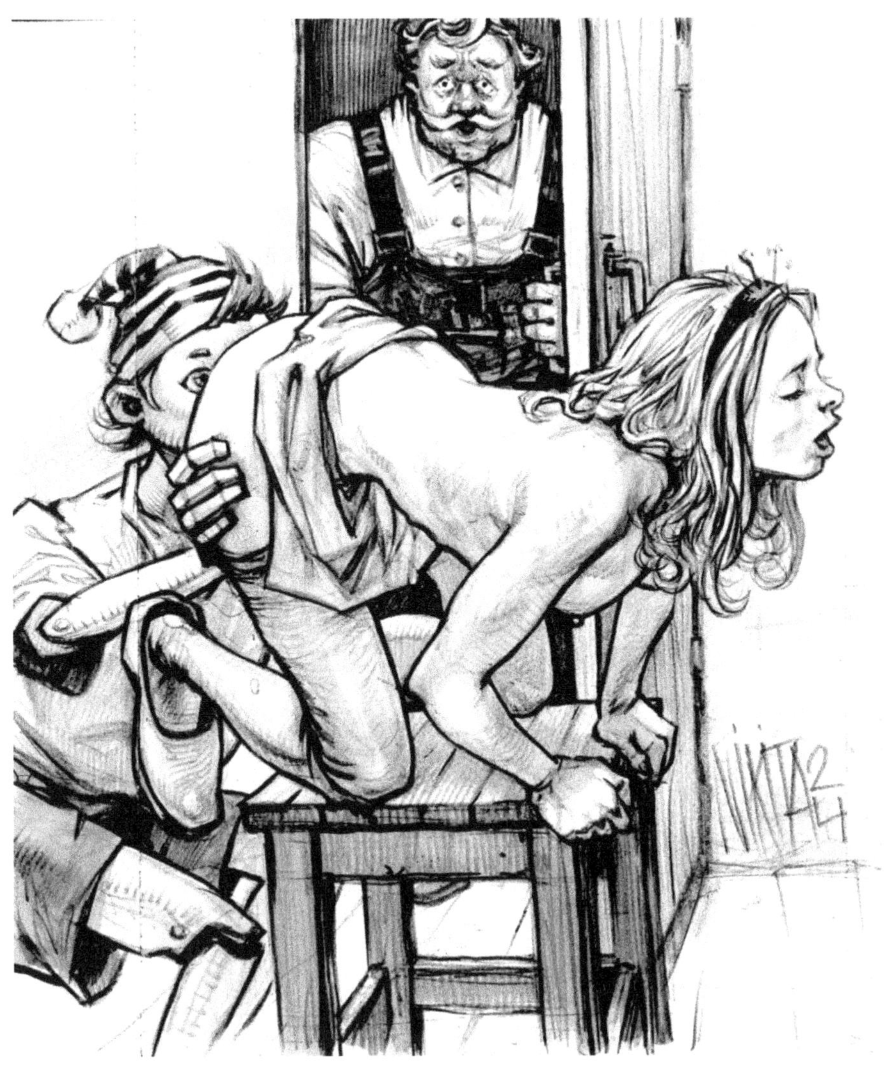

PINOCCHIO'S
FIRST CUCKOLDING

If his woman strays
It is not a disaster
Just bad for his nose

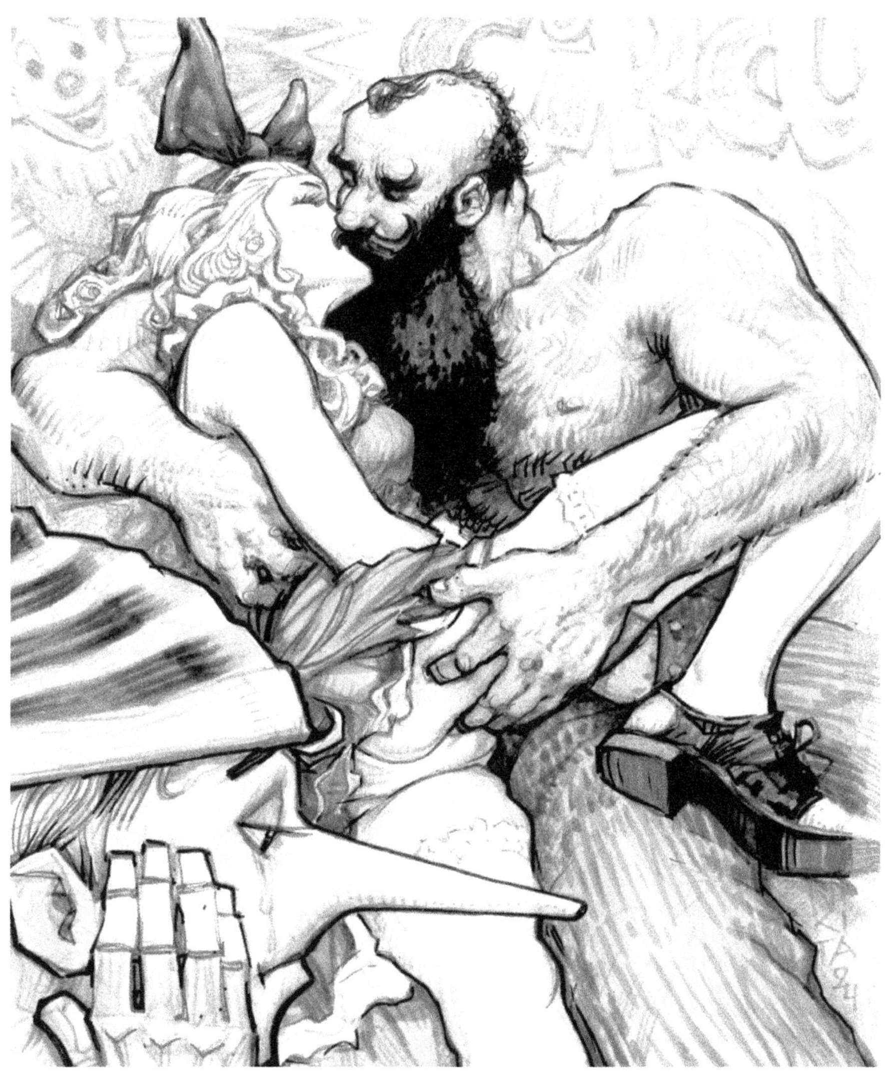

PINOCCHIO'S SECOND CUCKOLDING

Once was enough
For this sort of stuff
And yet they are at it anew
These two swarthy men
Have their way, and so then
Pinocchio 's a cuckold times two.

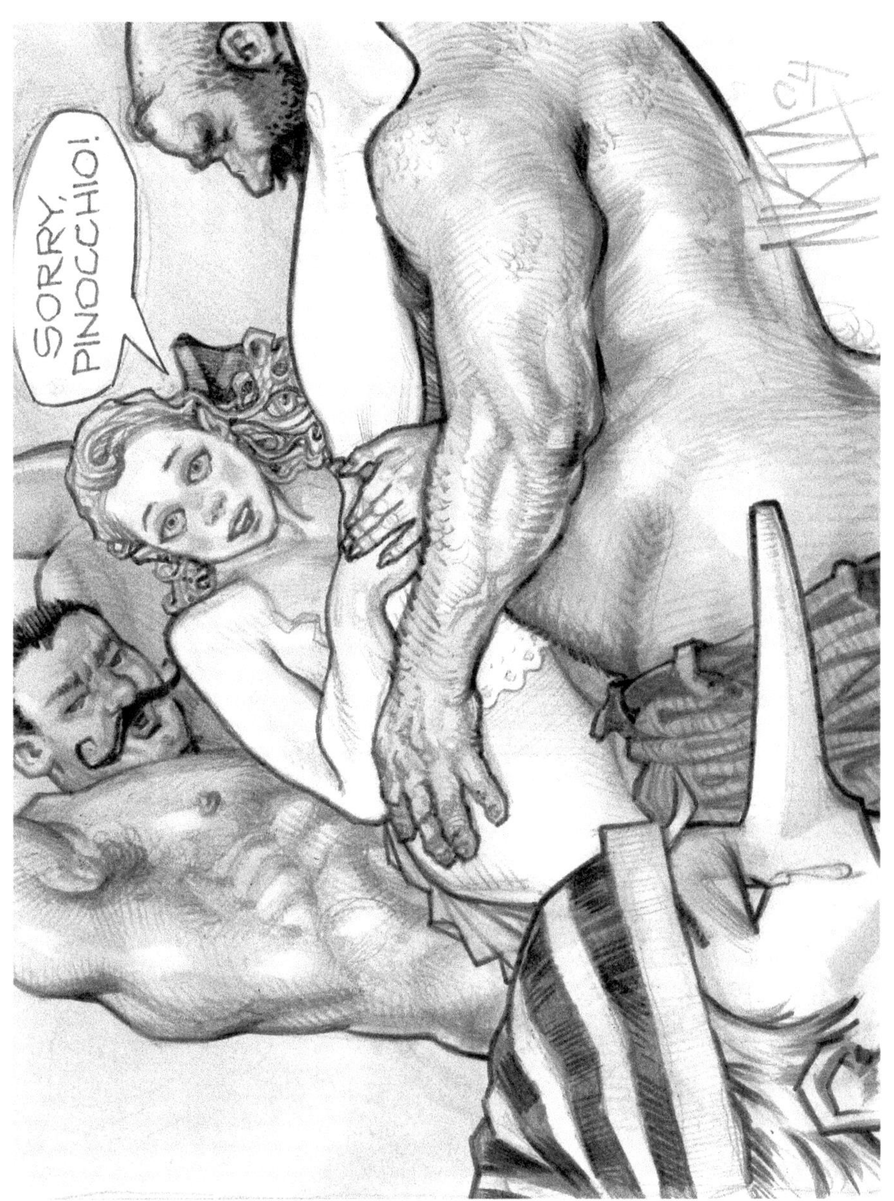
SORRY, PINOCCHIO!

10

THUMBELINA

Thumbelina is another character
who, although fictitious
we almost believe in as a living entity.
We have rather concentrated upon her
adventures with the toads. It will be helpful
to an understanding of the fair maiden if
the reader has a degree of empathy with toads!

THUMBELINA'S LEAF

It would be a bit silly
To sit on a lily
In this toad-infested water
As one of these creatures
With disgusting features
Wants you to be his new daughter.

His gormless young son
Wants to have lots of fun
With a gorgeous lady like you
With his knobbly face
And his clothes a disgrace
His positive features are few

If you stay on that leaf
It is my belief
That things will come to a head
There will come the sad time
When wedding bells chime
And you end up sharing his bed.

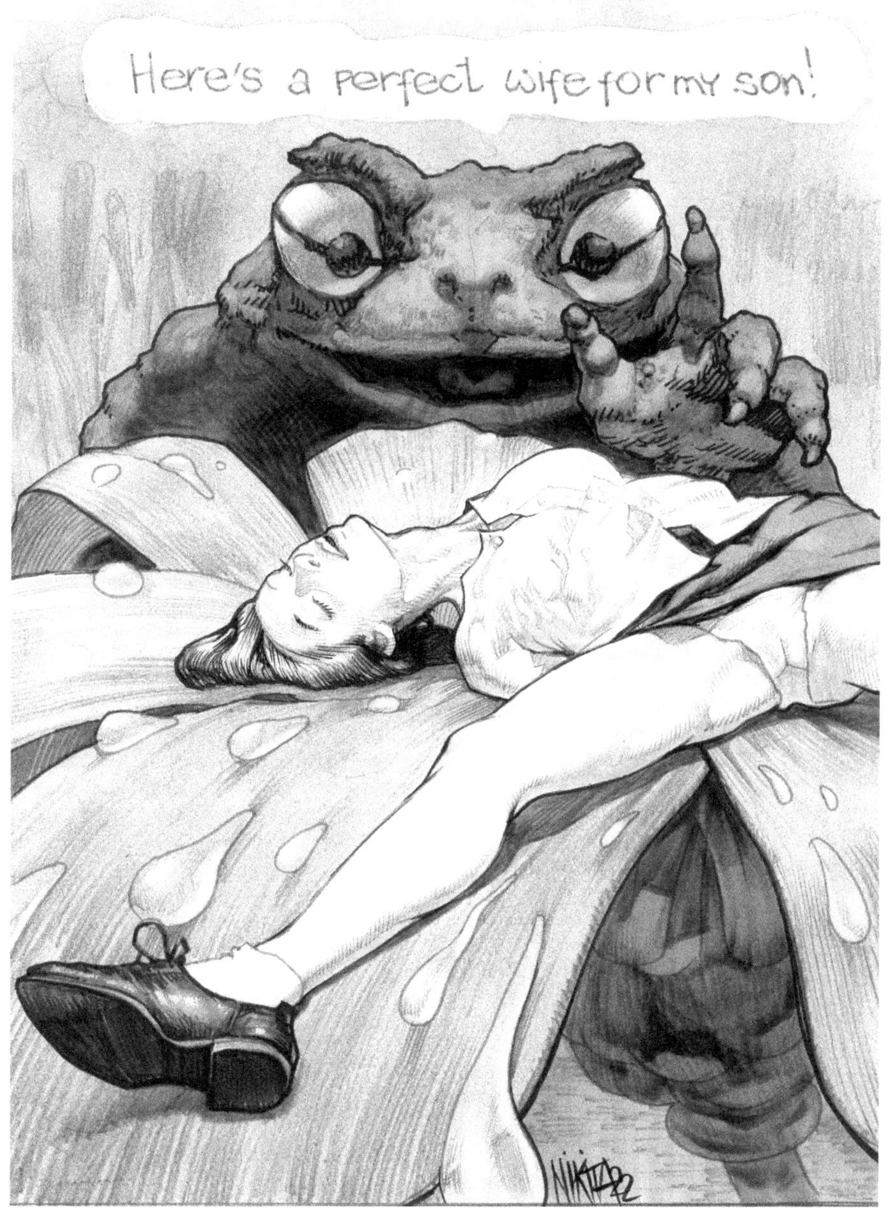
Here's a perfect wife for my son!

INVITATION

A strange young girl from Porthcawl
Partnered this toad to a Ball
For a do of that sort
Her skirt was too short
But the toad wore no clothes at all.

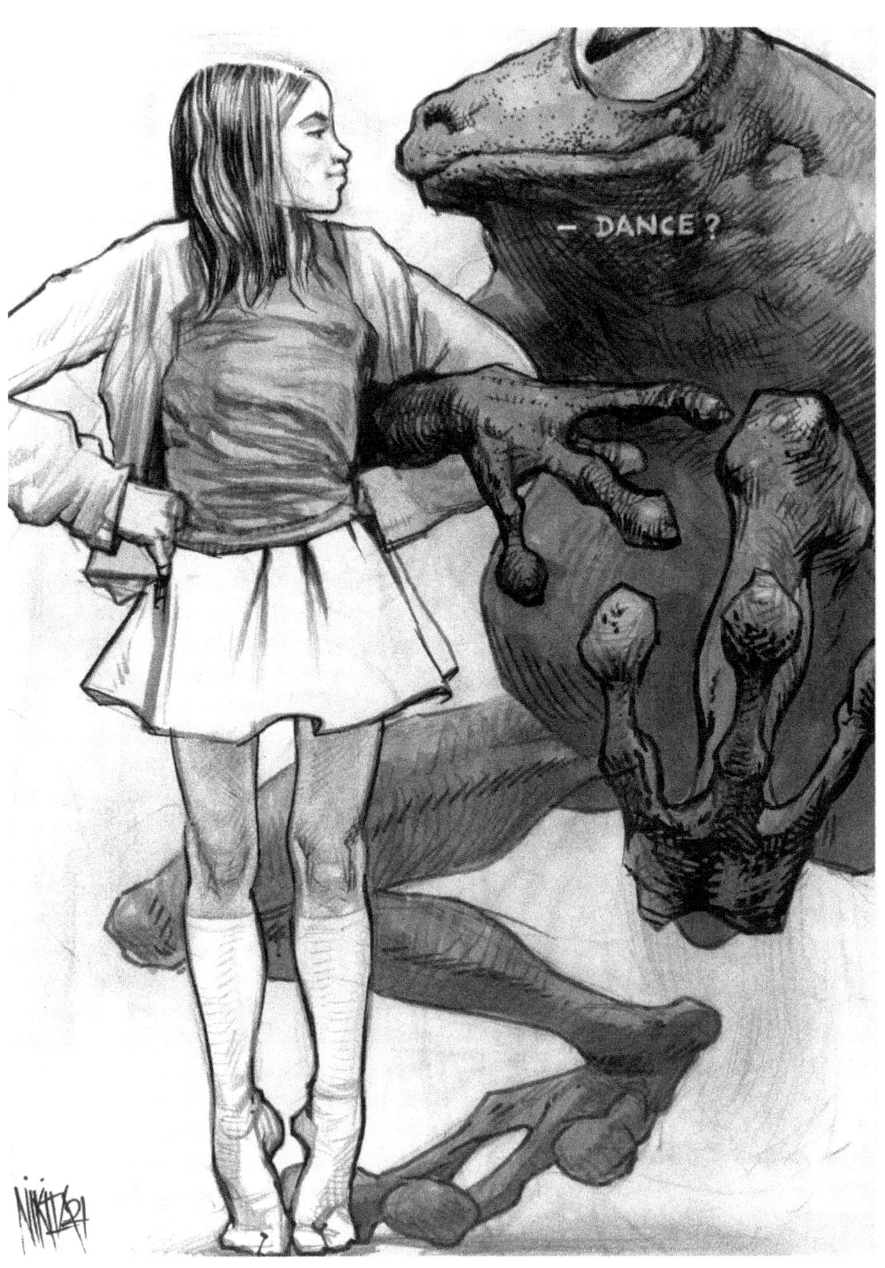
– DANCE ?

ENGAGEMENT

Savour the moment
Your swain produces the ring
Birds strip you naked
Beautiful bride for a day
Thereafter just a shag bag.

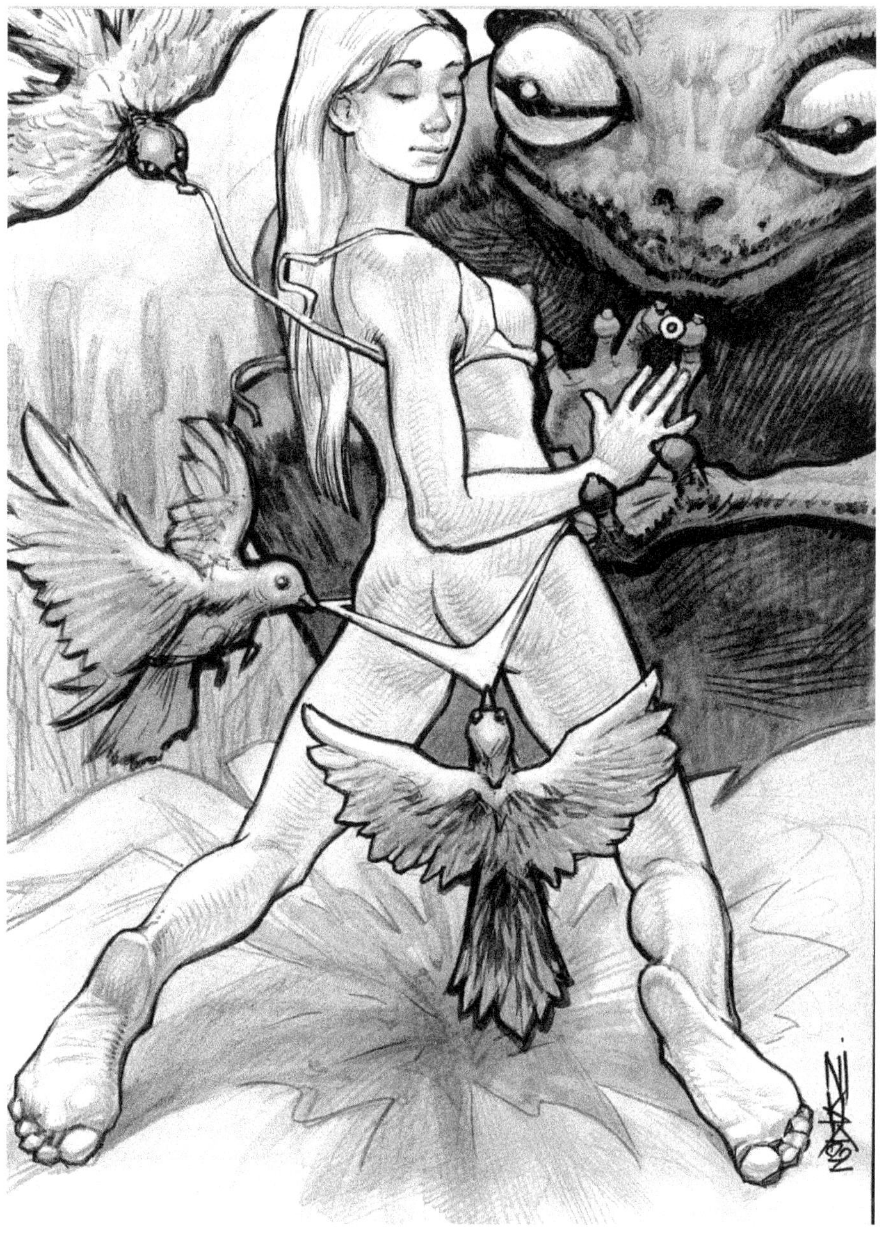

WEDDING NIGHT

Oh Thumbelina, Thumbelina,
What are you going to do
Your pulse is racing
Your toad is waiting
And everyone's come for the view

But Thumbelina, Thumbelina
Your wedding night won't rock
Because I fear
Something's missing here
For toads do not have a cock!

You see Thumbelina, Thumbelina
When toads are enjoying a date
He grabs from behind
And at the right time
Squirts sperm at the eggs of his mate

So Thumbelina, Thumbelina
Please forgive my heavy sarcasm
But you really must stop
Fucking him from on top
For there's no way you'll have an orgasm

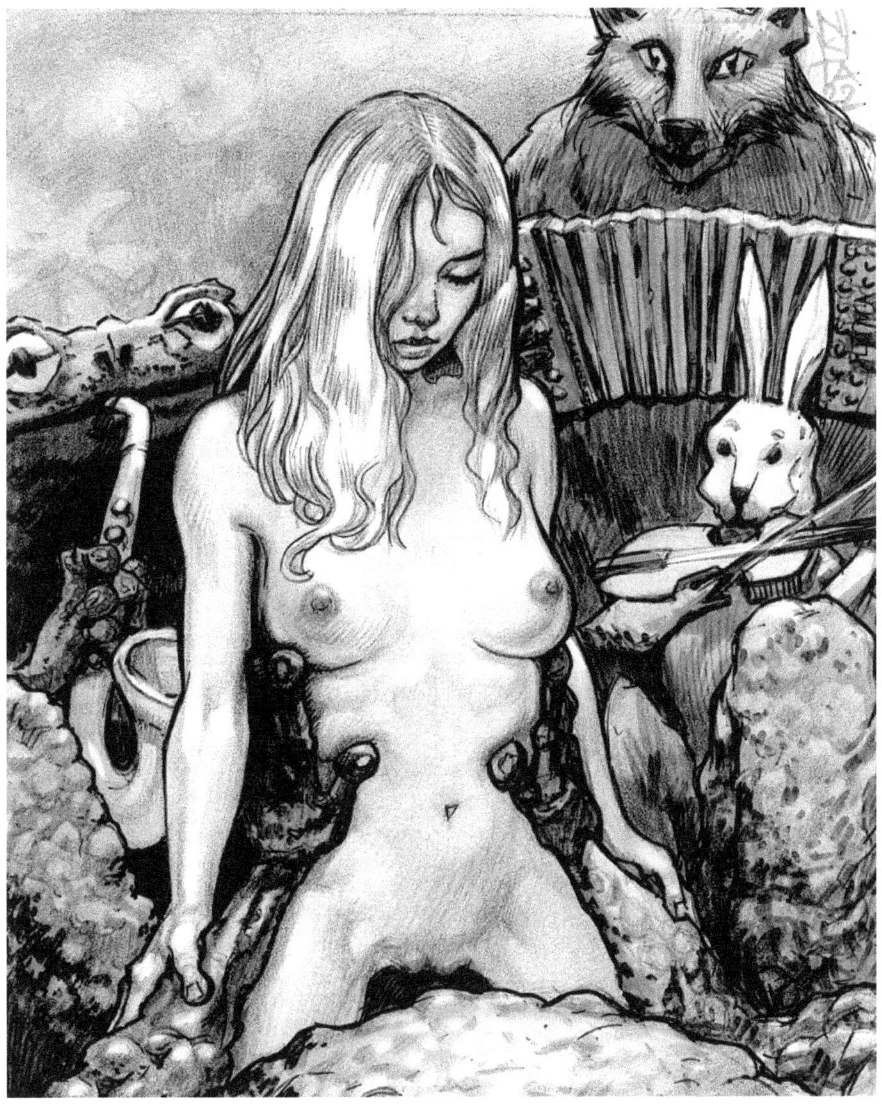

THUMBELINA DRUDGE

In these days when femicide
Is prevalent throughout the land
Women have to run and hide
Or wash and scrub the floor by hand

There's no relief from daily drudge
It's cook and wash clean
And if your supine male won't budge
It's because he's lazy and mean

So mop up his beer, stub out his cig
Bring him breakfast in bed
Make him think his libido is big
Because femicide means that you're dead.

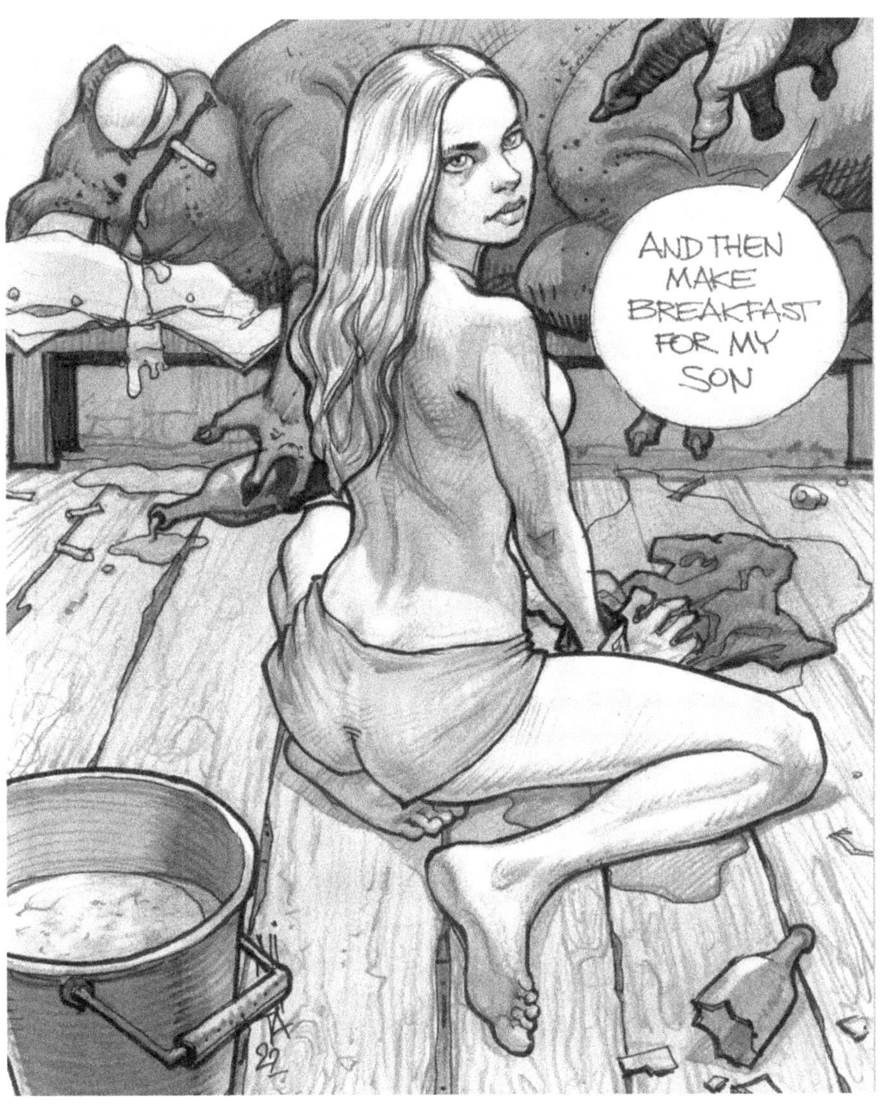
AND THEN
MAKE
BREAKFAST
FOR MY
SON

PROSTATE MASSAGE

Anal penetration
Is a subject most males rarely discuss
We like to pretend that in the end
It never happens to us

There's an unpleasant examination
For men with high PSA
That involves a doctor's fingers
In a somewhat intrusive way

Clearly Toad thinks he'll enjoy it
(He's a somewhat degenerate beast)
So instructs his friend to do his rear end
With long rubber gloves and some grease.

But as much as Toad may crave it
I am sorry to have to relate
That he won't get much stimulation
As toads do not have a prostate!

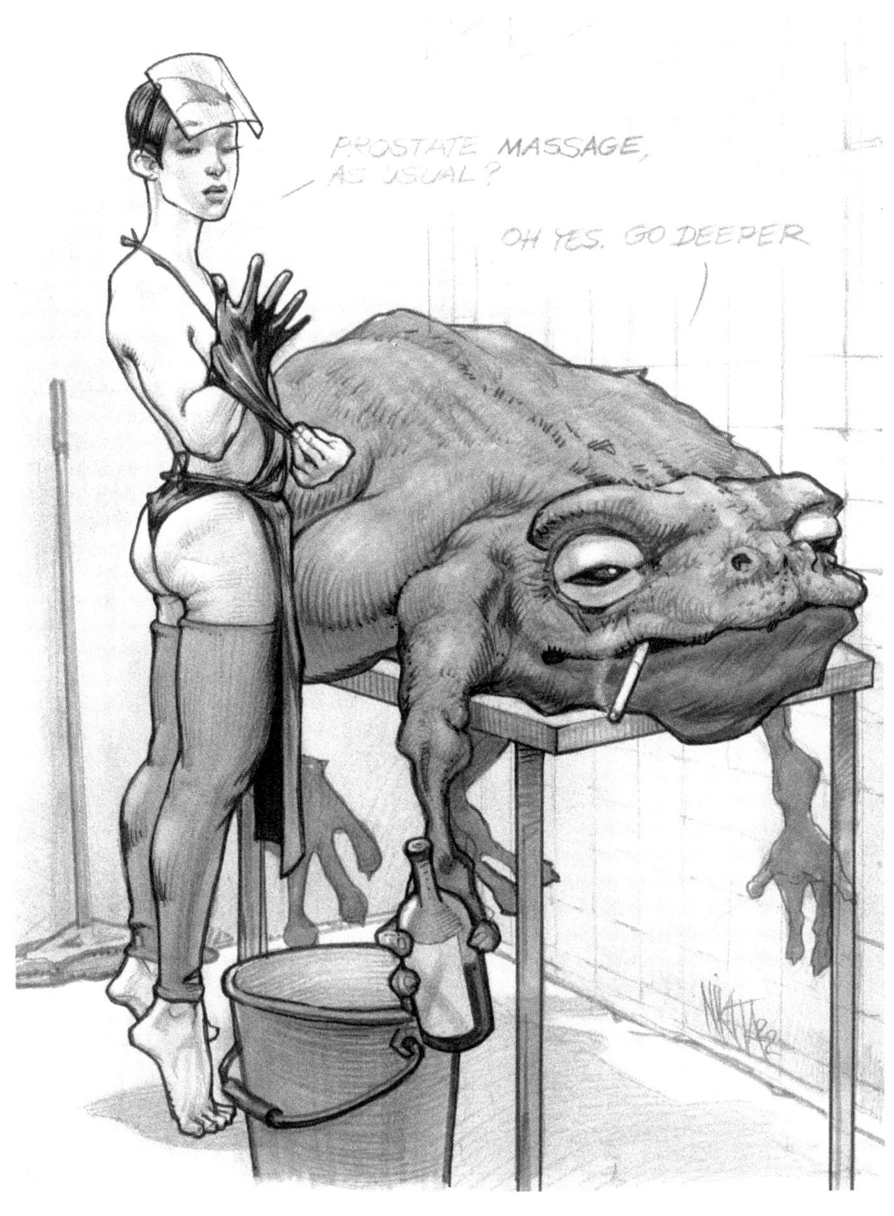
PROSTATE MASSAGE,
AS USUAL?
OH YES. GO DEEPER

11

TRAVEL

So many of us, when asked what we want to do,
say 'travel'. But what is this 'travel'. It can be jetting off
to somewhere warm where we are well fed,
provided with liberal quantities of alcohol,
and made very comfortable.
For the brave few it could be
thrashing through the Amazon jungle,
or stomping out in Antarctic blizzards.
For the more discerning it may well be
reclining at home and reading all about it -
such gentle fantasies are what we, and our
characters, will try to provide you with.

SMOKE BALLOON

Soaring in the sky
Peacefully puffing away
Corrupting her lungs

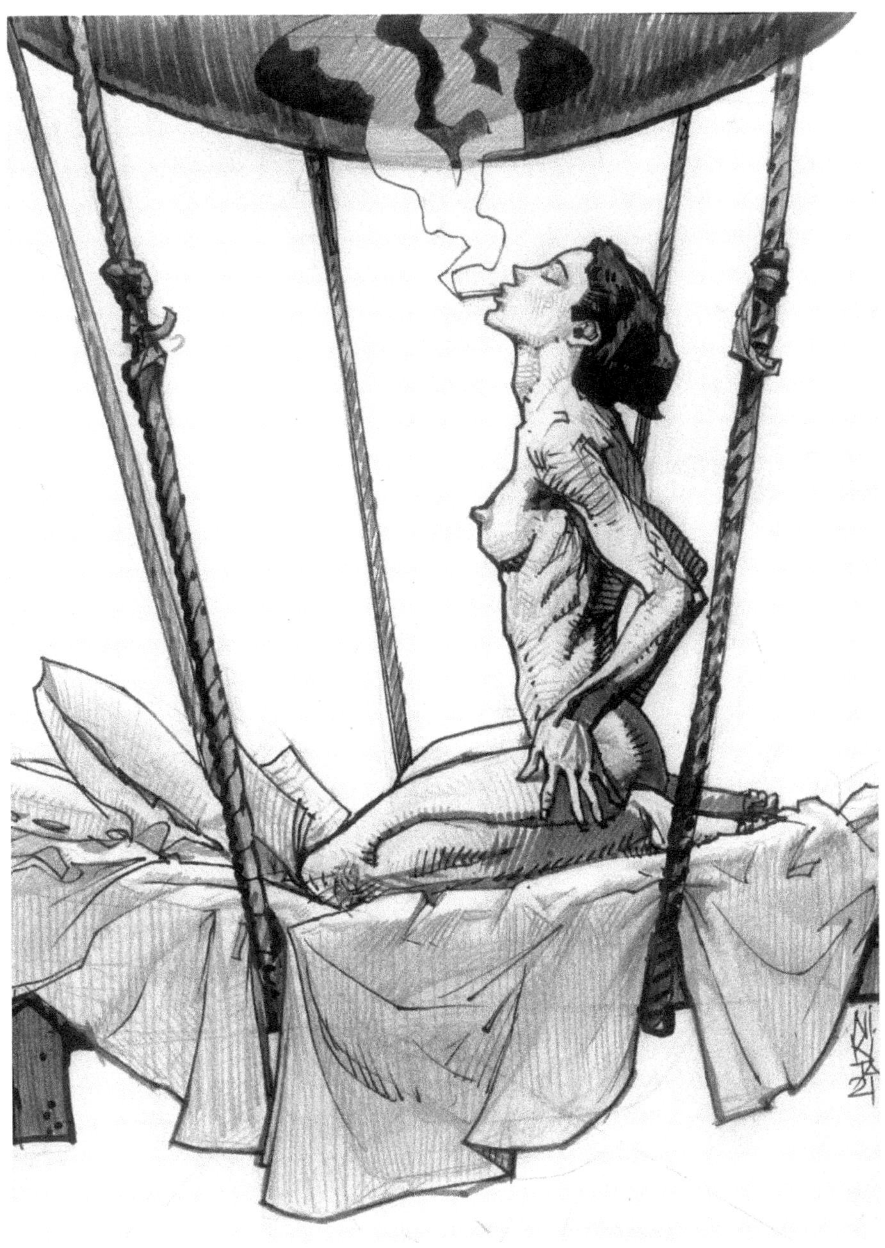

PASSENGERS

There was a young woman called Jane
Who hitched a lift on a plane
But clinging there
With her doll and her bear
She waited for breakfast in vain

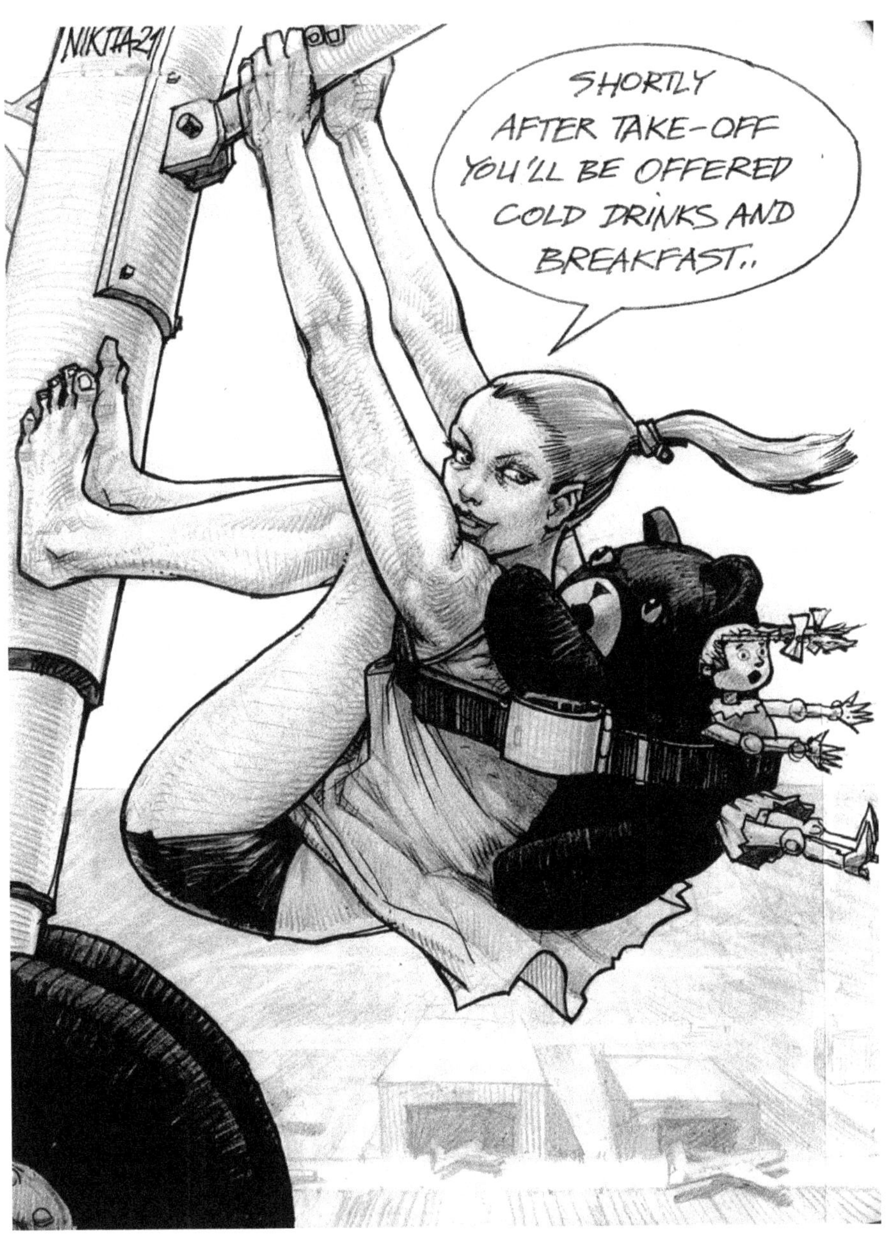
NIKITA21
SHORTLY AFTER TAKE-OFF YOU'LL BE OFFERED COLD DRINKS AND BREAKFAST..

PASSENGER'S CAT

There was a young lady from Chester
Who trained her cat to protect her
It grew such a size
That to his surprise
It ate the ticket inspector!

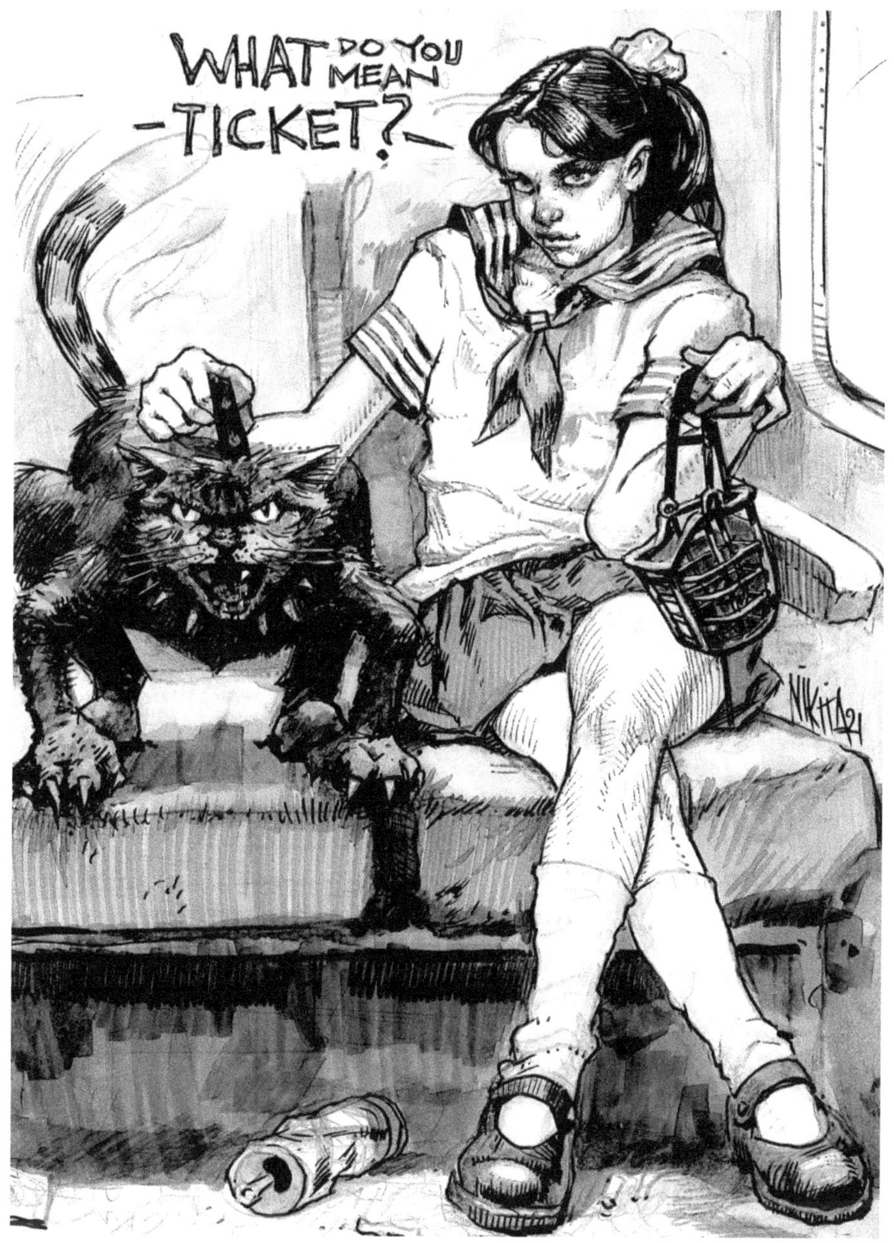
WHAT DO YOU MEAN
-TICKET?-
NIKITA 21

ESCAPE THRILL

On occasion it is best
To flee
To put as much distance
As is possible
Between yourself and
Your tormentors, be they
Physical or psychological.
You will use dreams,
Those cruel mimics
Of waking life,
To escape tedium.
So you witness
Your subconscious self
Running oh so fast to nowhere.
Conjuring:
The speeding train
The grasping arm
The naked girl
The dangled ladder
And, that ubiquitous white knight,
A helicopter. And as you travel
Through this unrequested fantasy
Fear terrifies
Illusion besets
The unattainable beckons
And you can only pray that
This cacophony of experience
Will enrich and pleasure
Your mundane life

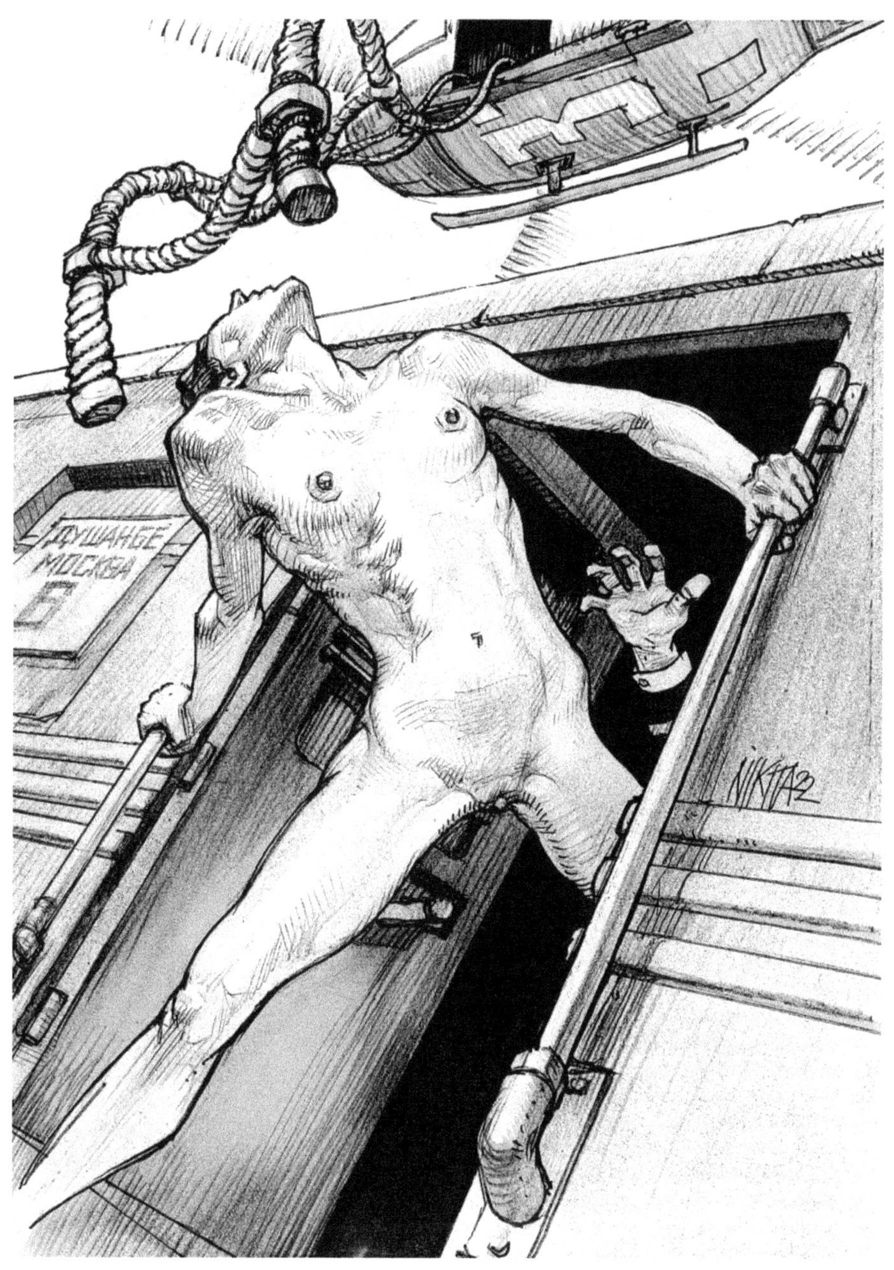
ДУШАНБЕ
МОСКВА
6

PAY TOLL

If you're here for a while - pay me
If you like my style - pay me
If you're feeling virile - pay me
For this is your lucky day

If you're car or truck - pay me
If you're down on your luck - pay me
If you're here for a fuck - pay me,
And then be on your way

If you'd like to stray - pay me
If you're straight or gay - pay me
If you want to lay me - pay me
Check out my rates for today

This Toll is a Single fee
So be sure to understand
So whatever you do with me
All returns are banned

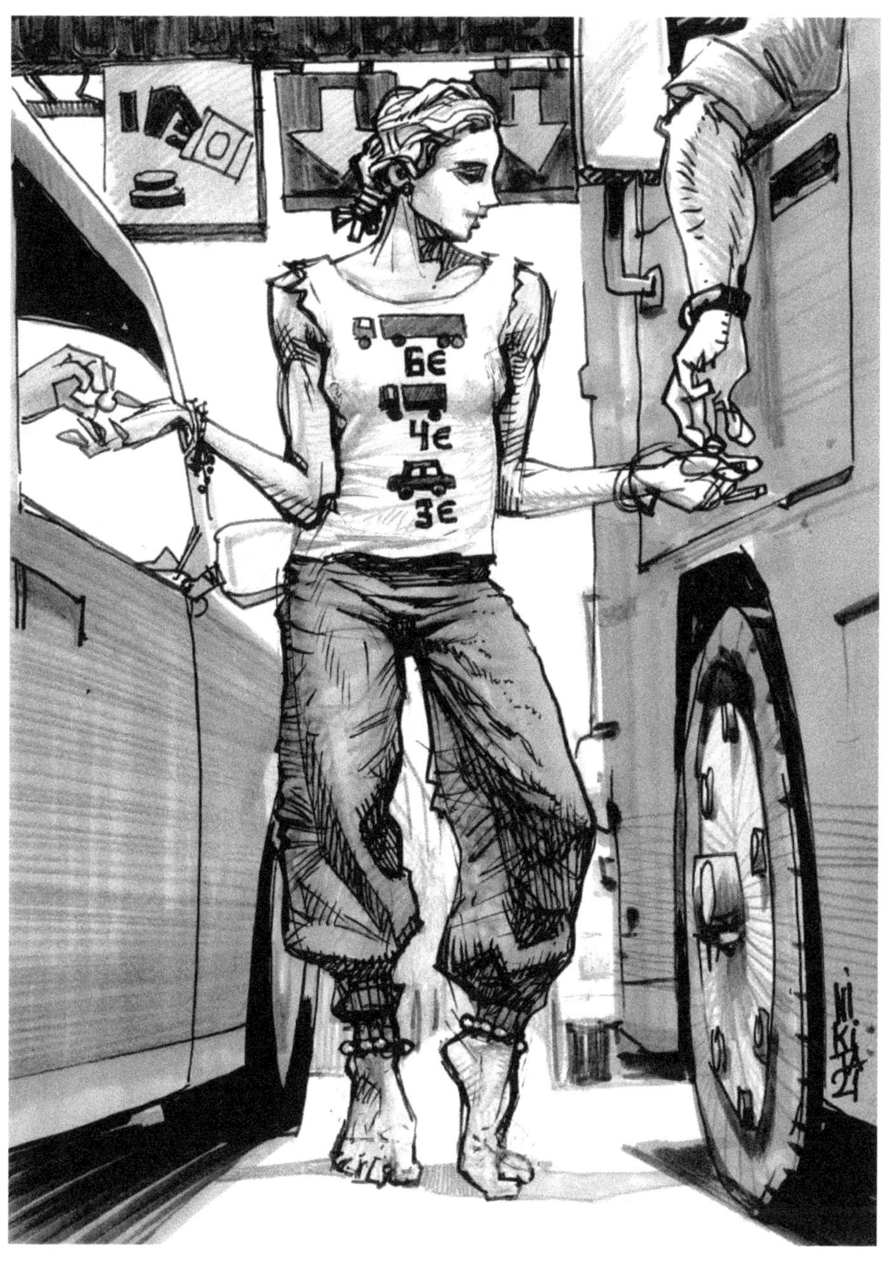
БЕ
ЧЕ
ЗЕ

EXHIBITIONIST

Quietly living our lives
Perhaps on a train
Or a park bench
We may suddenly be confronted
By something that is
A bit scary
On occasion this
Might be a cock or cunt
Being exhibited by
A mildly deranged individual
It is probably best
Not to make a detailed study
Of the anatomy involved
However much it might
Disgust or appeal to you.
Better by far to continue
To read your newspaper
Or immerse yourself
In your mobile phone
Thereby pretending
That your own genitals
Are bored by such a spectacle.

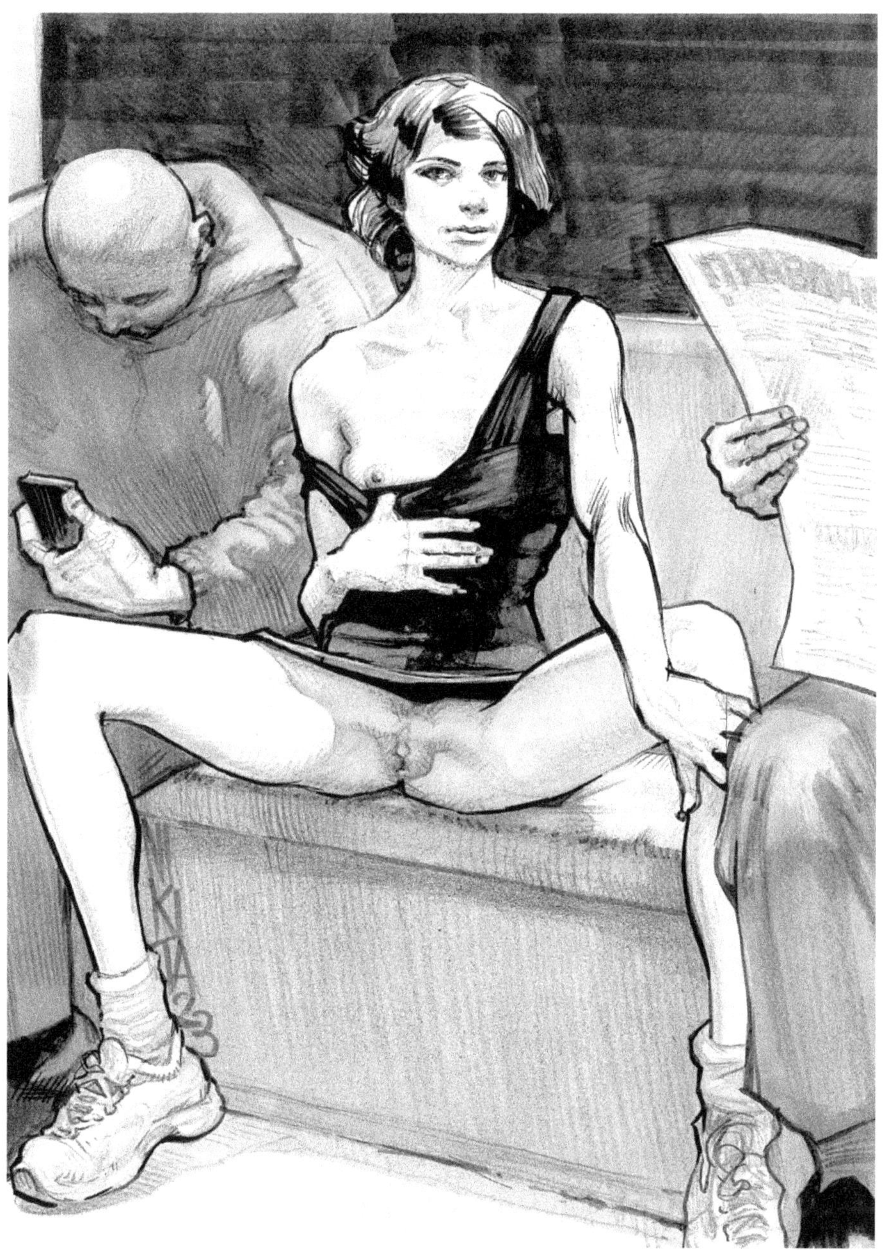

PICKPOCKETS

You don't have to look very far
To realise that we are all
Ripping each other off.
If only it were just a matter
If picking pockets
It would be simple
And not so very damaging.
To lose your wallet,
Perhaps a few euros
A credit card or two
Is annoying
But it is not life-threatening
Just the outcome
Of petty-thievery.
Other thieves steal from
Our emotions
Leaving heart rending gaps
In our psyche
It is so much harder
To protect oneself against
Such cruel robbery.
And the most horrible thing is
That we do this unwittingly
To others.

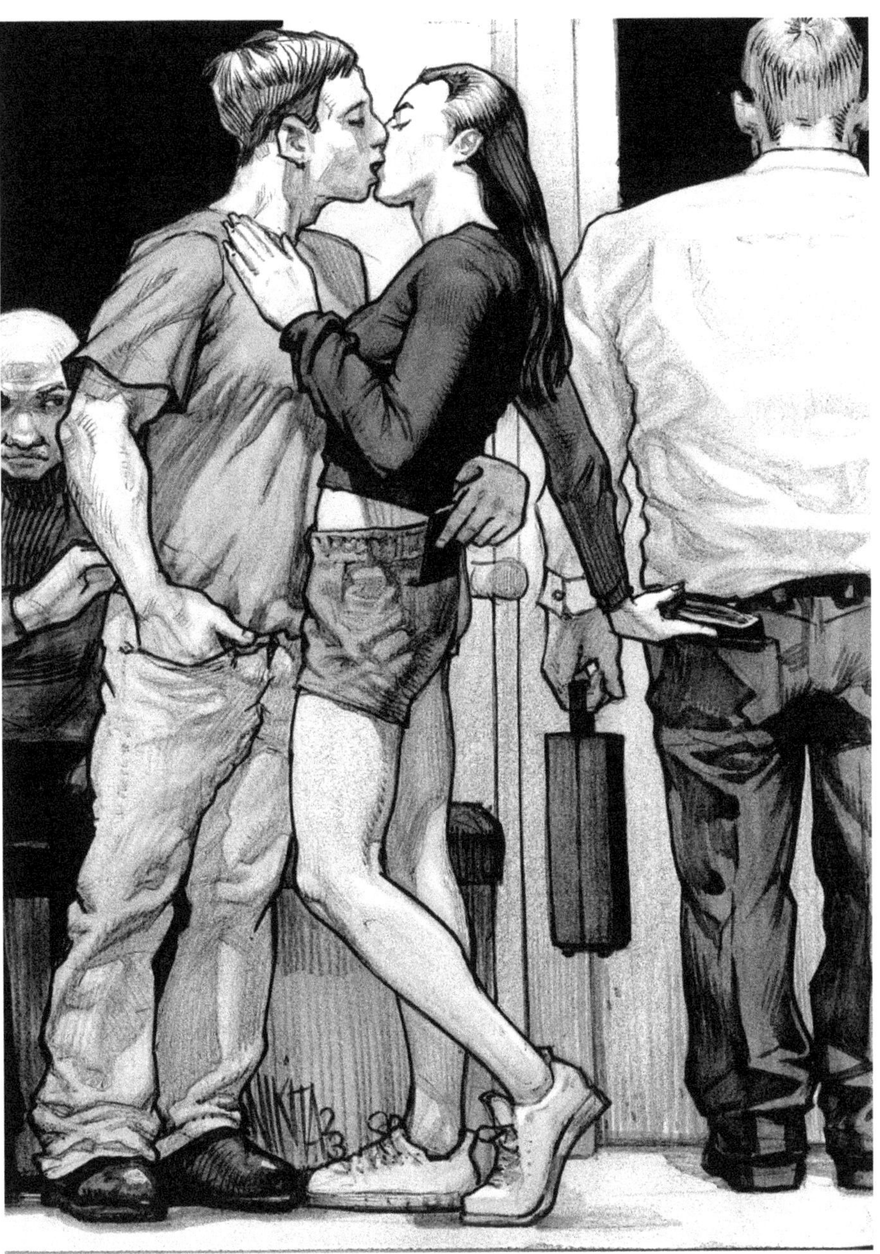

PASSENGER ANNOUNCEMENT

Be it in body, or in your mind
Turbulence of any kind
Can disturb things and cause a fuss
Whilst you enjoy cunnilingus

It is certainly best when you're in flight
Not to obscure the captain's sight
But ensure he always looks to the front
Before he navigates to your cunt.

To this end I would advise
Not to take him by surprise
But encourage your would-be Don Juan
To fly with his auto-pilot on

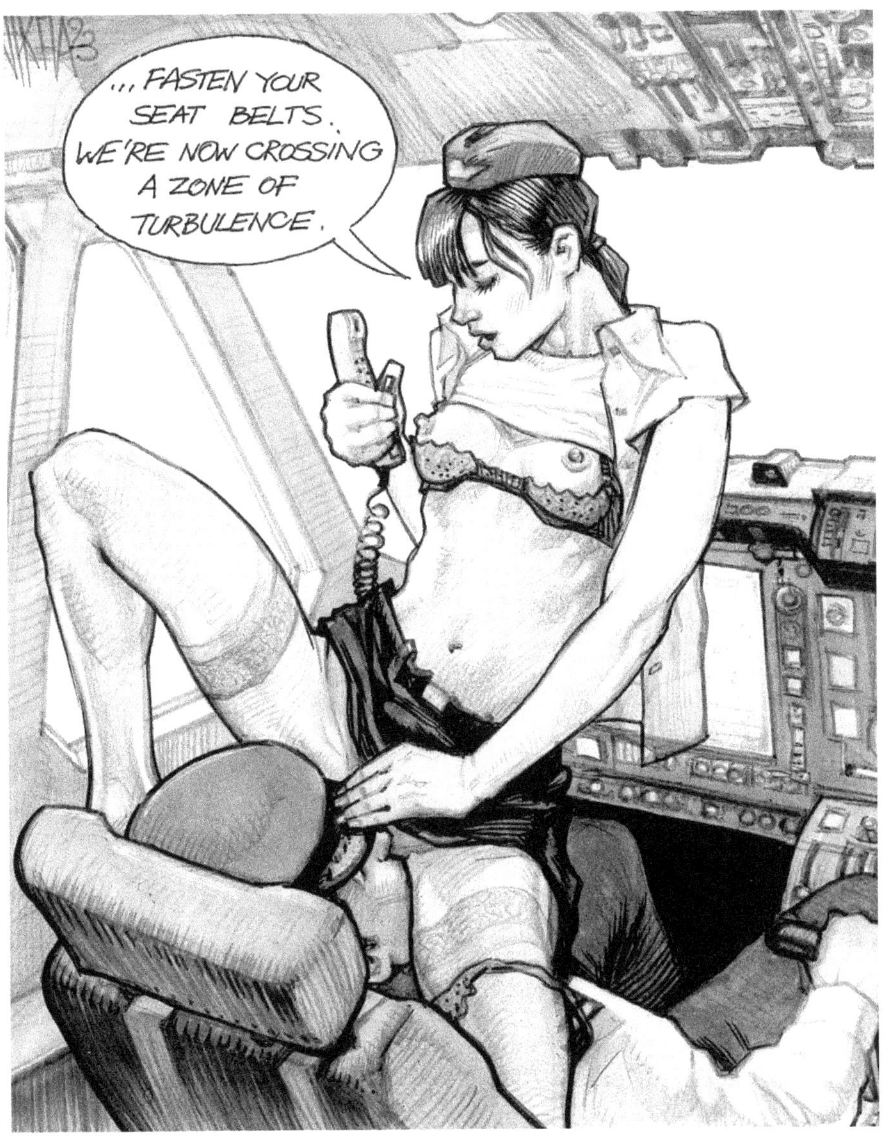
..., FASTEN YOUR SEAT BELTS.. WE'RE NOW CROSSING A ZONE OF TURBULENCE.

FULL THROTTLE

A stewardess known as Kate
Thought she and the captain should mate
So she revealed both her tits
And her juiciest bits
For a full throttle conjugate.

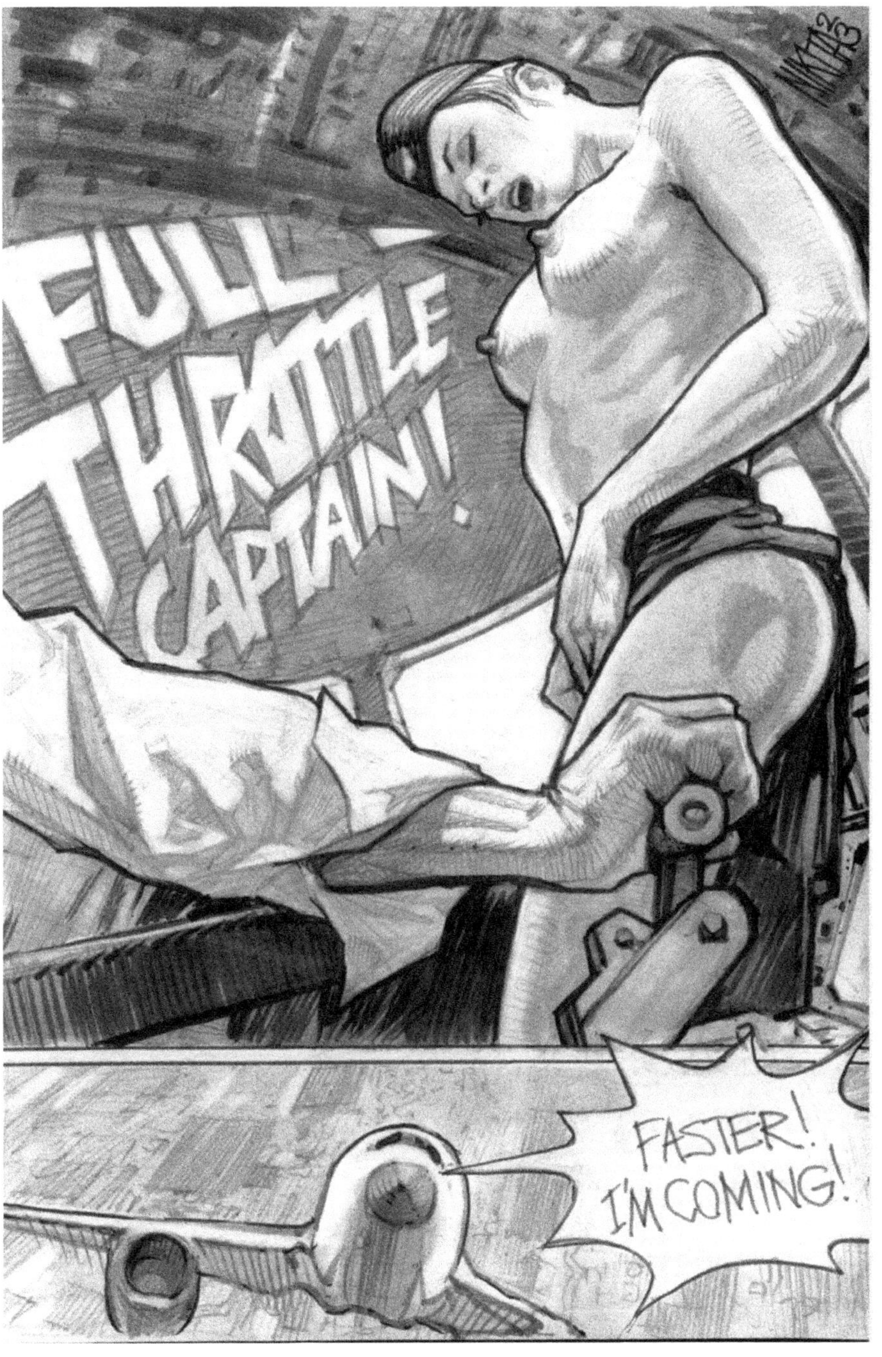
FULL THROTTLE CAPTAIN!
FASTER! I'M COMING!

REFILL

Your tank must be full
When you start your adventure
So you can push on

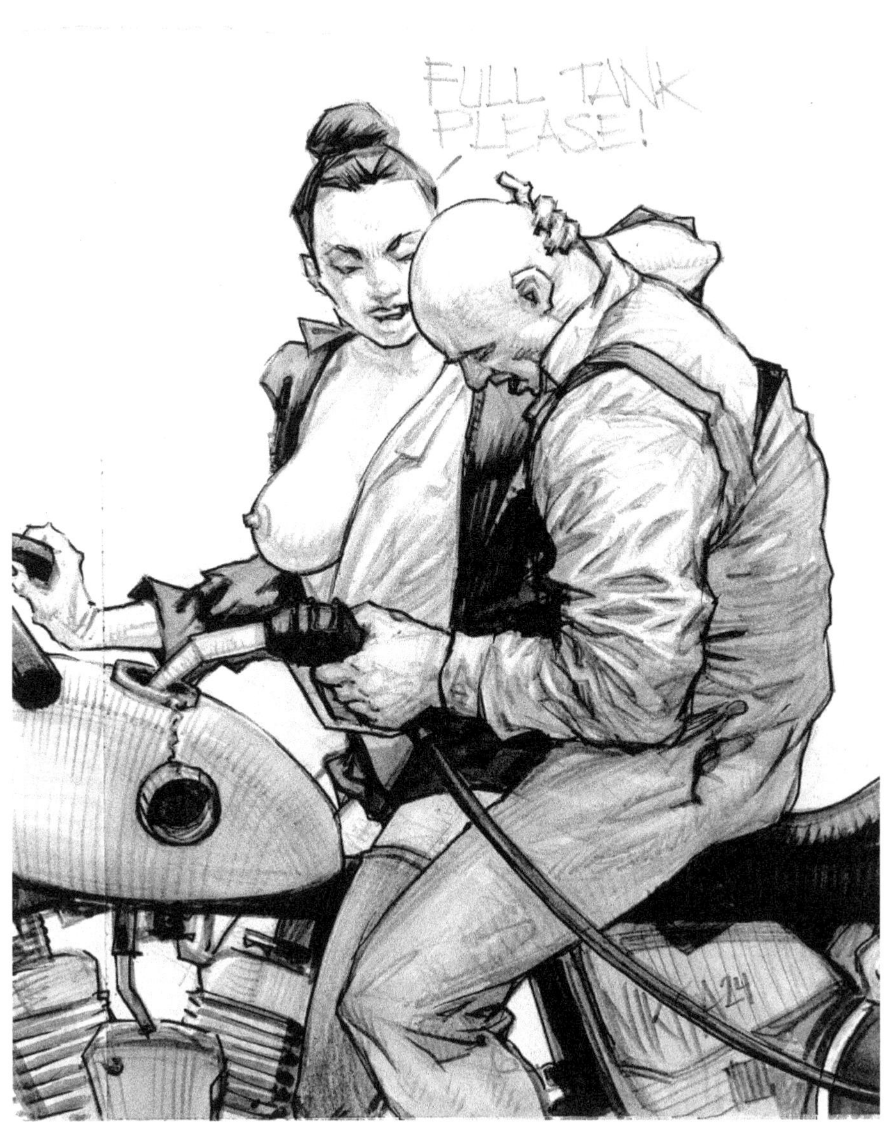
FULL TANK
PLEASE!

ENVY

The throb and the thrust
Are an absolute must
If you want to go biking today
Be ahead of the curve
And be ready to swerve
If anything gets in your way

Enjoy the thrill
Of using your skill
To put on a decent display
Just turn up the wick
And ride hellish quick
And strip off your clothes on the way

There are people who see you
Who just want to be you
Although you would lead them astray
Of course part of the thrill
Is she's not on the pill
So you might be a father one day!

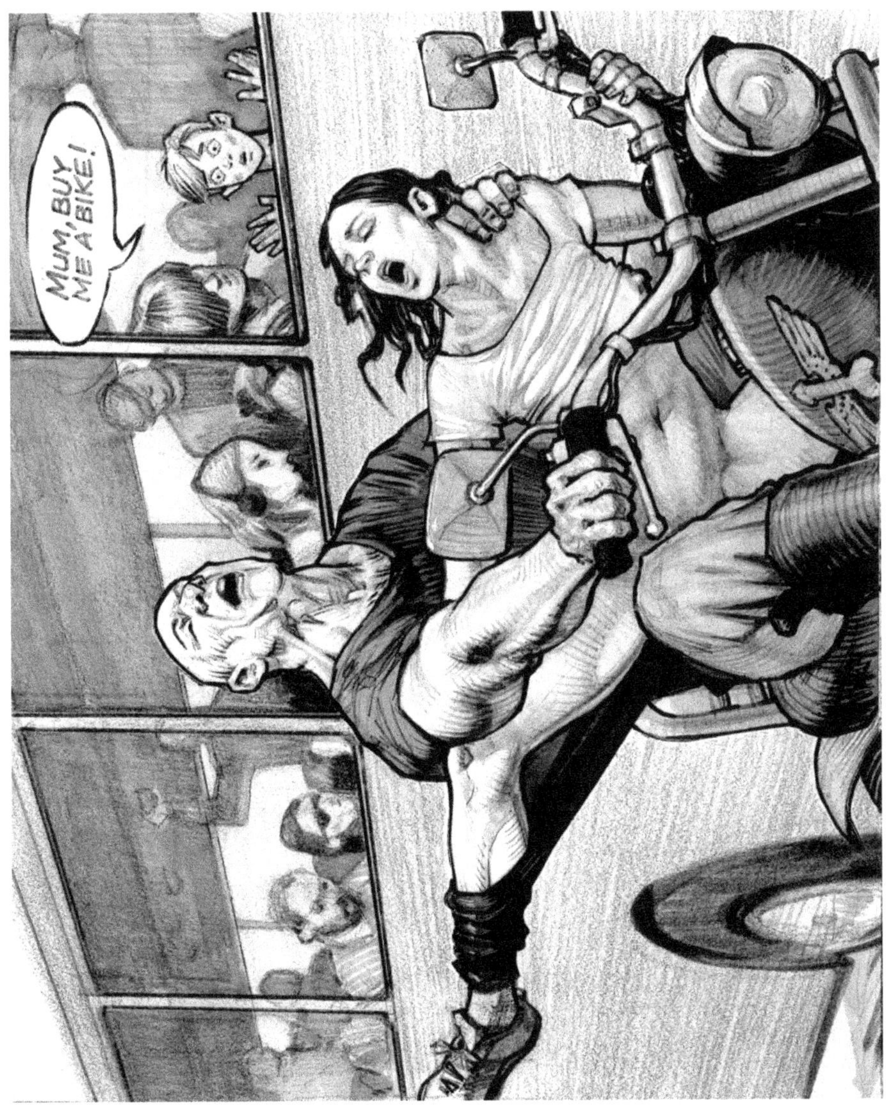
MUM, BUY ME A BIKE!

NIGHT DREAMS

Be very careful
With your subconscious
And treat it kindly
For it is best that
It is not ignored
Or worse still thwarted.
We can build a relationship
With the subconscious
More often than not
Through our dreams.
Not just the deep sleep dreams
Of our nightly slumber
But also those fleeting
Moments of daydream.
It can take a minor incident,
Combine it with
Something evil
Then twist the brain
Into generating weird
And sometimes fearful
Non-sequiturs.
Accept these for they are
Part of us.
Such mental imagery
Is an important addition
To our innate character.
So welcome the beasts
That prowl your head

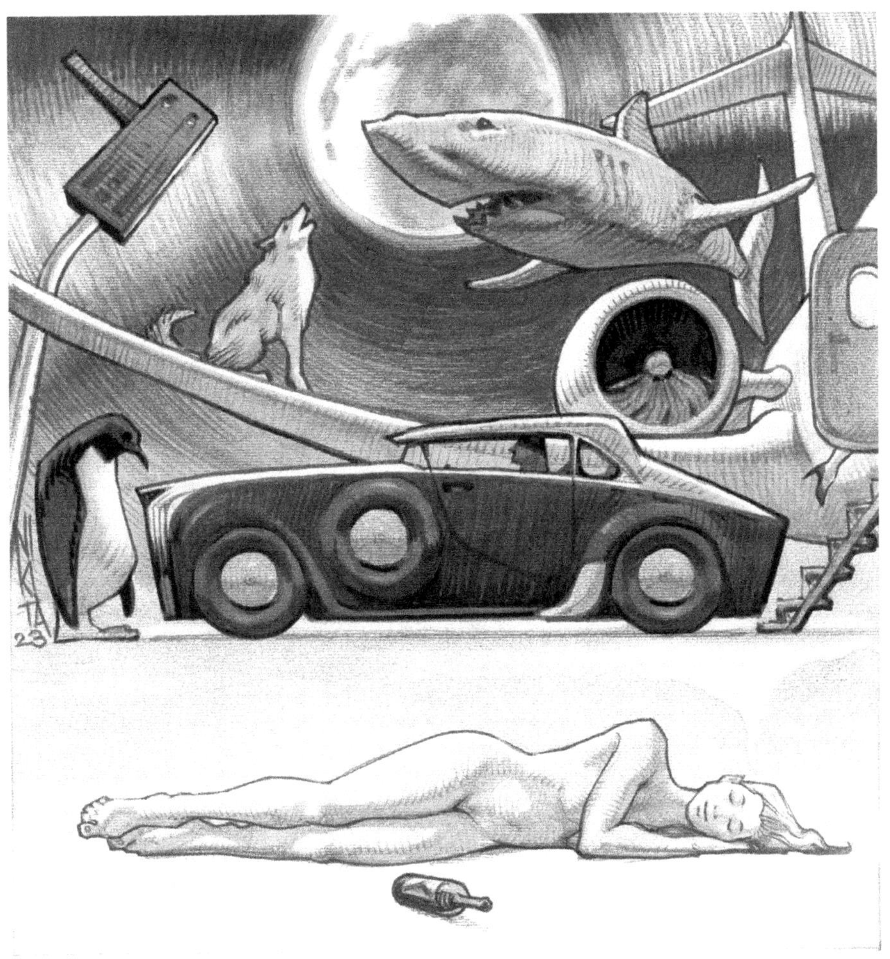

12

BEAUTY AND BEAST

It is a two-sided coin is it not?
On one side we have 'Beauty'.
often depicted as a gorgeous young maiden,
whilst on the other there lurks
something dismal, dark, and dangerous.
Whilst we are happy to promote
the above-mentioned maiden and her ilk
we need to be cautious in that
her Beauty may be no more than skin-deep
whereas the Beast may possess a heart of gold!

QUEEN

Not quite mythology
Nor harsh reality
A respected ancient monarchy
Far from banality

Its own lore and customs
Attuned to its history
Proud of its lineage
Wrapped about in mystery

Beast and Beauty present
In confusing dichotomy
Bound together mentally
But exhibiting autonomy

In this alien presence
There is a synchronicity
The Queen and Brute within us
Bonding subliminally

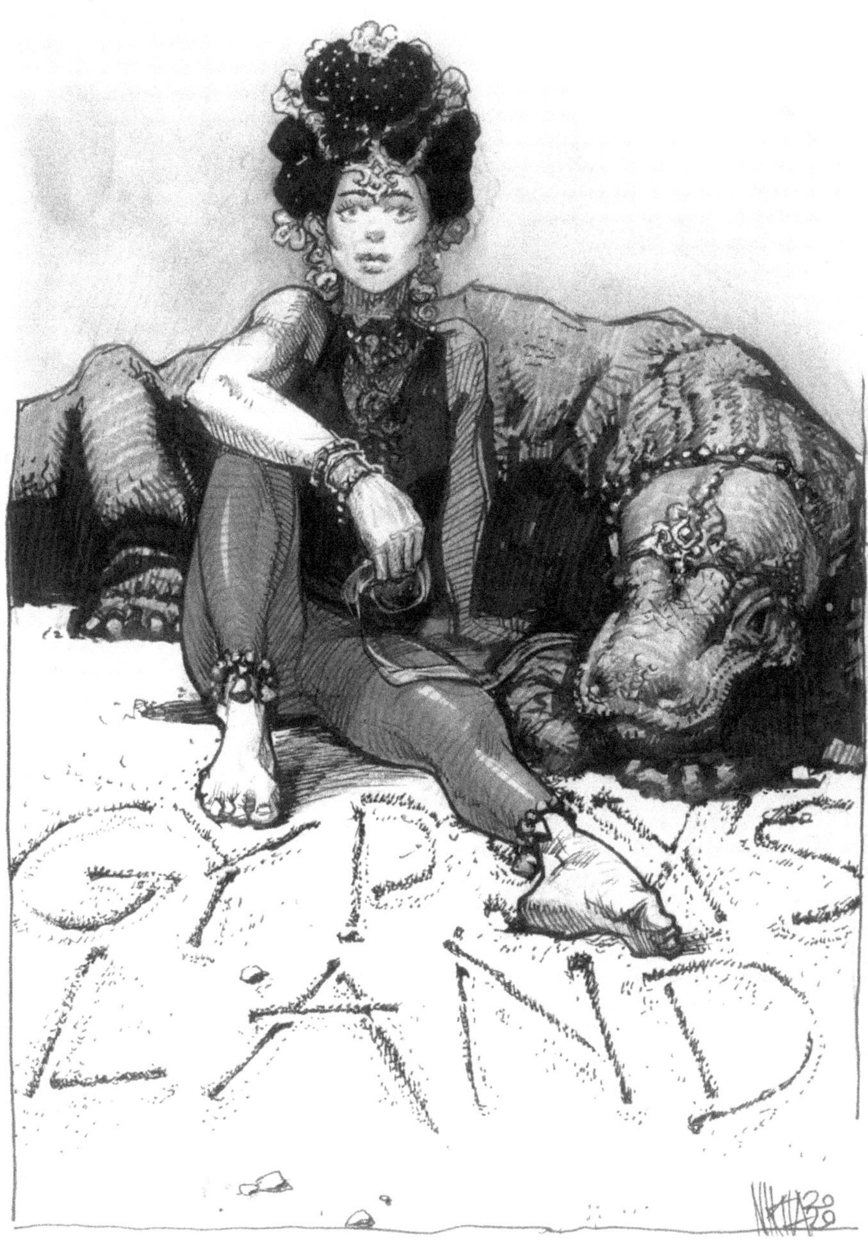

NUTCRACKER

Both Prince and Mouse King
Move from Story to Ballet
To enjoy Marie.

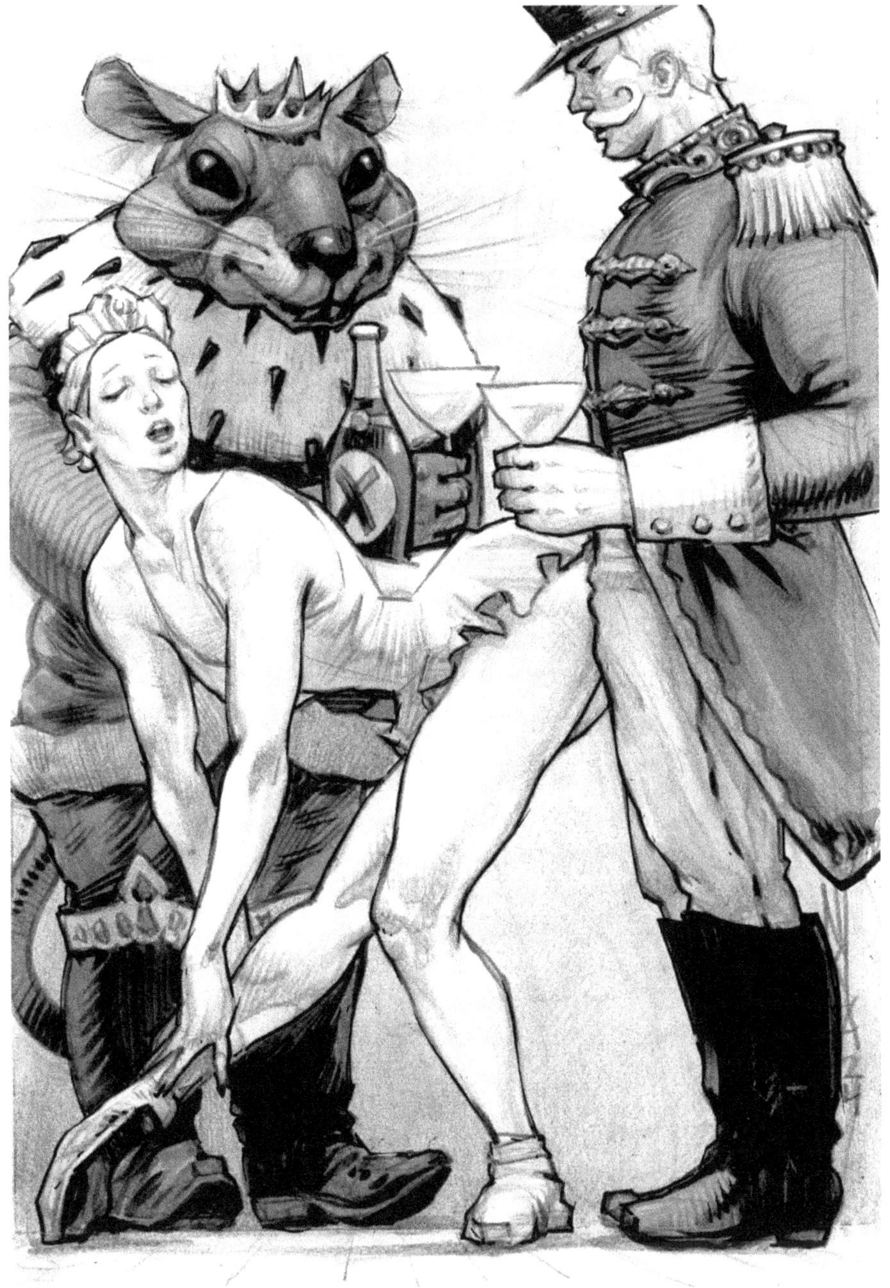

GYPSIE'S LAND

She didn't dislike him,
On the contrary,
Nor was she afraid,
Not in the least,
But he was a big ugly bugger
Difficult to take anywhere.
Large social events
Railway carriages
Shopping malls
Were out of the question.
Best to keep him at home
To herself,
Behind closed doors,
Where physical traits
Do not matter

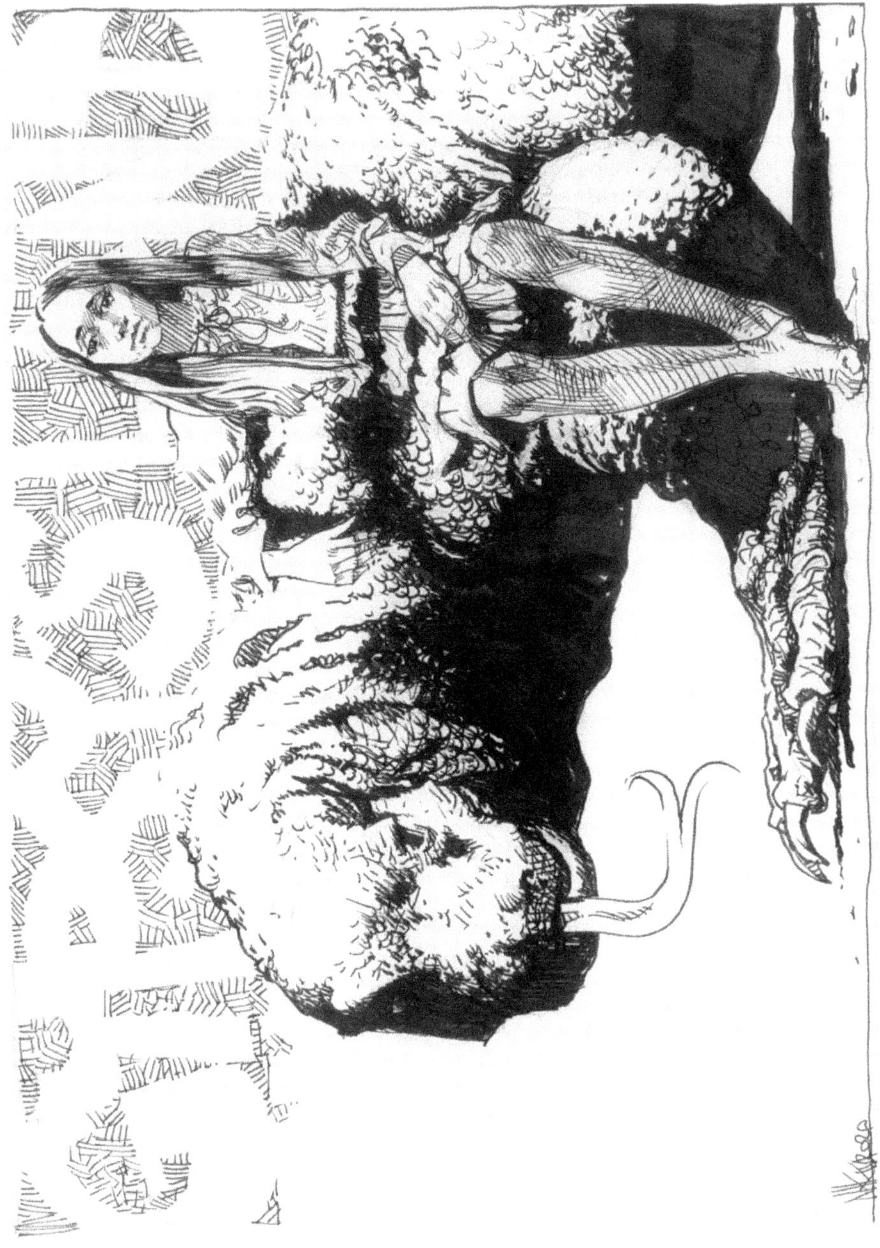

WHALE RIDE

There was a young lady called Gail
Who liked to ride a great whale
The naughty cetacean
Gave her much stimulation
By blowing itself off on her tail

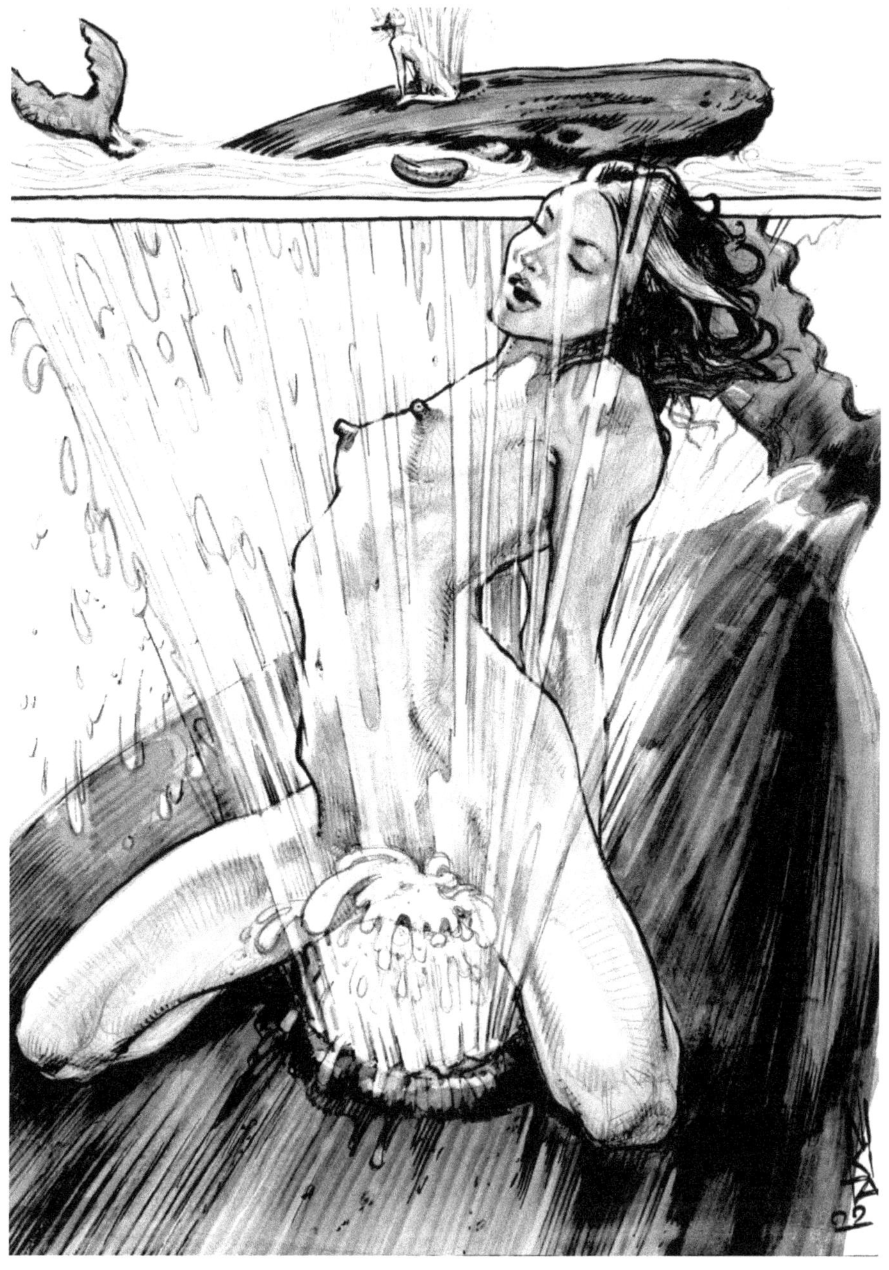

TORERO

Timing perfection
Dancing their destiny
Balance macabre

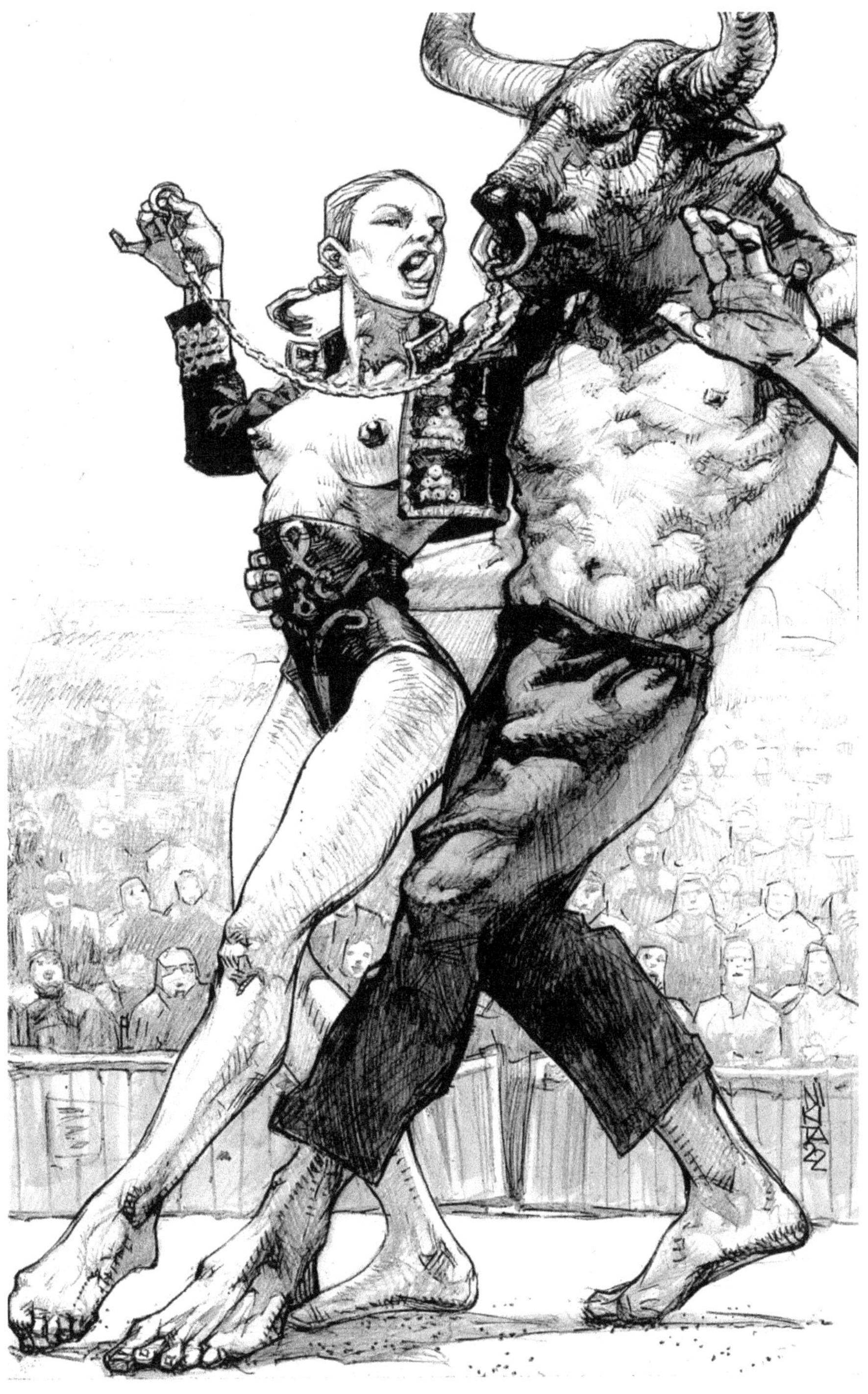

APPEARANCE
IS DECEIVING

The outer tiger
Stripped of all its stripes
Waiting to have you

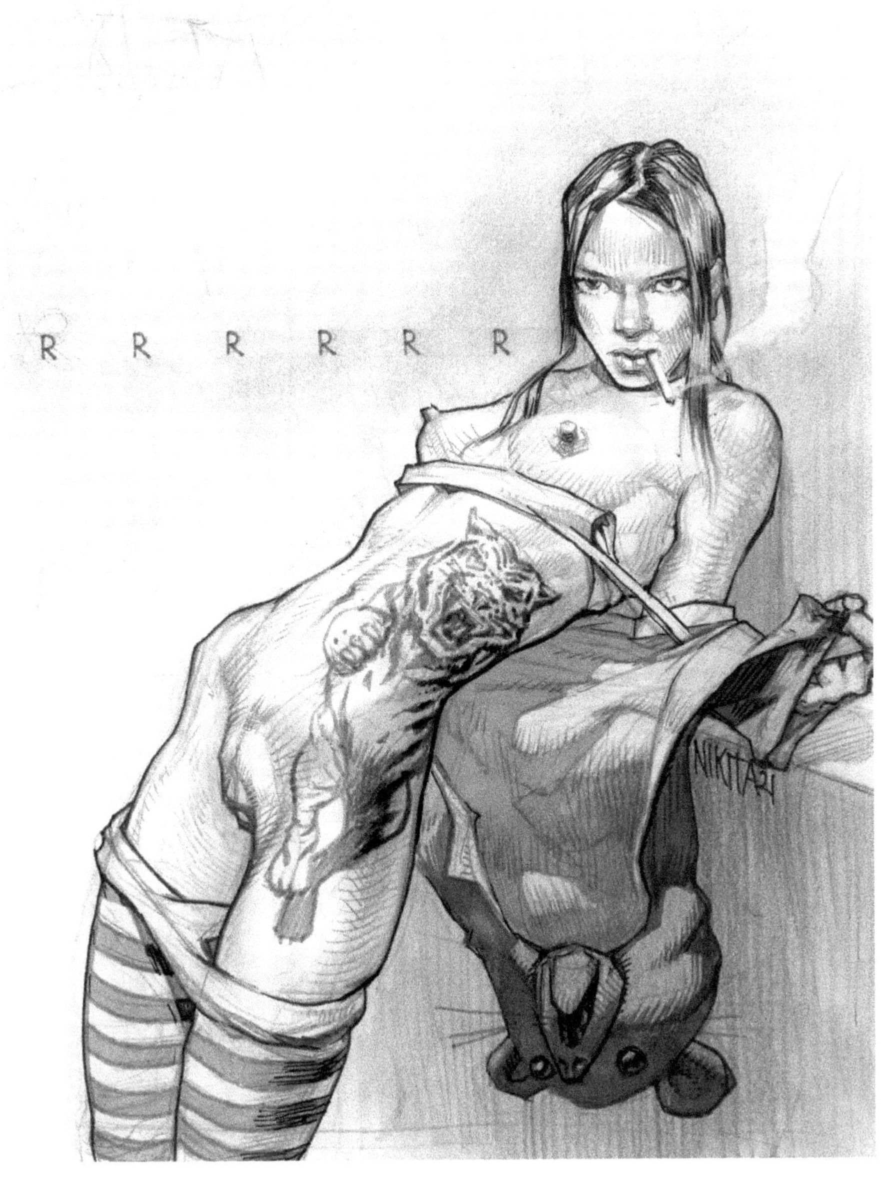
R R R R R R
NIKITA21

AMPHIBIAN MAN

It must be a dream
She is tingling all over
The pleasure is hers

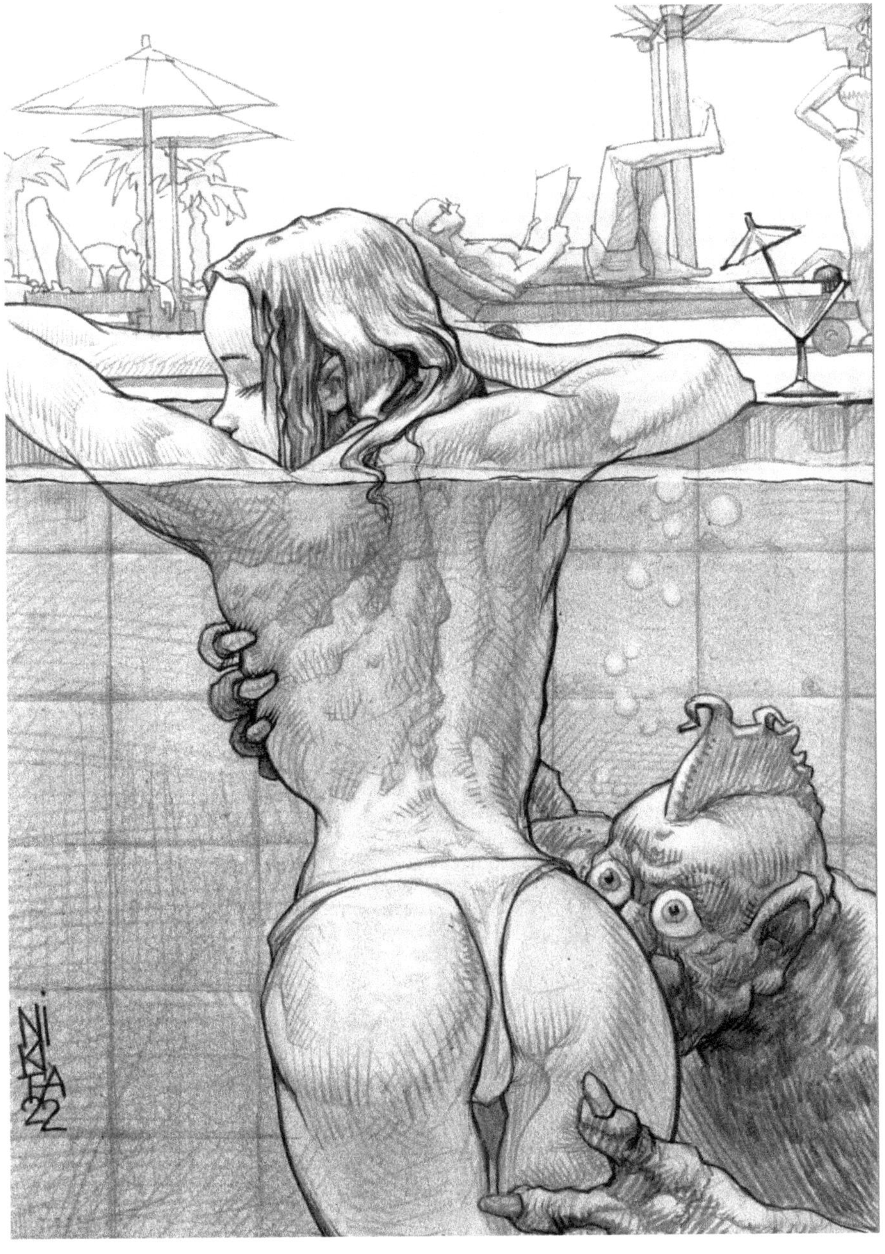

ICHTIANDRES

In the Upper World
All is serene
And she manages to maintain
An attitude of
Sweetness and calm
But underneath
In her hidden world
The daemons of lust
Assail her
So that she
Holds them to her
Unable to resist
Their subversive
Ministrations

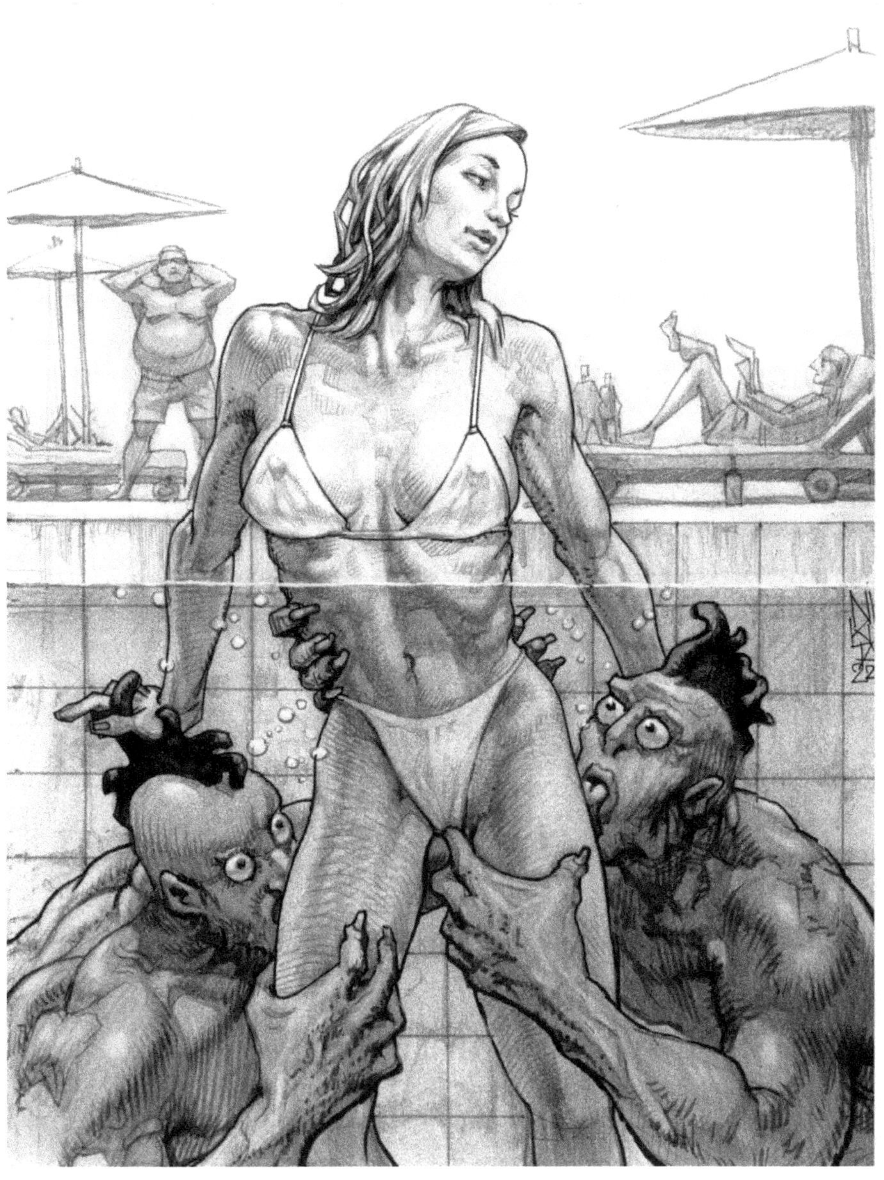

GENIE

If you release your Genie from his bottle
Make sure he is just what you require
For a tiny mistake in the summons
And things could go seriously haywire

One thing that can cause you problems
Is if he is not the right size
Too small and there's no satisfaction
Too big – that I wouldn't advise!

Genies are such wonderful creatures
They ripple with muscles, all tanned,
They are there just to do your biding
To follow your every command

But even if you are a princess
Both refined and very well-bred
You might find your Genie is too boring
And opt for a humanoid instead.

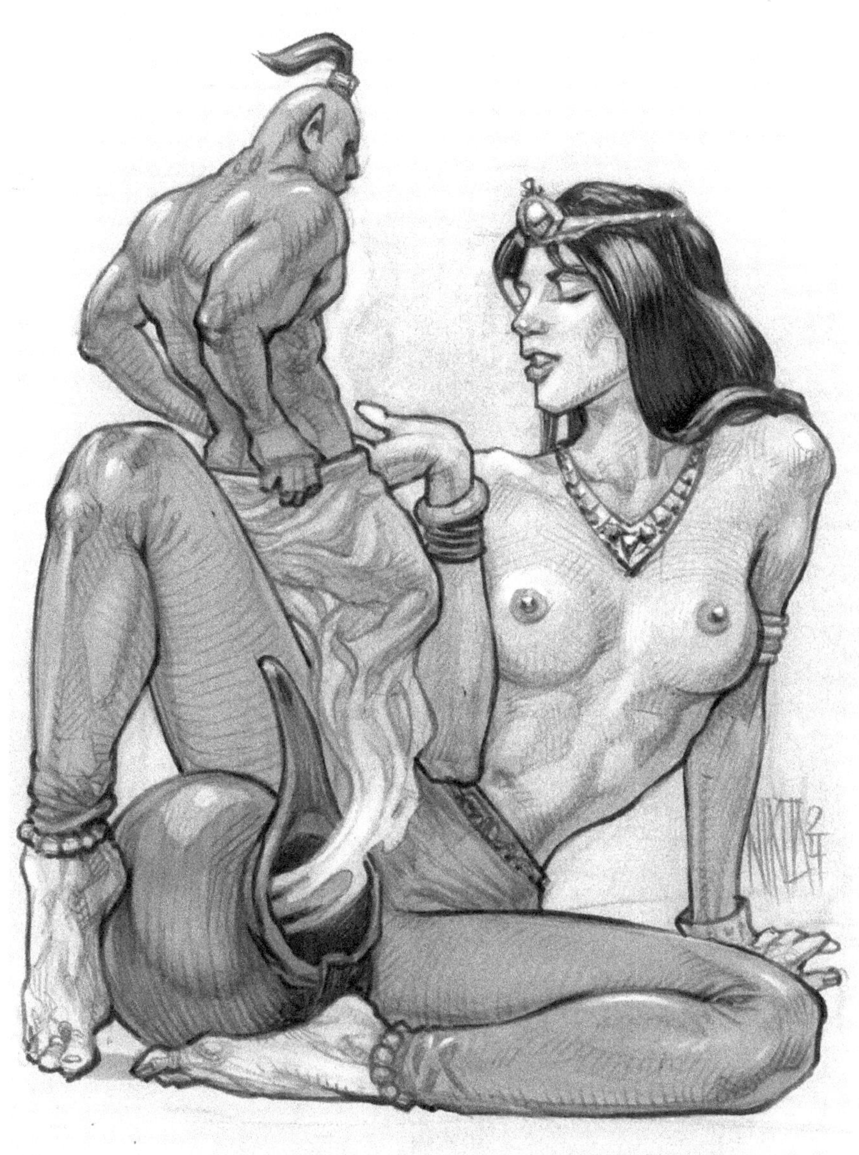

PICNIC

There are occasions when
Spreading a tablecloth on the grass
Of a buttercup-laden meadow
And disgorging the contents
Of your wicker hamper
Leaden with viands
And cucumber sandwiches
Pretty pastries
And a bottle of or two
Of Bolly
There are occasions when
This is not enough
When the cry of the wolf
Within your imagination
Reaches out towards
It's corporeal kin.
At such a picnic
The hunger for food
Is a secondary desire
So you cannot help but
Lay down your trug
And enjoy to the full
The sensory experience
Of fur
And claws
And wolf!

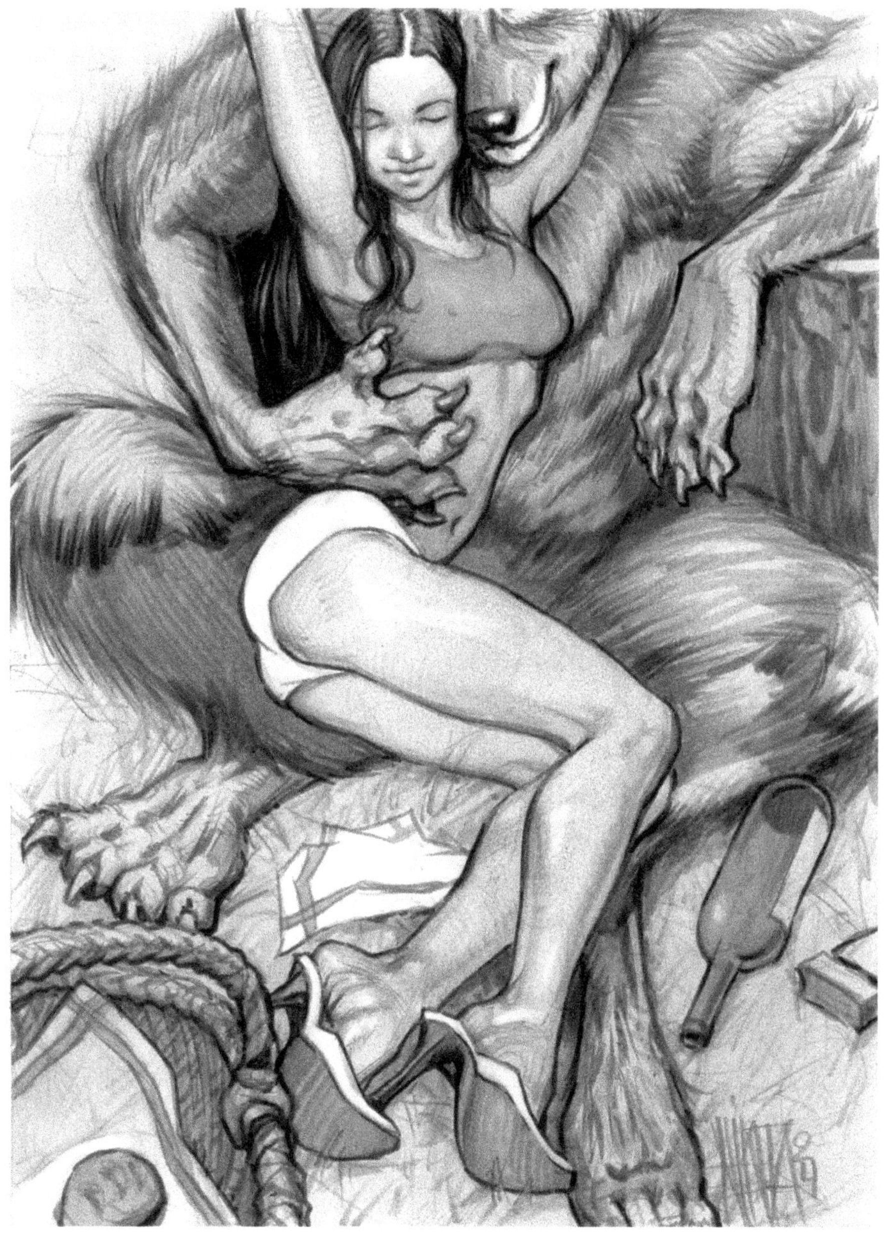

DIVERS

With two randy toads
The happy freedom of a swim
Such simple pleasure

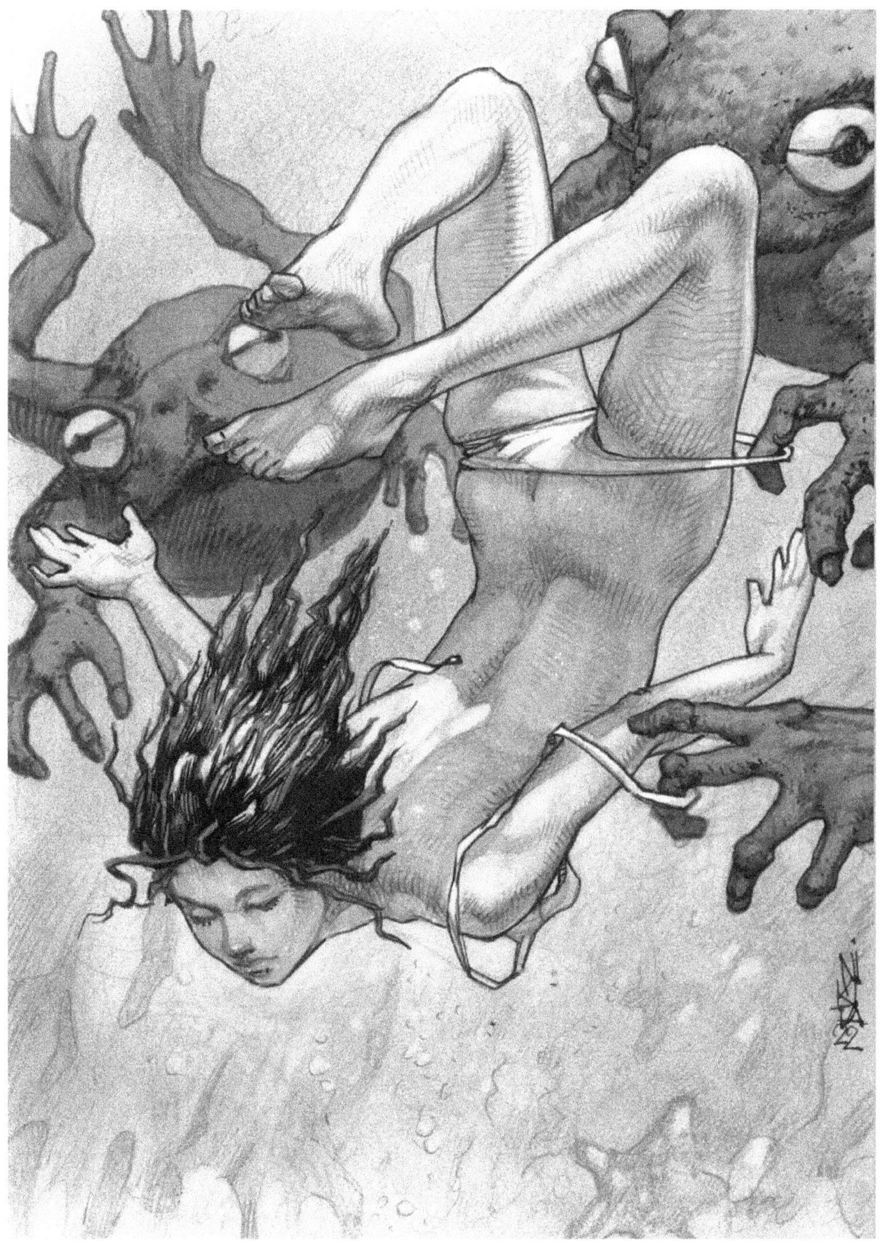

SEA STAR

A certain young fisherman's daughter
Enjoyed feeling life underwater
Most exciting by far
Was a randy sea-star
Whose leg went where it just didn't oughter.

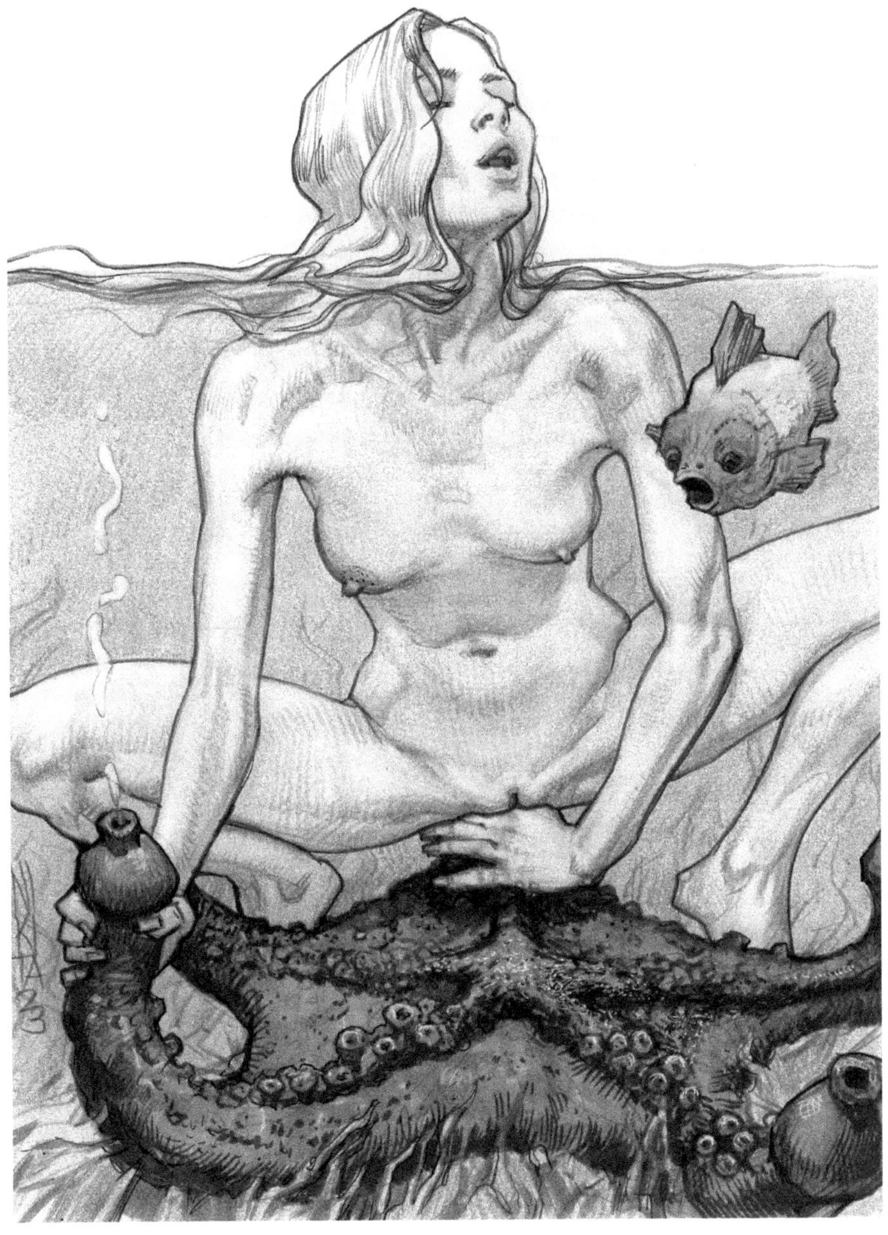

NAVIGATOR

The story has changed
No longer the innocent
You are in control
That wolf you know
May have breakfasted
On Grandmama
But he is yours now
Using technology
GPS and Dashcam
You know where you both
Are going
And if the outcome
Is not very pretty
Then be aware that the end
Justifies the means
Even if those means are
Sharp teeth.

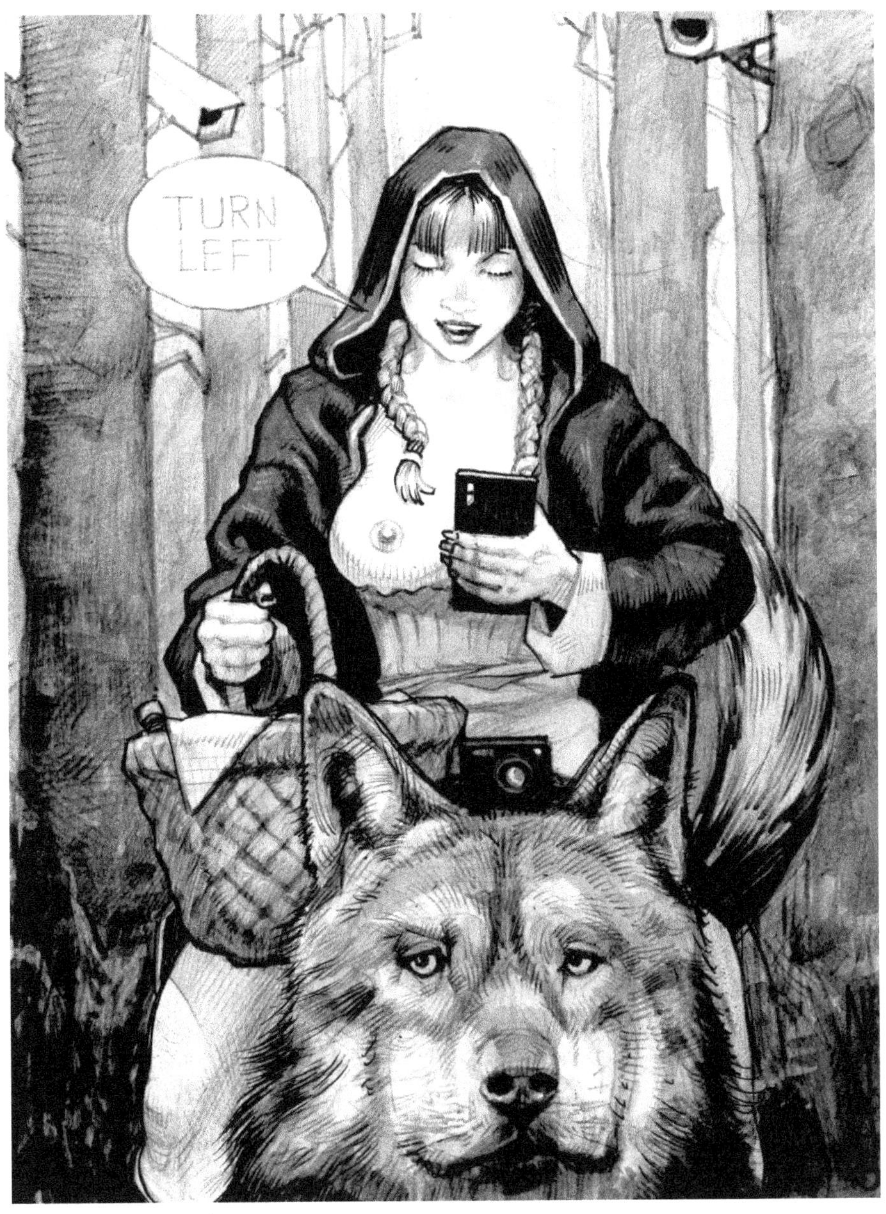
TURN
LEFT

ANIMUS

Do you see me?
Really see me?
For there is more to me
More me than you might see
When you first see me
Look not at me
But into me
Can you see me now?
Just as Jung saw me
The me of femininity
Lurks in the male me
The masculine me
The me that yells
"Fuck Off"

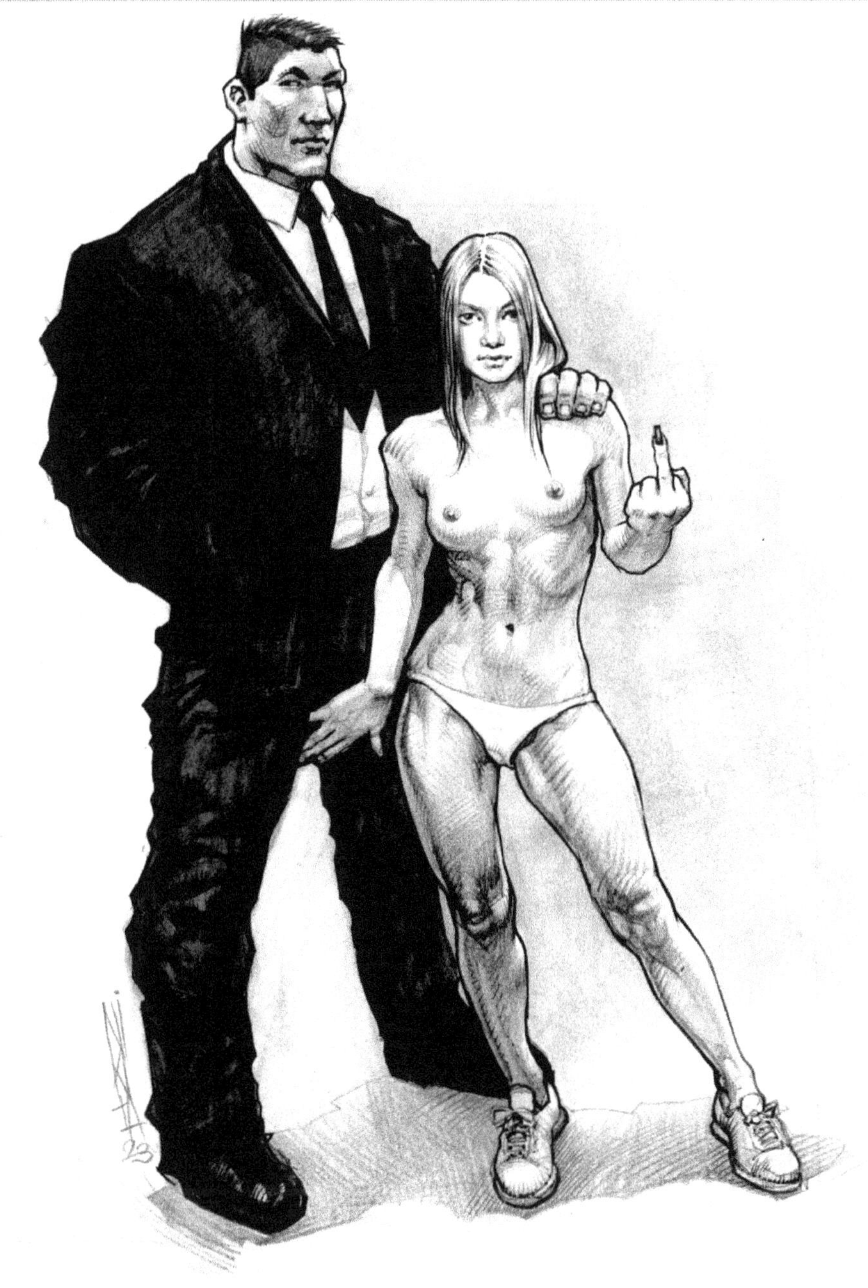

YETI CATCH

Your common or garden Yeti
Likes to live in the snow
He prefers to stay well hidden
Where humans never go

But sometimes just for amusement
He'll reveal himself to surprise
Some unsuspecting person
Who cannot believe their eyes

For the Yeti is very hairy
And undeniably massive
He is quite a frightening monster
And his roars are far from passive

But despite his forbidding looks
His is a wonder to behold
For he has the kindest of natures
And his heart is purest gold.

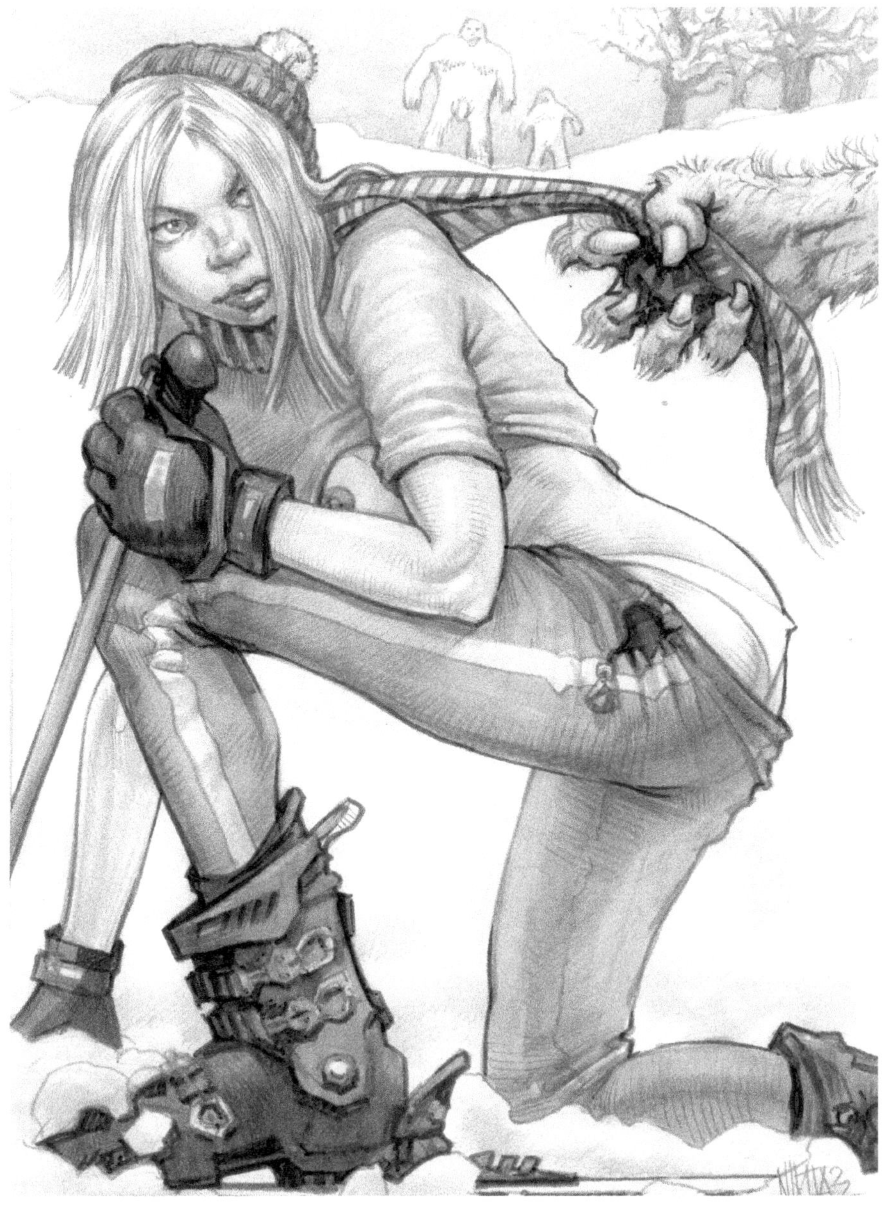

YETI AROUSAL

Yeti are ready
Standing firm for action
Pure male fantasy!

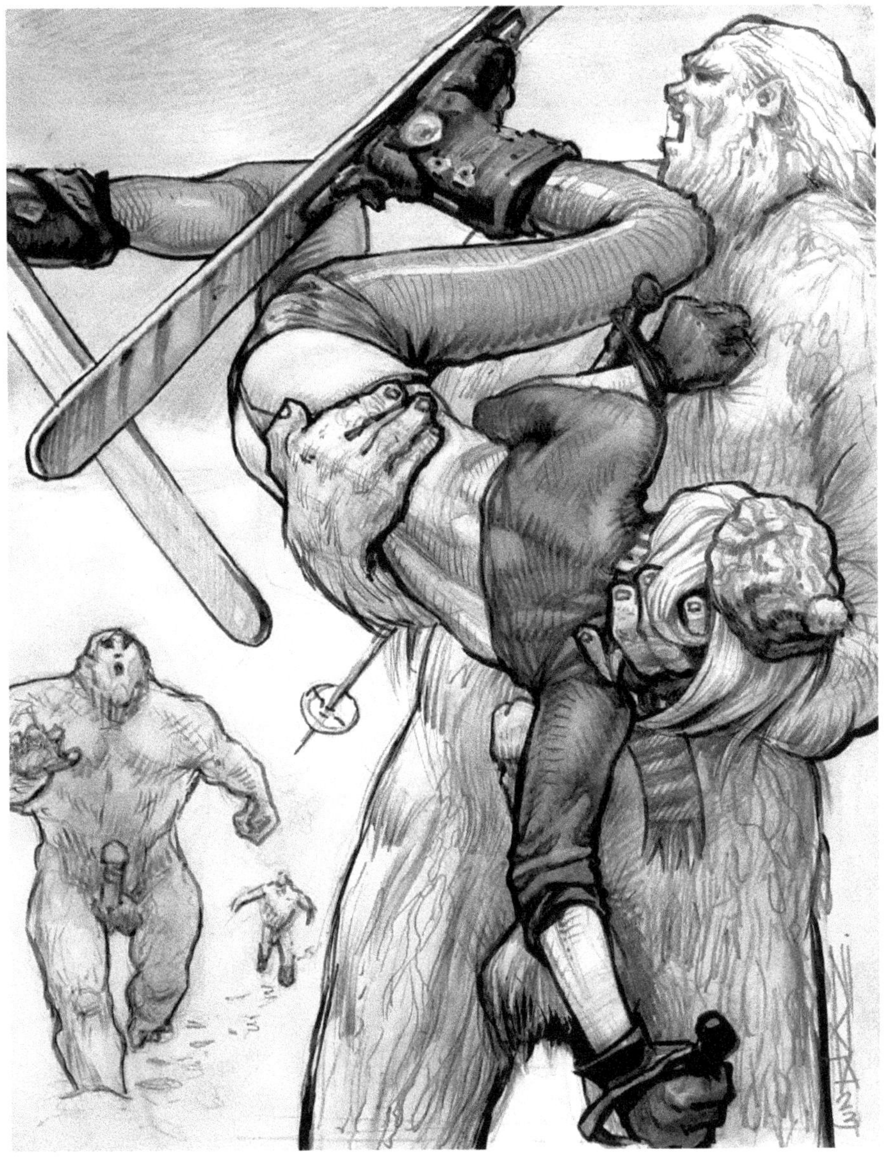

YETI MULTI

There was a young lady called Pru
Who enjoyed a Yeti, or two
She said "two or three
Would satisfy me
But four would be too much to screw."

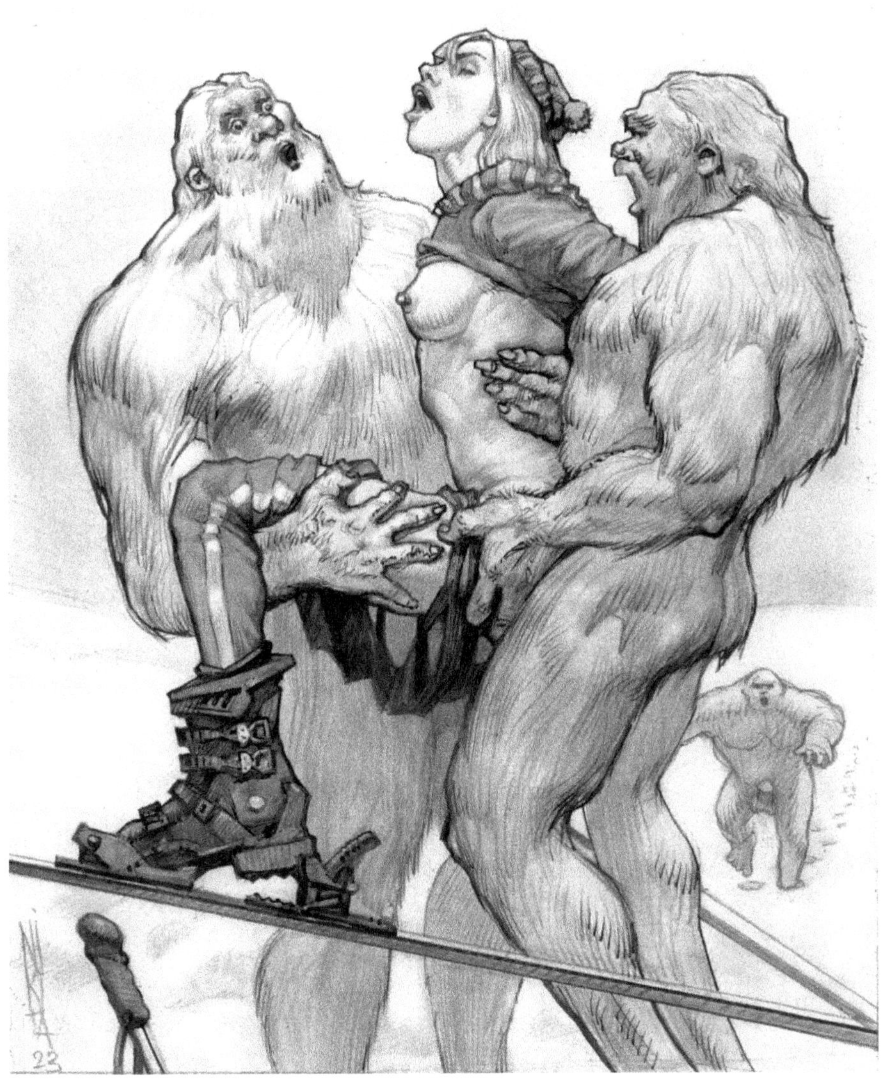

YETIS DONE

Two Yeti are done
Third Yeti performing well
Do not think, just shag.

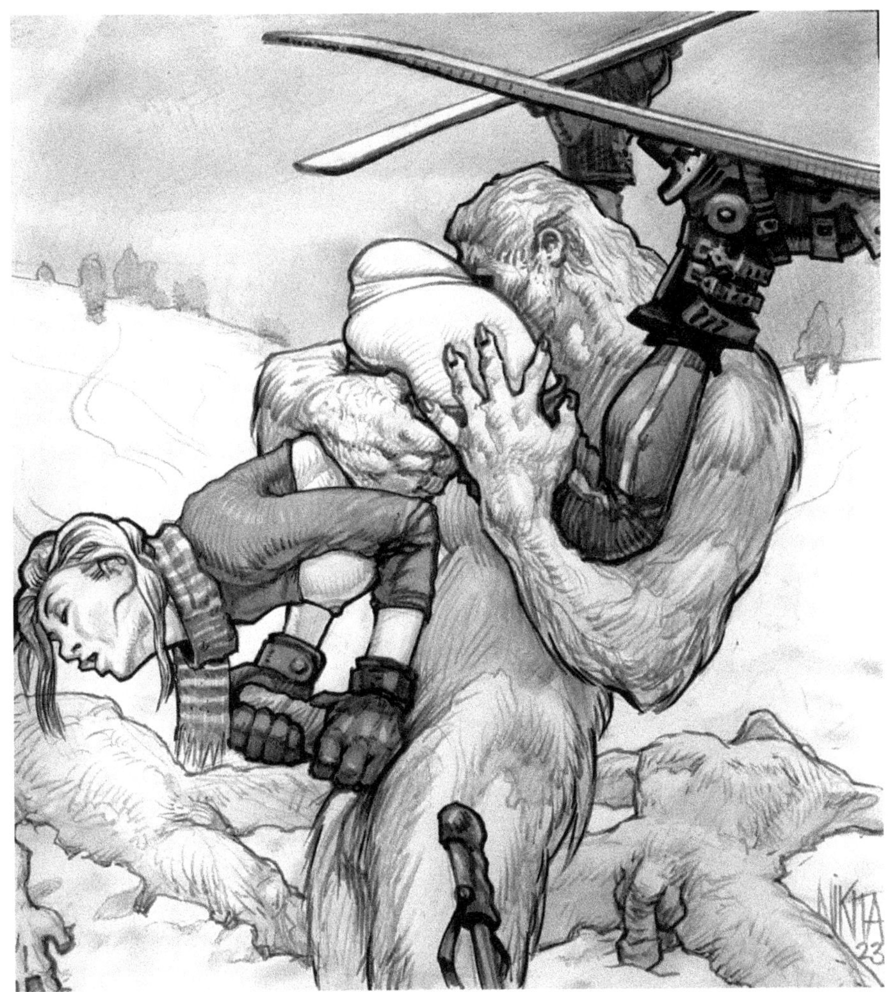
NIKITA
23

WINNER

The battle's won
The enemy dead
Your flag should be flying
At their masthead

But both ships are shattered
And instead
All your brave shipmates
Have joined the dead

A pyrrhic victory
It is for you
For you can't sail the ship
Without your crew

So lie yourself down
On a chest that you saved
And use your great cutlass
In a manner depraved

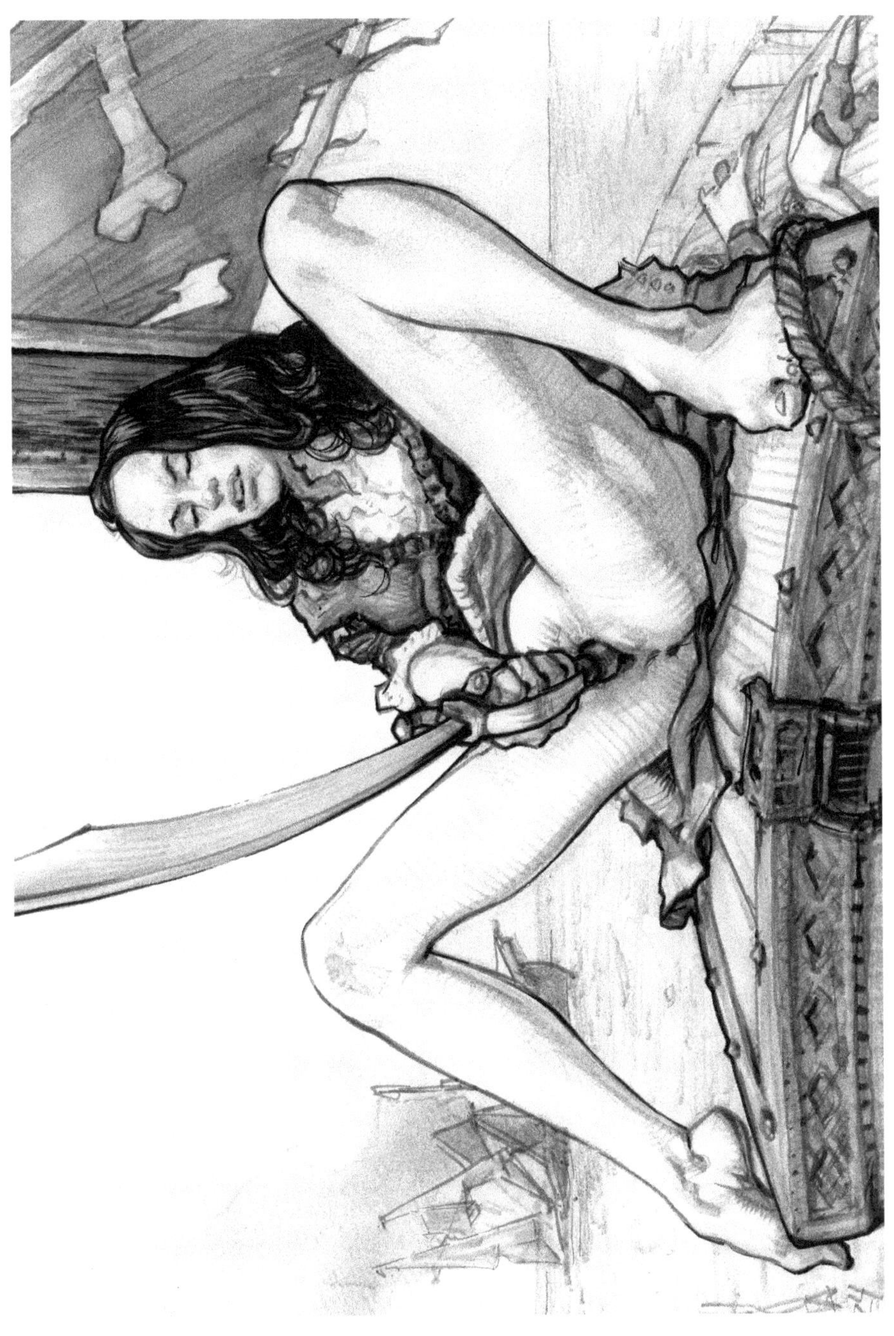

13

WORK AND REST

There are those of us who positively enjoy the work that we do and who are happy to jump out of bed on a Monday morning with the prospect of five, or six, or even seven days of 'work' ahead of us. Sadly the majority of the working population do not see it that way - and would much rather opt for a day or two of rest. Having said that 'Rest' is not just slouching on the sofa, rather it includes all those wonderful activities that we indulge in - except of course 'Work'.

LUMBER-JILL

Her axe fells forests
She wields it stark naked, so
Men are also felled

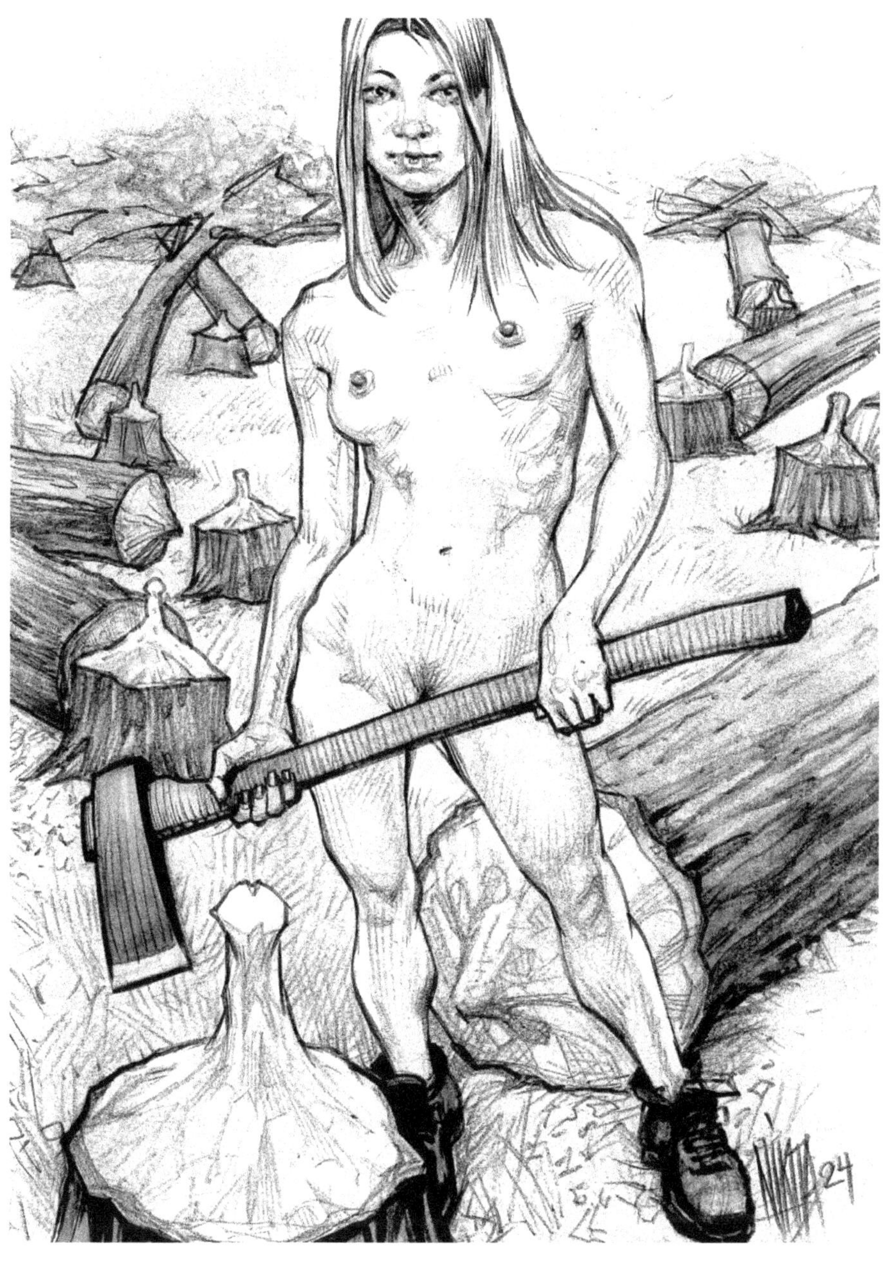

BARBER

Razor is too suave
Angle-grinder does the job
Head must not be lost

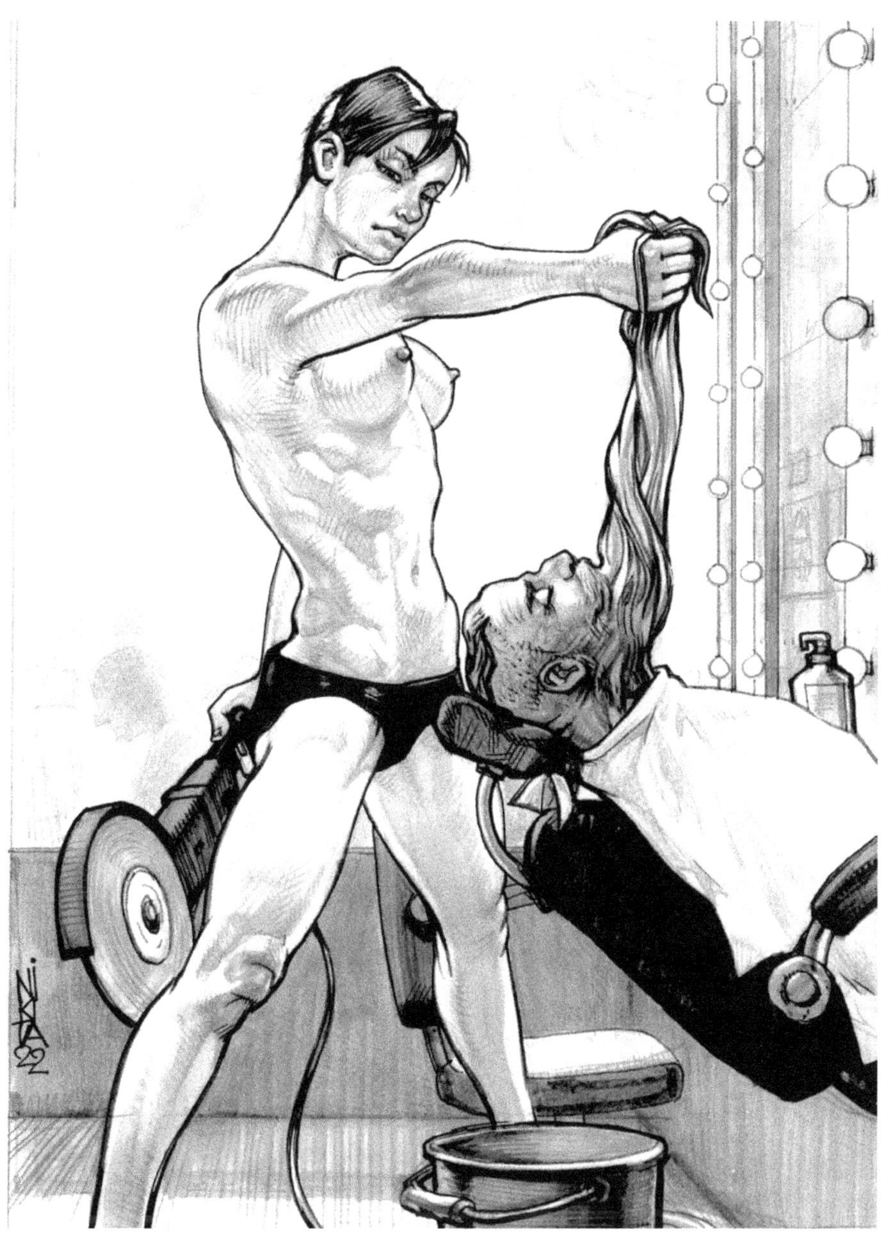

CINDERELLA

No charming Prince,
No fancy slipper
No horses, coach no dance
Nothing that a girl can do
To grab a fighting chance
Just slave all day
In all that heat
And try to keep her cool
But Cinders has a special treat
For Buttons is no fool
Her scanty dress
Her wayward sprawl
Her blue 'come hither' eyes
Tease, stimulate, enthral
Which surely is not wise
For who may come
And may make free
With this enticing pose
The Prince and Buttons both can see
She wears few underclothes

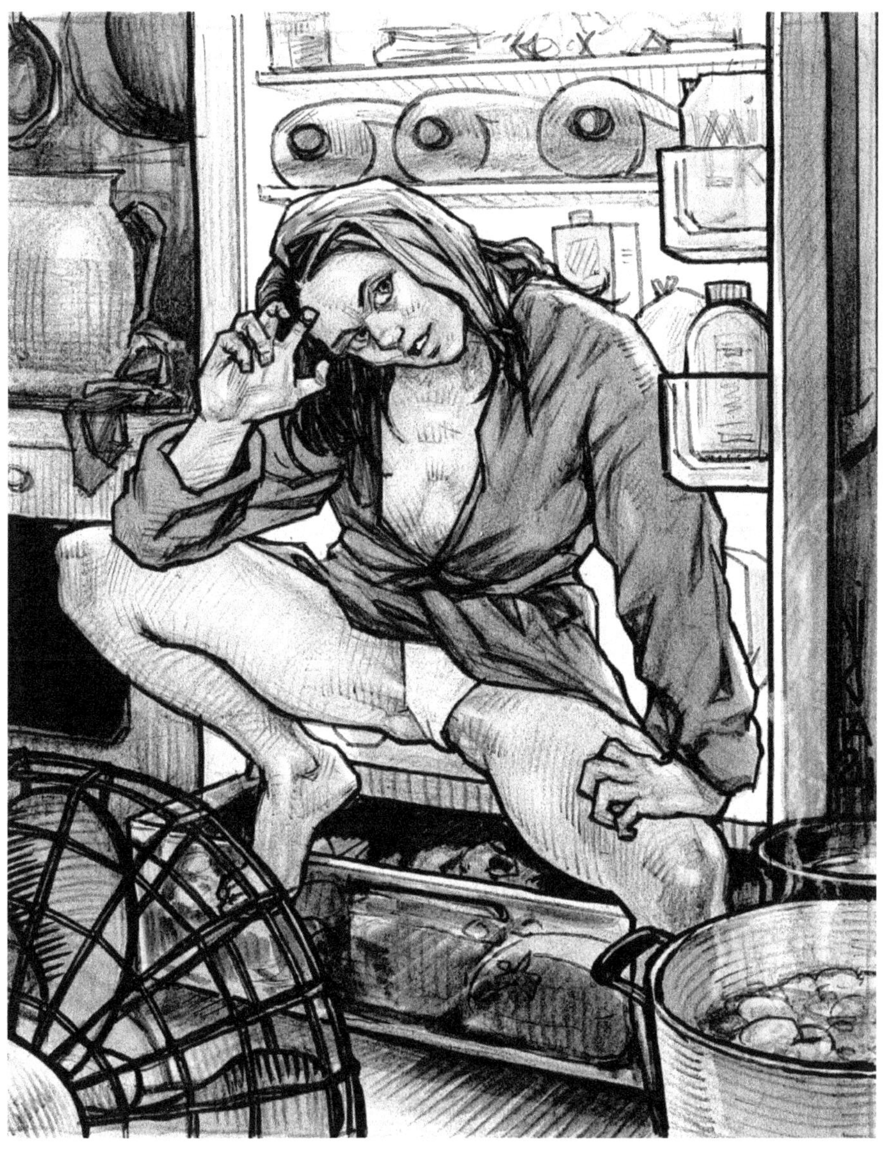

REFRESHMENT

A delightful young lady called Ann
Was prepared when the heatwave began
She stripped to the buff
Which was not quite enough
So she tickled herself with a fan

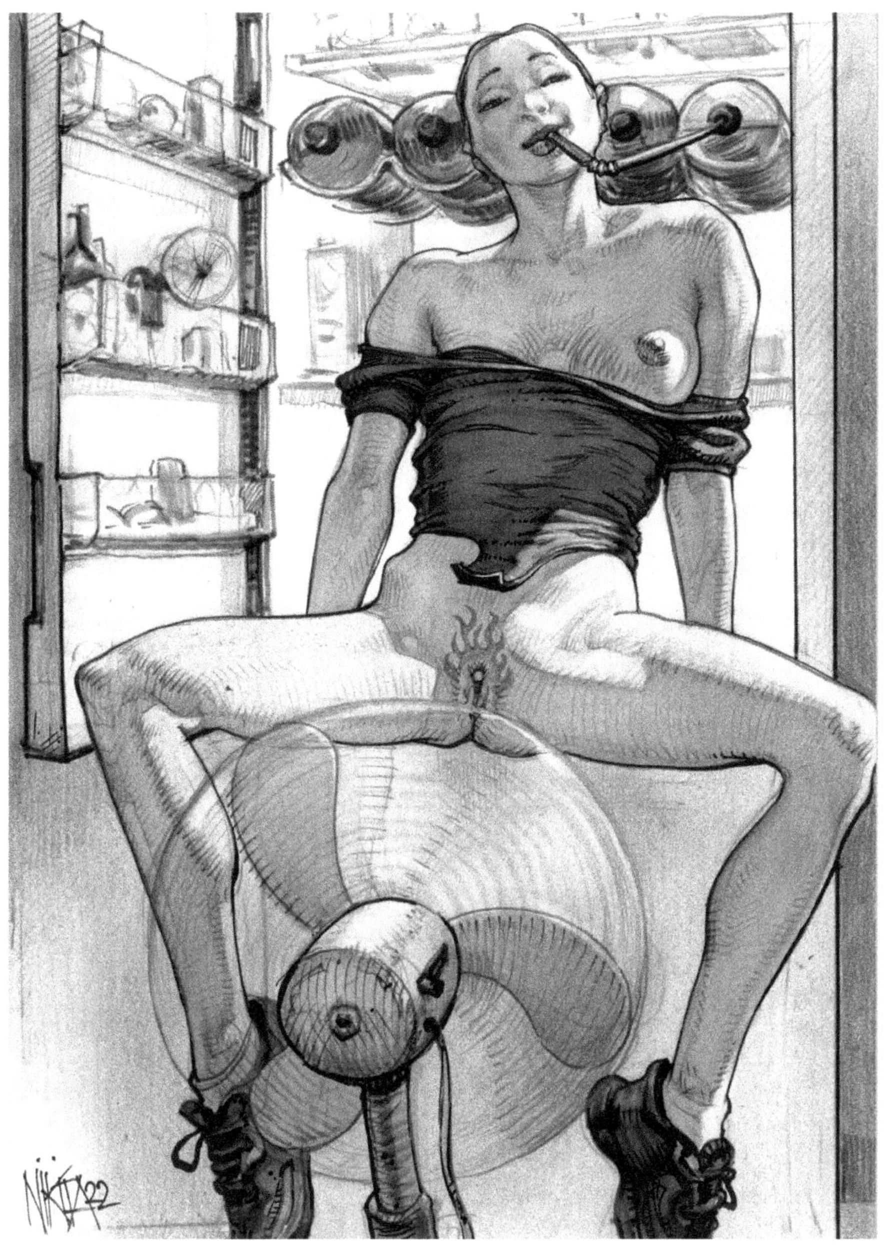

LAUNDRY

A pretty young girl, Bernadette
Charmed everybody she met
But a problem arose
When she stripped off her clothes
And sat naked in the launderette

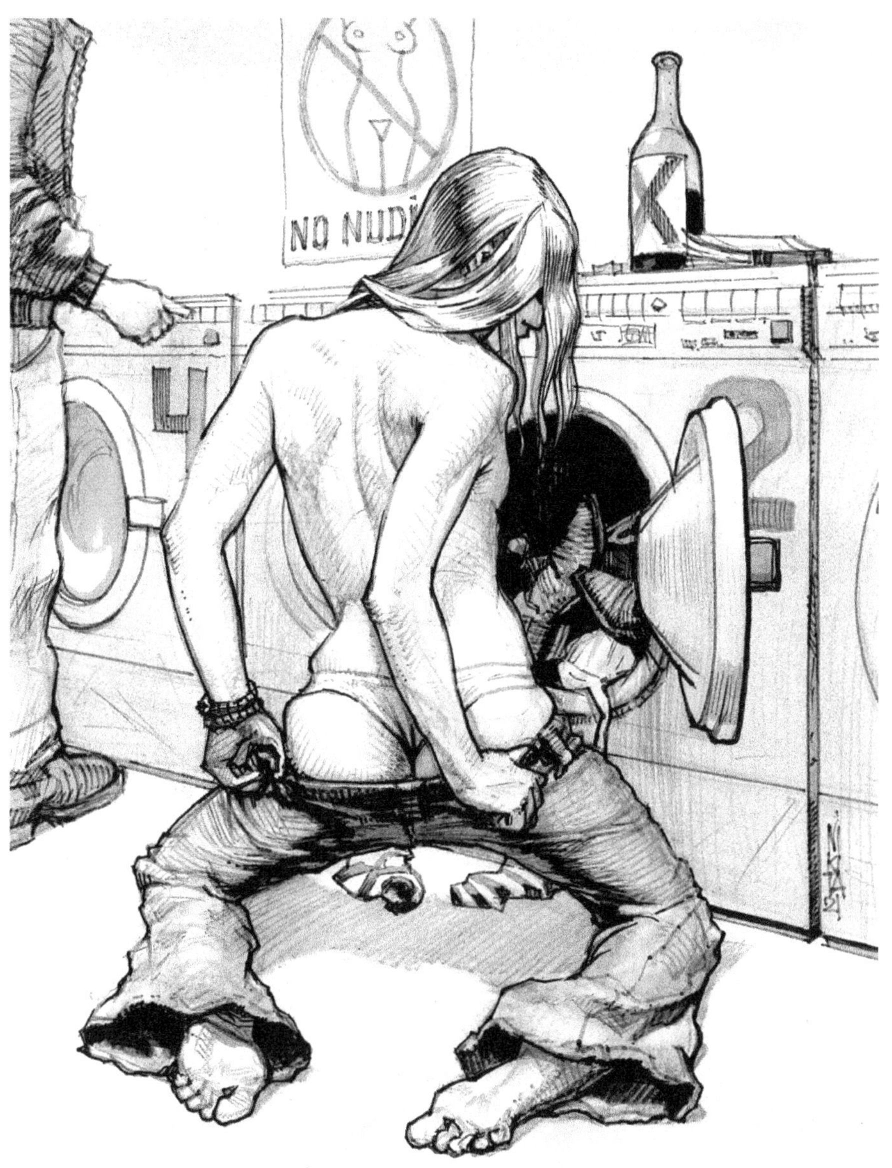

CASTING

Displaying charms without inhibition
They come in their hundreds searching for fame
Their future fixed on this one audition
Willing and eager and heedless of shame
Nakedly kneeling as caster requests
Exposed in this way they are well portrayed
With their crotches shaven and enhanced breasts
The casting couch culture must be obeyed

No more should such things be managed this way
Following Weinstein we know what to do
A hopeful actress should not be man's prey
But proud of her talent, shouting 'Me Too'

Men are to blame, as for them it's a wrench
To stop lusting for a pretty young wench

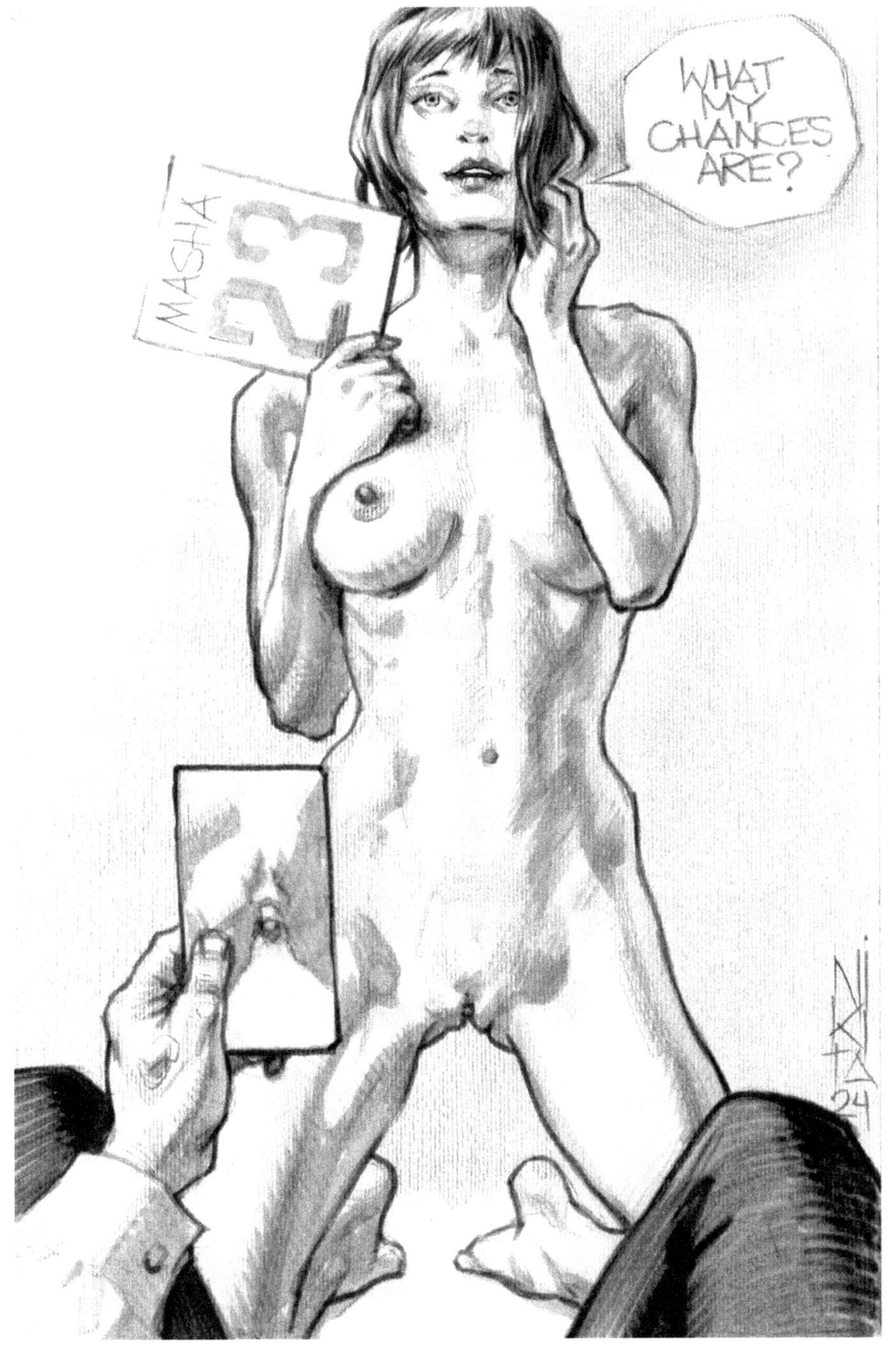
WHAT MY CHANCES ARE?
MASHA
23

WEBCAM PUPPET

Puppet for delight
Long distance pornography
Excites her as well

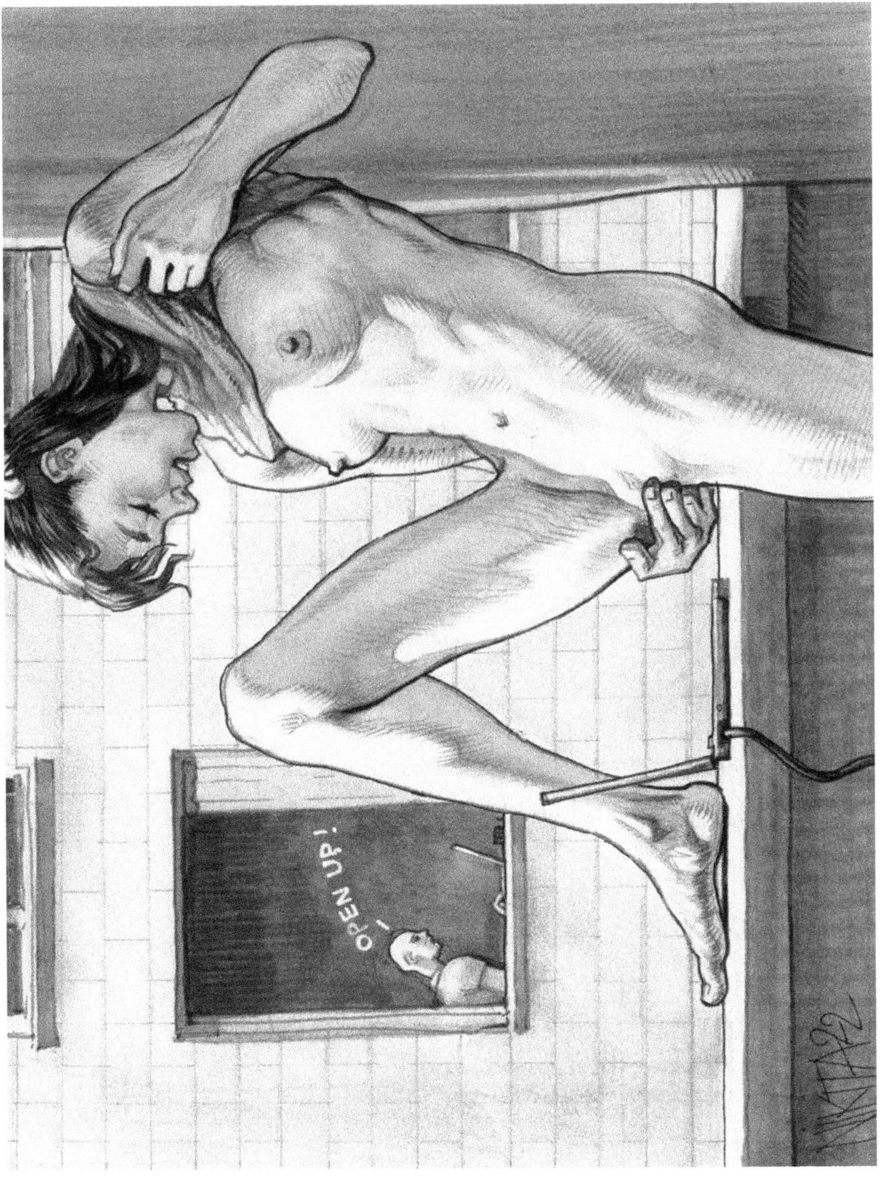
OPEN UP!

WEBCAM MODEL

Exposure for pleasure
Is no way to measure
The morals of modern man
Indeed such delights
And arousing sights
Have existed since time began

In the past things forbidden
Were carefully hidden
But now they are all on webcam
All you could desire
For ten euros an hour
Or a monthly subscription plan

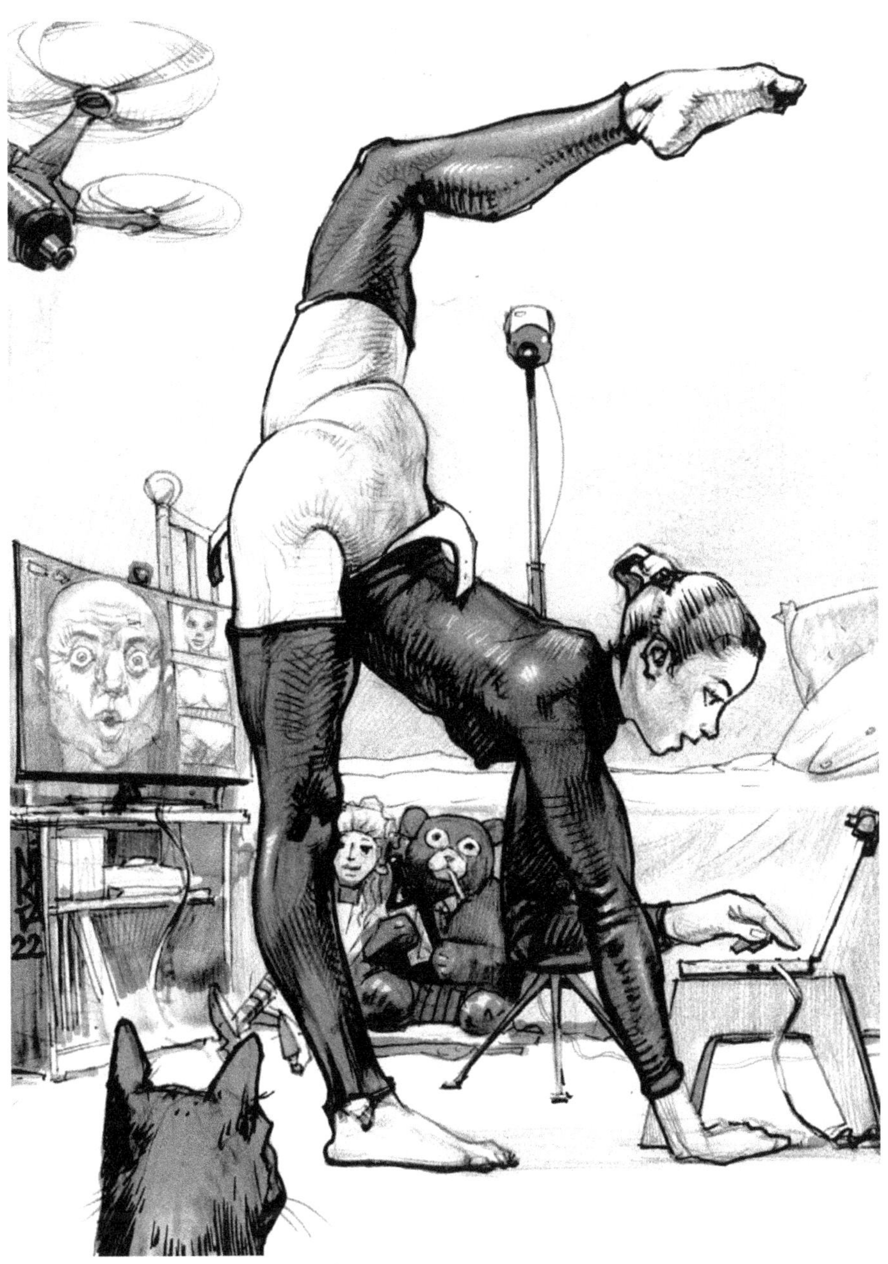

STATEMENT

I need to make a statement
That I want the world to see
So I wrote it very large, and
Scrawled it over me!

Most moral themes are baseless
Their proponents only chatter
Their idea of action
Is to 'escalate' the matter

So I stand up here before you
You moral bad misfits.
If you want to learn how to behave
Just read between my tits.

If the message does not reach you
You poor immoral cripples
Then re-read the words I've written
Right between my nipples

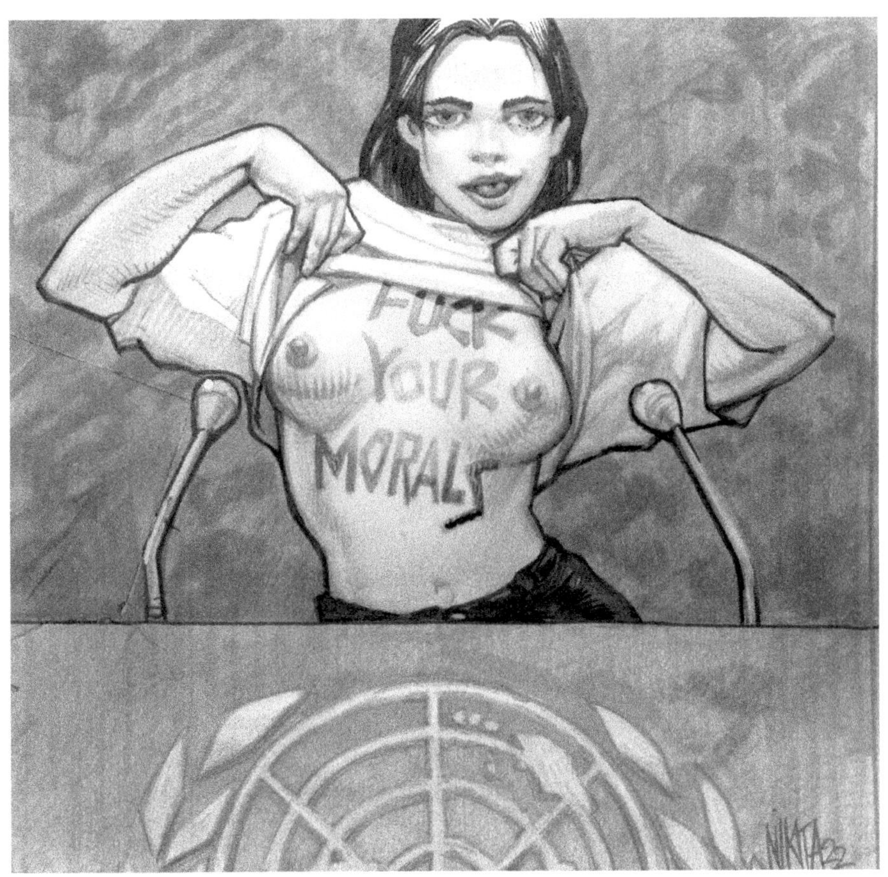
FUCK
YOUR
MORALS

PIN CODE

A lovely young lady called Gwen
Stooped low at the ATM
And the fun would begin
As she entered her PIN
And exposed the way to get in

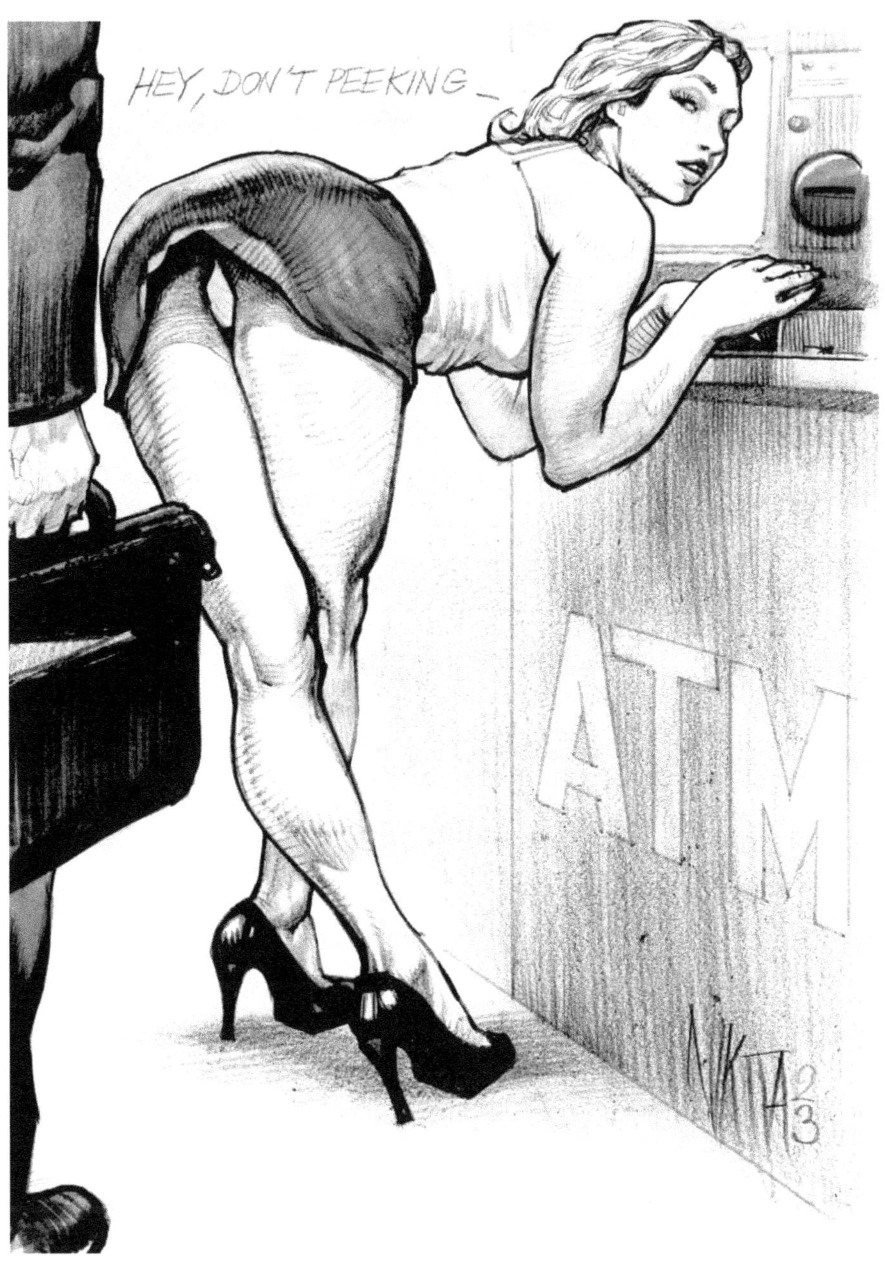
HEY, DON'T PEEKING_
ATM
NIKITA 23

CONTACTLESS

In this modern age we say
It is safer if we pay
By credit card, or else by debit
But sometimes it is hard
To remember you card
And it's useless if you do not have it!

Implanting is a way
That may just save the day
As it will be hard to lose
But where it should go
I really do not know
What intimate place you should choose

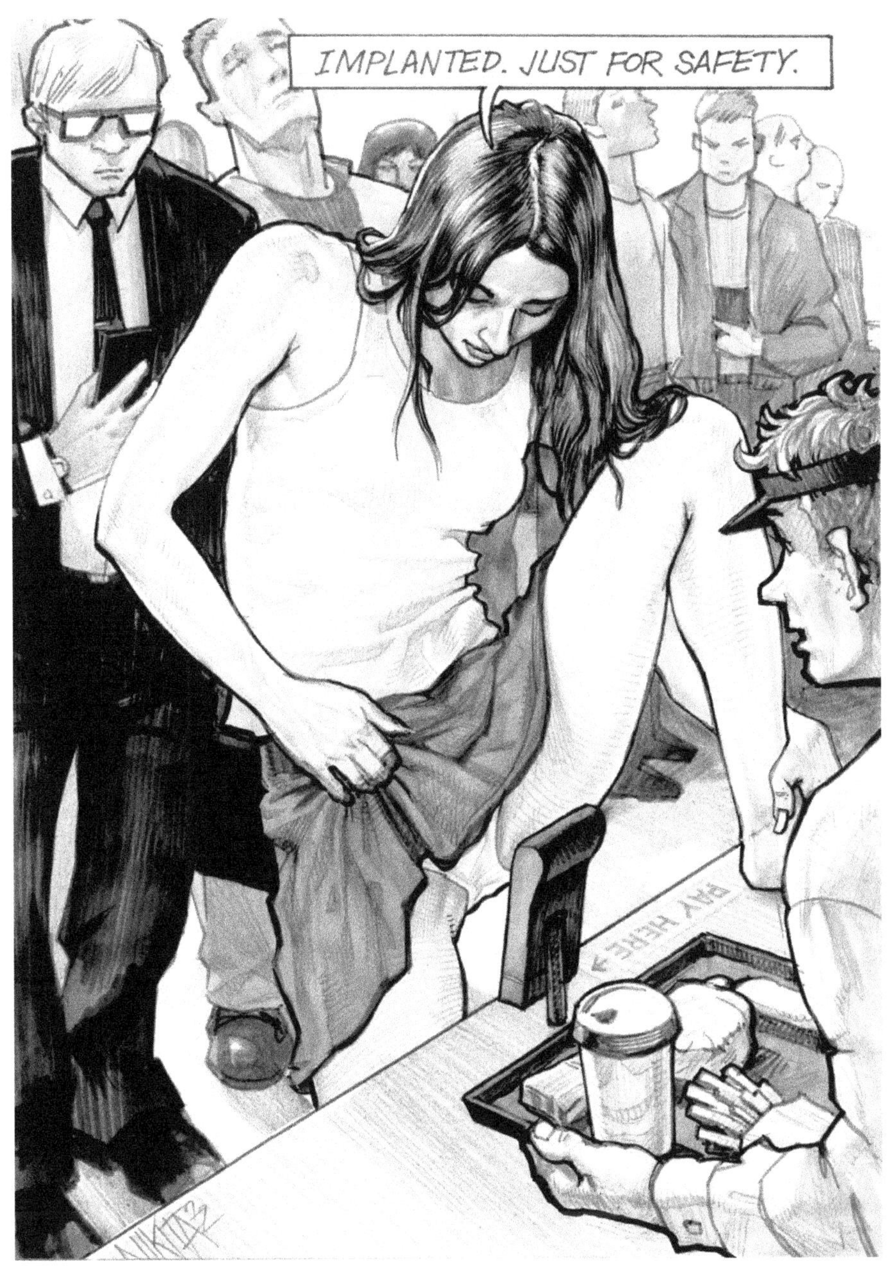
IMPLANTED. JUST FOR SAFETY.
PAY HERE

ELEVATOR

There was a young lady from Bude
Who rode the lift in the nude
How she opened the door
As she reached every floor
I will leave it to you to conclude

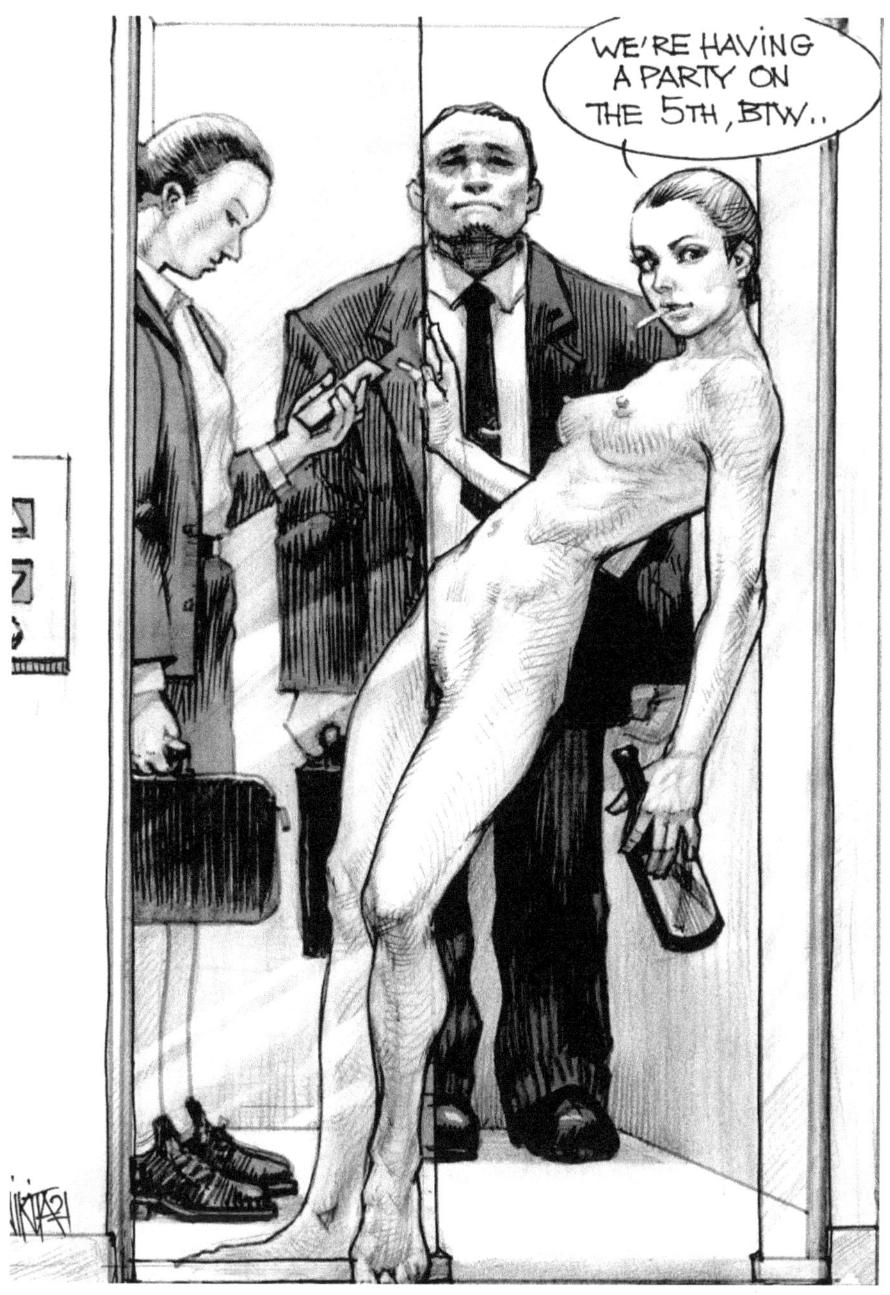
WE'RE HAVING
A PARTY ON
THE 5TH, BTW..

RECIPE

If the sauce tastes great
You ask for the recipe
And they take the piss

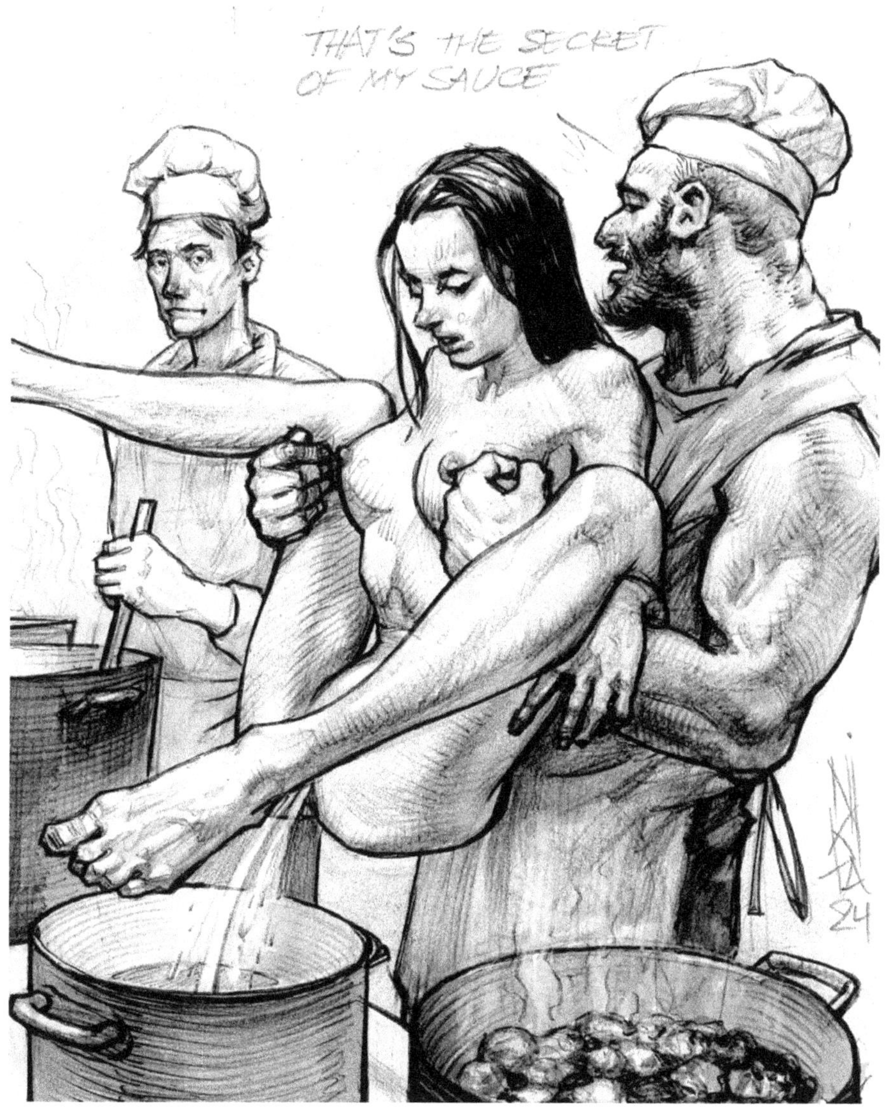
THAT'S THE SECRET
OF MY SAUCE

SCYTHIAN PRINCESS

There was a young lady called Bess
An olden-day gorgeous princess
She ruled the Crimea
By force and with fear
Which is why it is still such a mess.

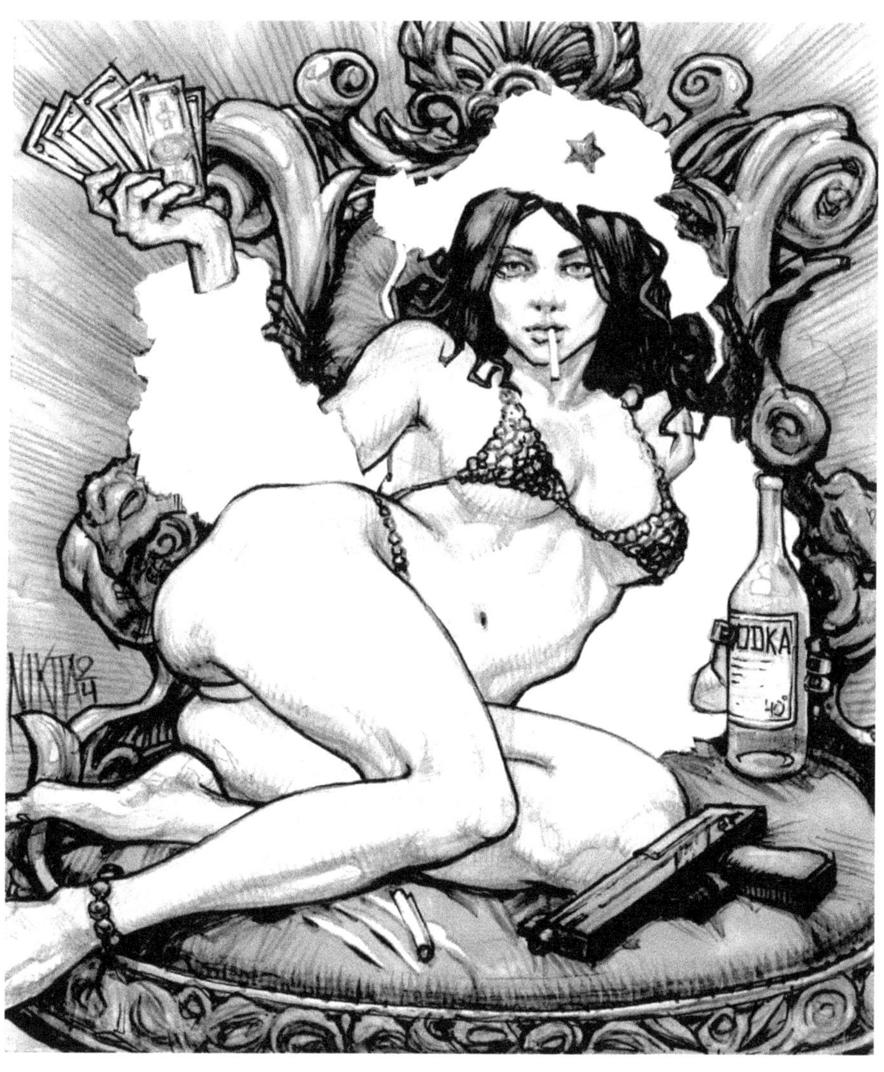
ODKA
40°

EGGPLANT

An Urban Myth says
Aubergines need hatching
Which delights the cook

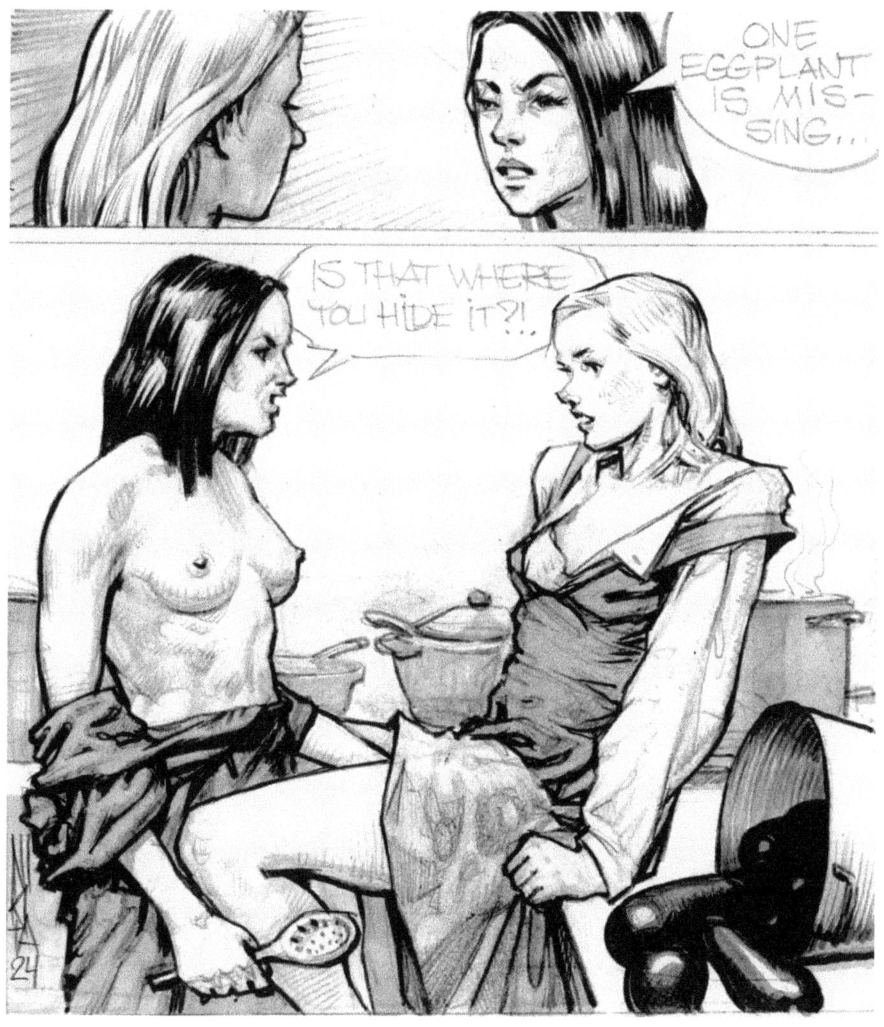
ONE EGGPLANT IS MIS-SING...
IS THAT WHERE YOU HIDE IT?!..

BANANA SHAKE

There are times in life
When, despite your sunny nature,
Depression sets in
How to rid yourself
Of this imposter
Is a very personal matter.
Some people take exercise
Others over-indulge in alcohol
There are just a few
Who prefer to plug themselves in
To a liquidiser
Grasping it firmly between their legs,
So that the vibrations
Resonate in all the right places,
Then waving an errant banana
In the air, in the forlorn hope
That passers by
Might be fooled into thinking
That all ailments can be cured
By creating and ingesting
A banana-shake.

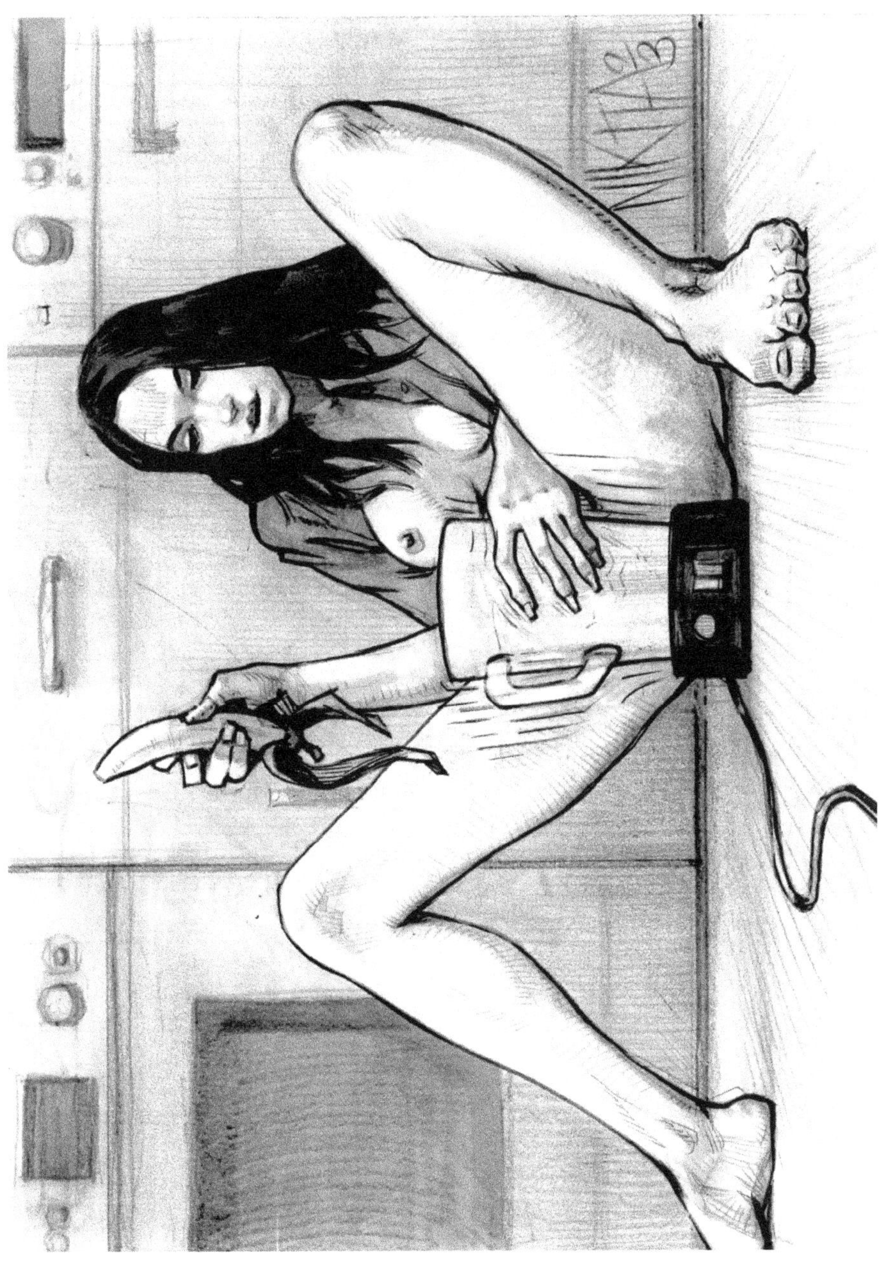

DRIVING SCHOOL

Two mechanisms
Working to enhance our lives
Offer speed and sex

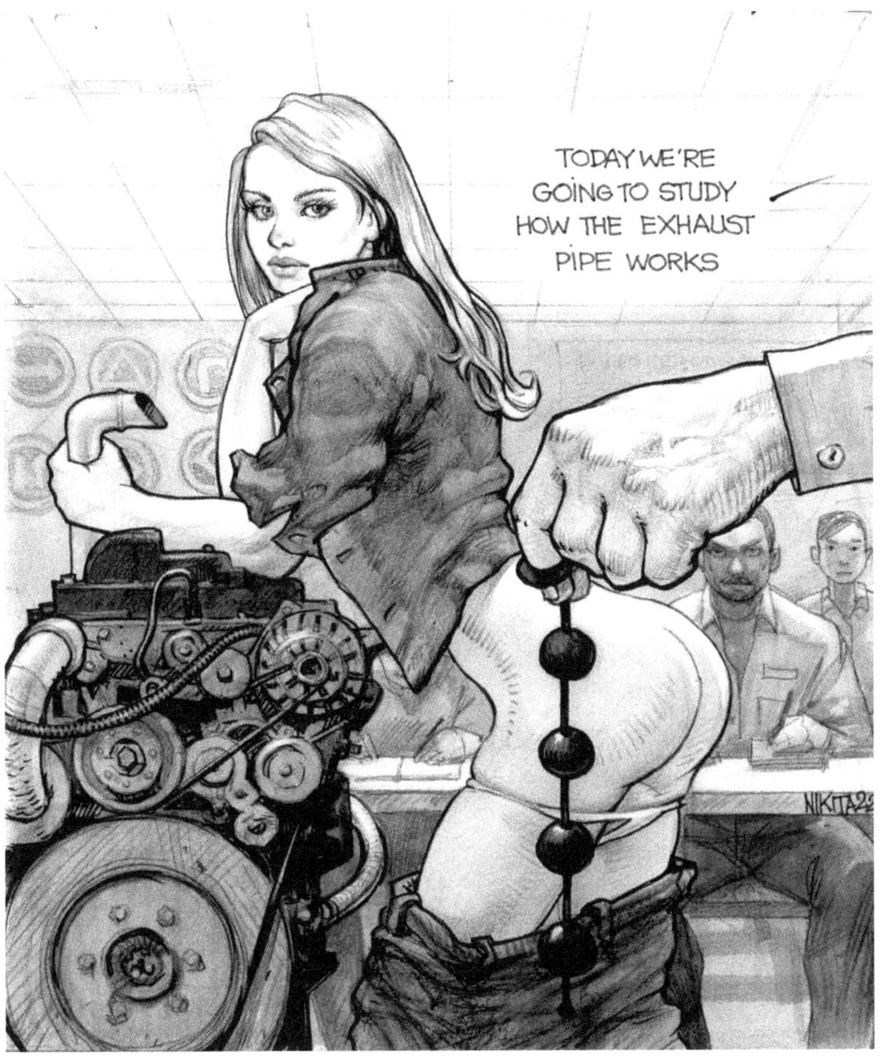
TODAY WE'RE
GOING TO STUDY
HOW THE EXHAUST
PIPE WORKS
NIKITA22

ELECTRICIAN'S DAUGHTER

A sparky's daughter, Camilla
Wanted something to thrill her
She put clamps on her nips
So the charge through the clips,
When she clutched at her crotch, would fullfil her

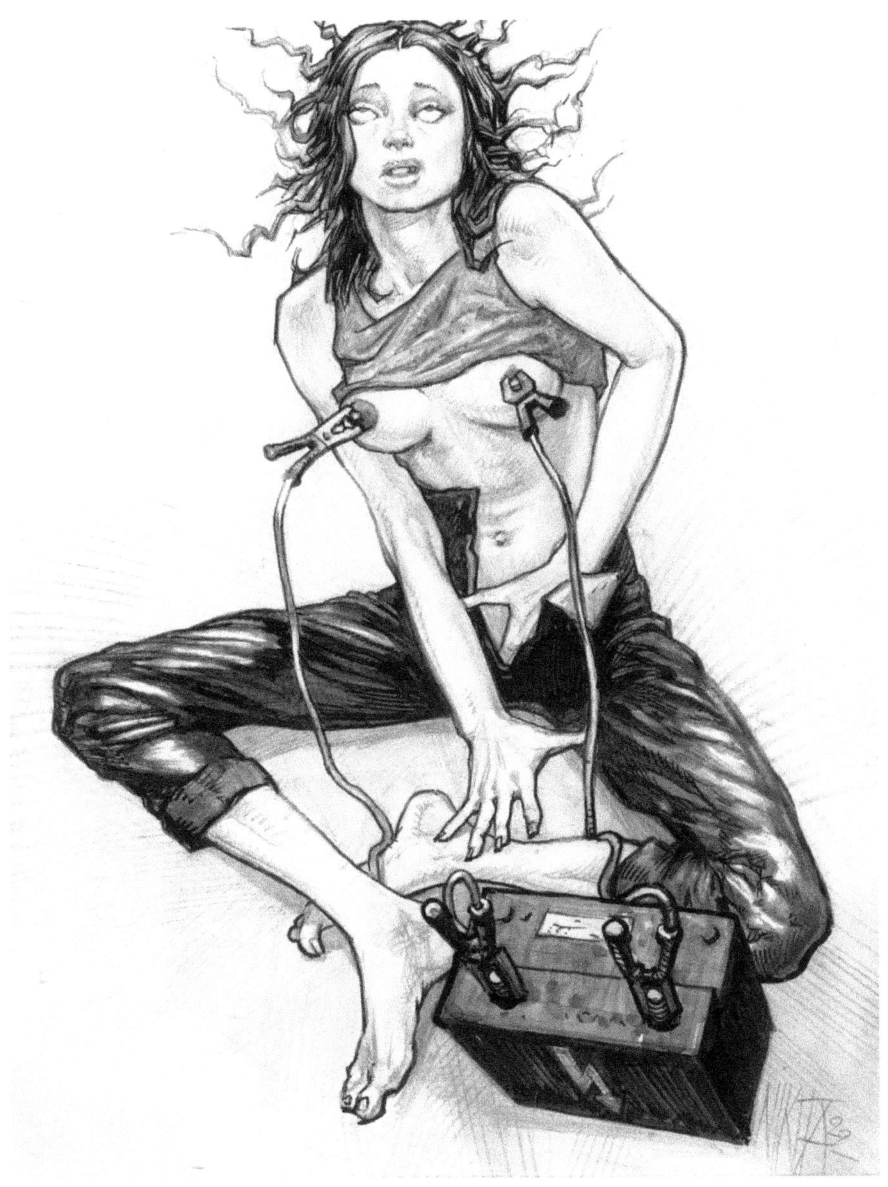

WORKING CLASS GIRL

For a destitute girl they call Fay
It is, sadly, all work and no play
What with substance abuse
Cigarettes and strong booze
She can't celebrate Labour Day.

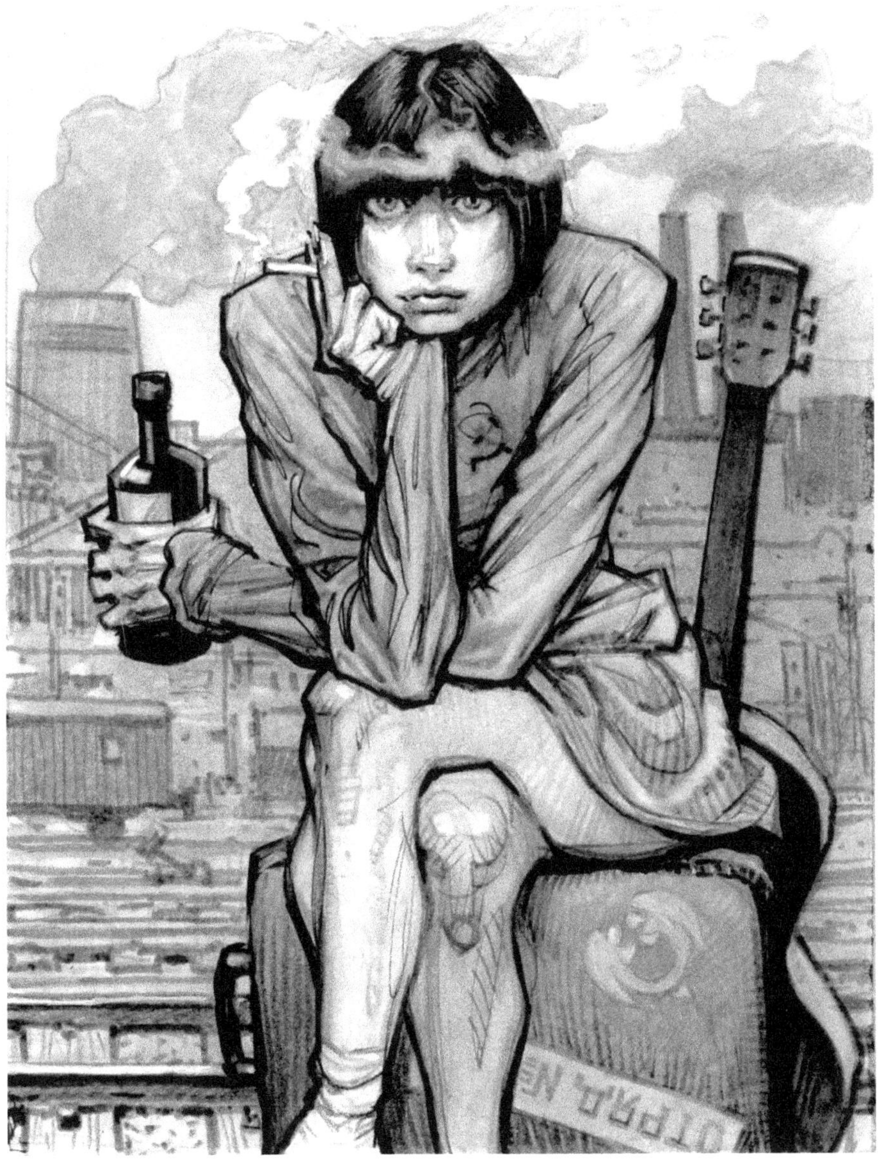

GARDENER

In very hot weather
Watering is essential
In shady places

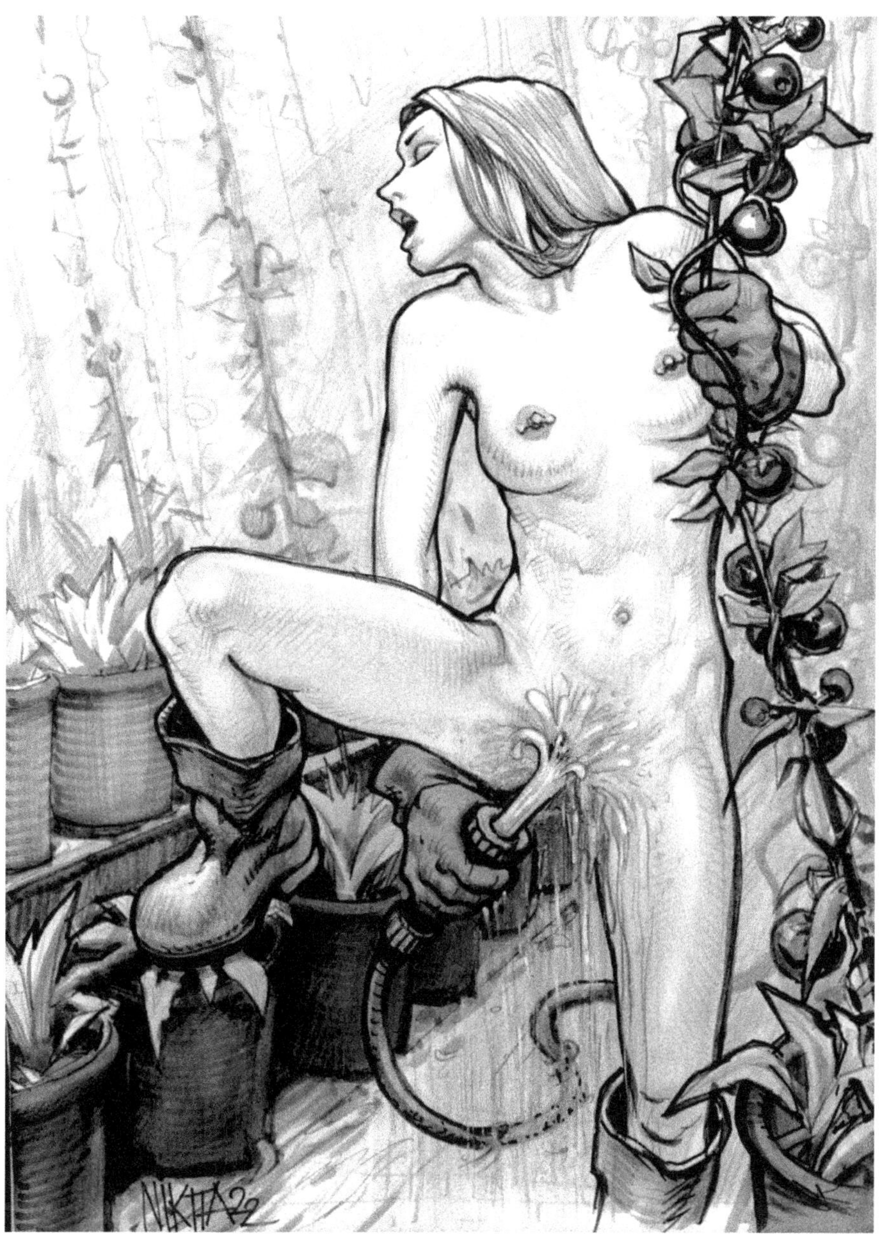

FUCK WORK

There was a young lady called Chris
Who decided to give work a miss
So she stripped to the buff
And that was enough
To give her a life full of bliss

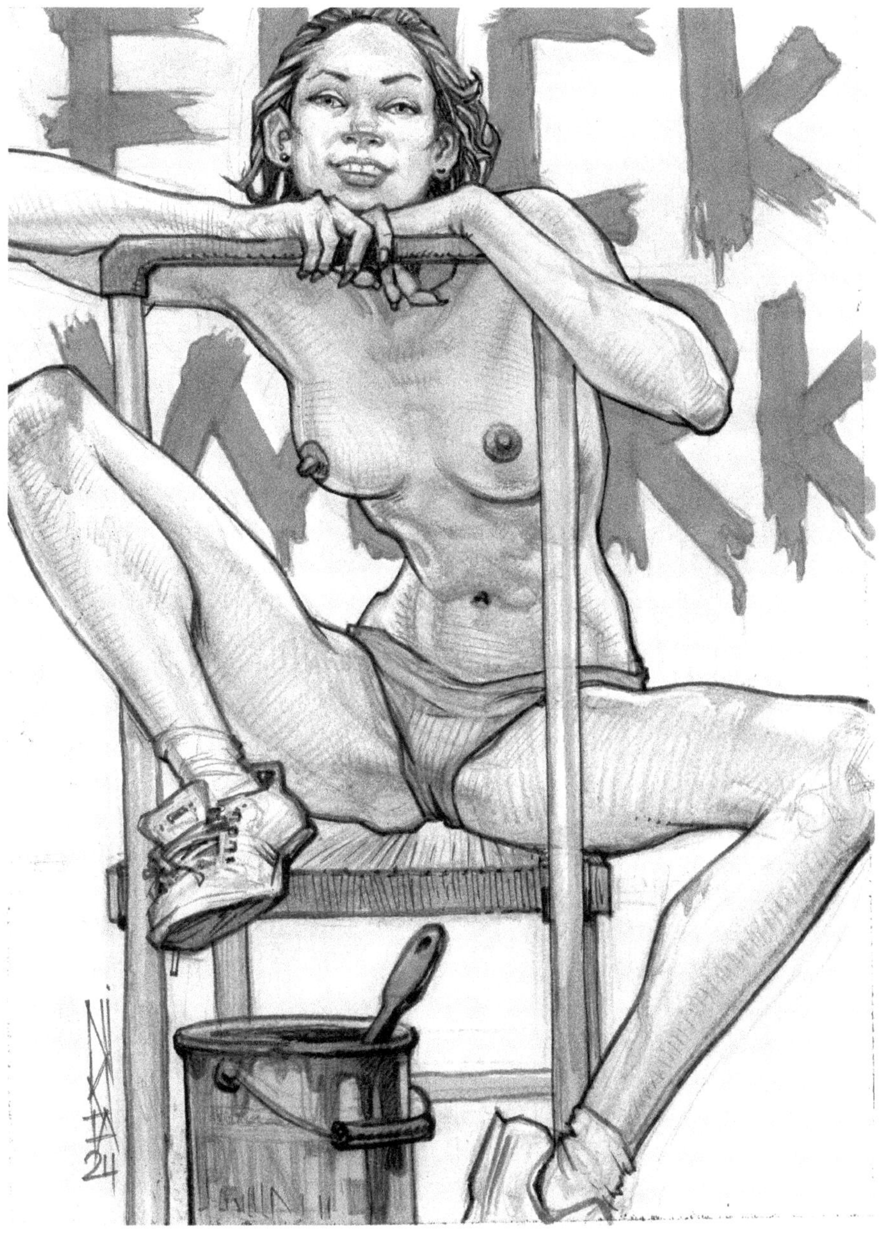

14

ART

In some circles the word 'Art' is a turn-off,
not a subject that more than a few people
would wish to be associated with.
However we have tried to portray it in
a sometimes gritty, often humorous, way,
and hope that by doing so we are encouraging people
of all types to gain pleasure from the images and
words in this book, and in the wider world.

YOUNG SCULPTOR

Tools ready for work
Naked model waiting now
Sculptor has it all

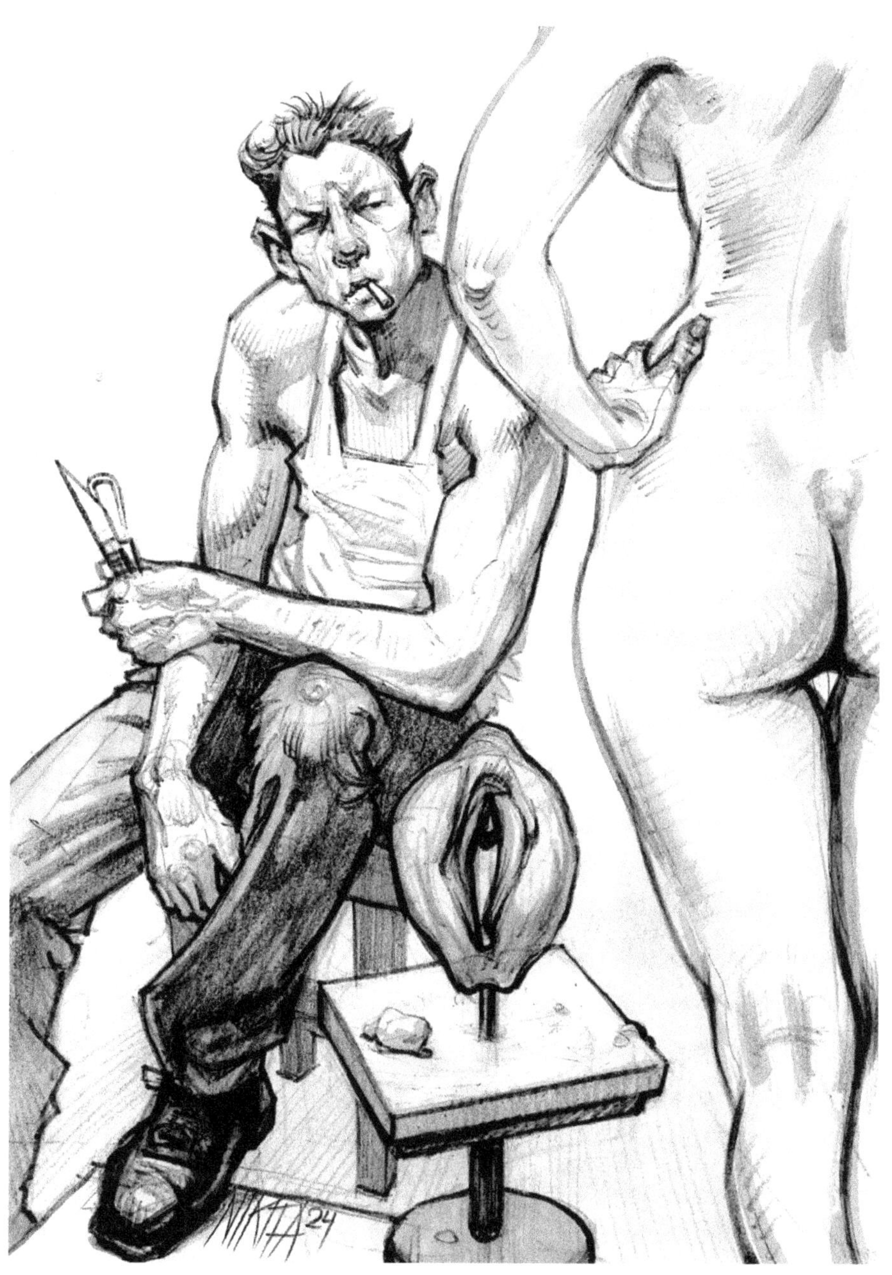

PICASSO & MODEL

Now leaving the Blue
Picasso paints his model
Enjoying her curves

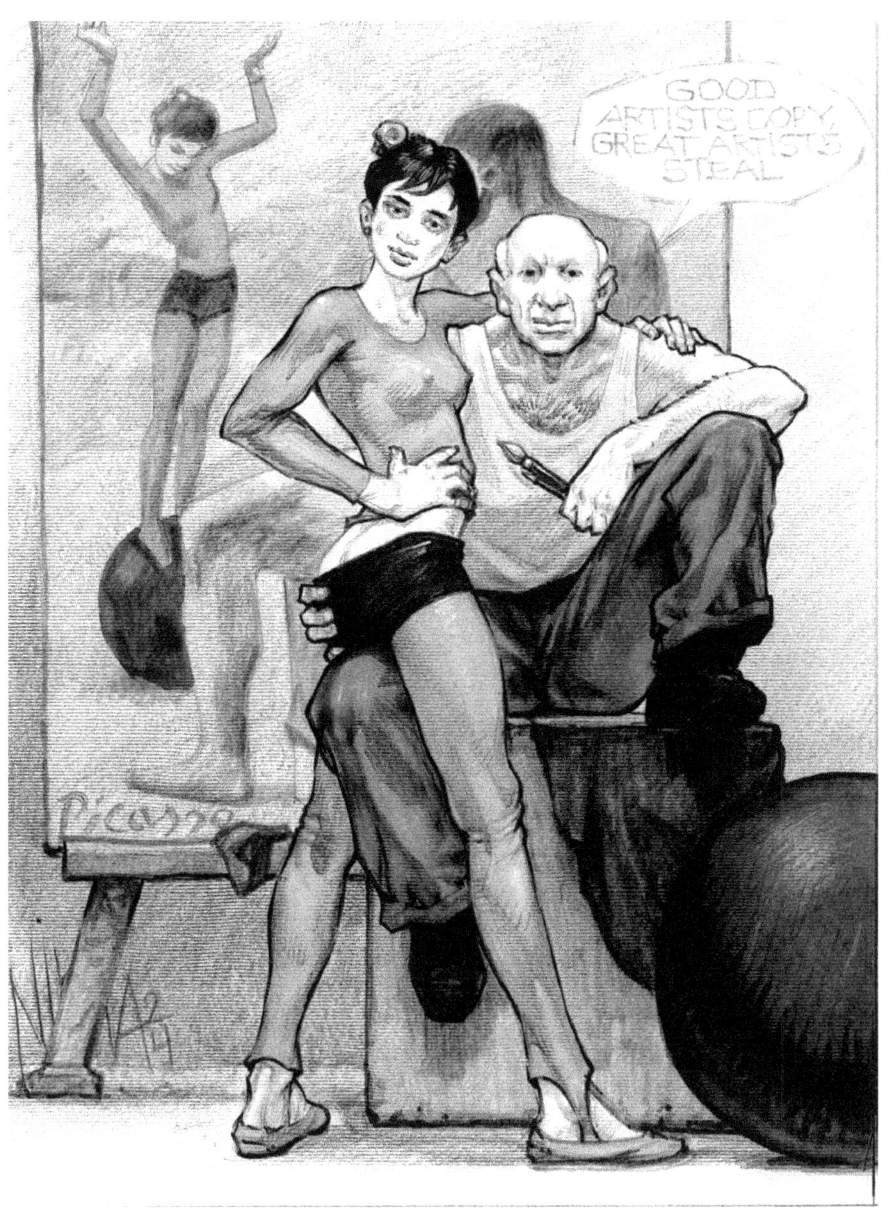
GOOD ARTISTS COPY, GREAT ARTISTS STEAL

GALA

Surrealism rules
Transposing weird images
Like Dali's moustache

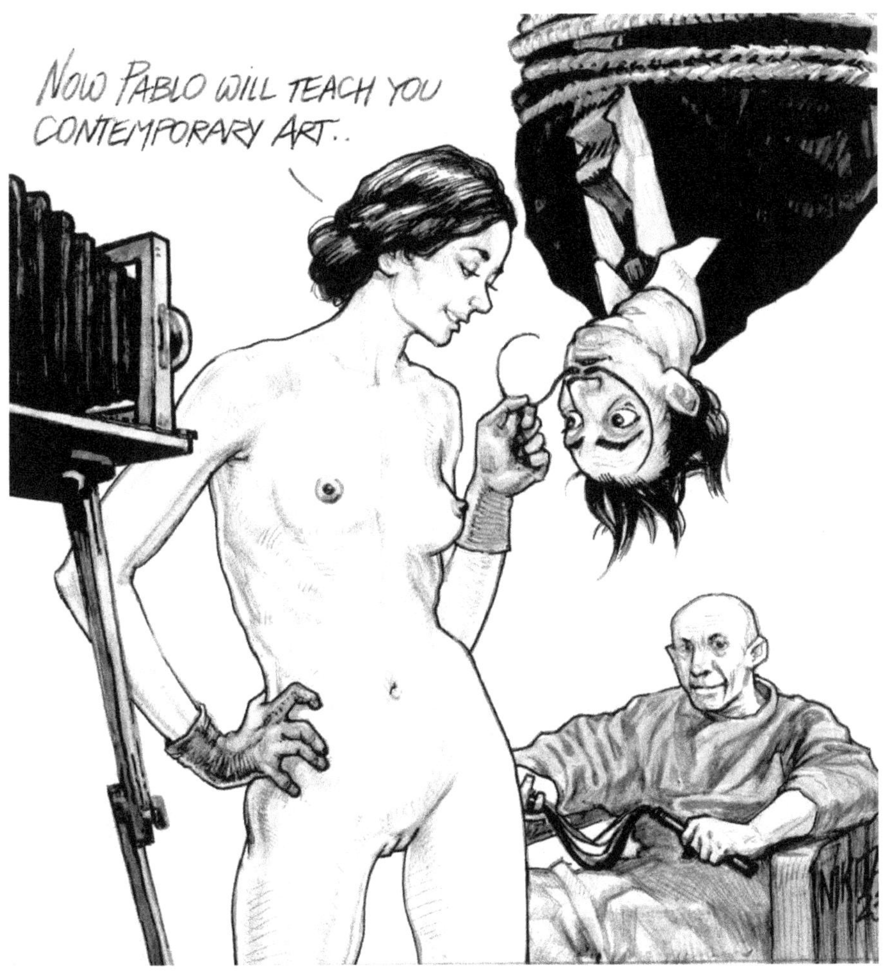
NOW PABLO WILL TEACH YOU CONTEMPORARY ART..

CELEBRATION

A naked young lady from Rome
Liked to drink on her own
She knew what to do
With her handy corkscrew
So the cork found itself a new home

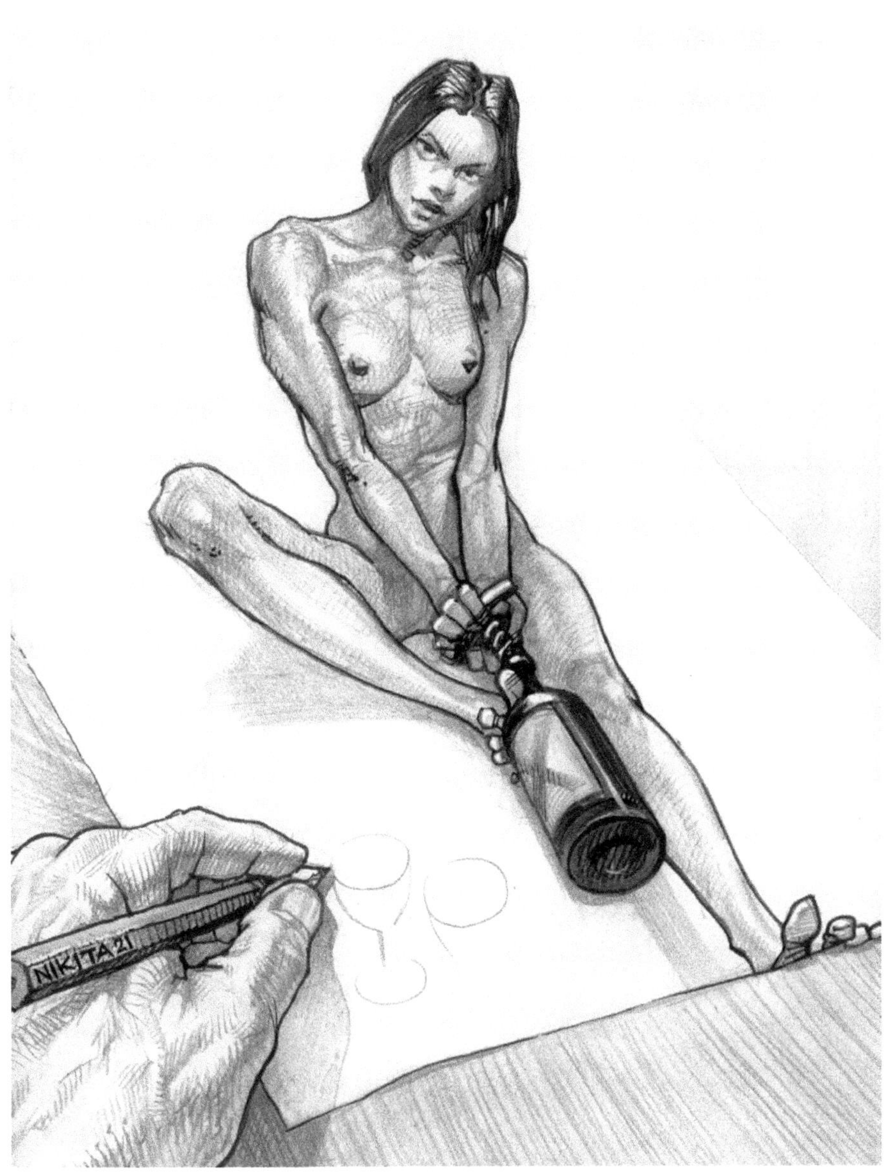
NIKITA 21

FURIOUS MODEL

There was a young model called Grace
Who could never remain in one place
She could not stay still
But wanted the thrill
Of a truly artistic embrace.

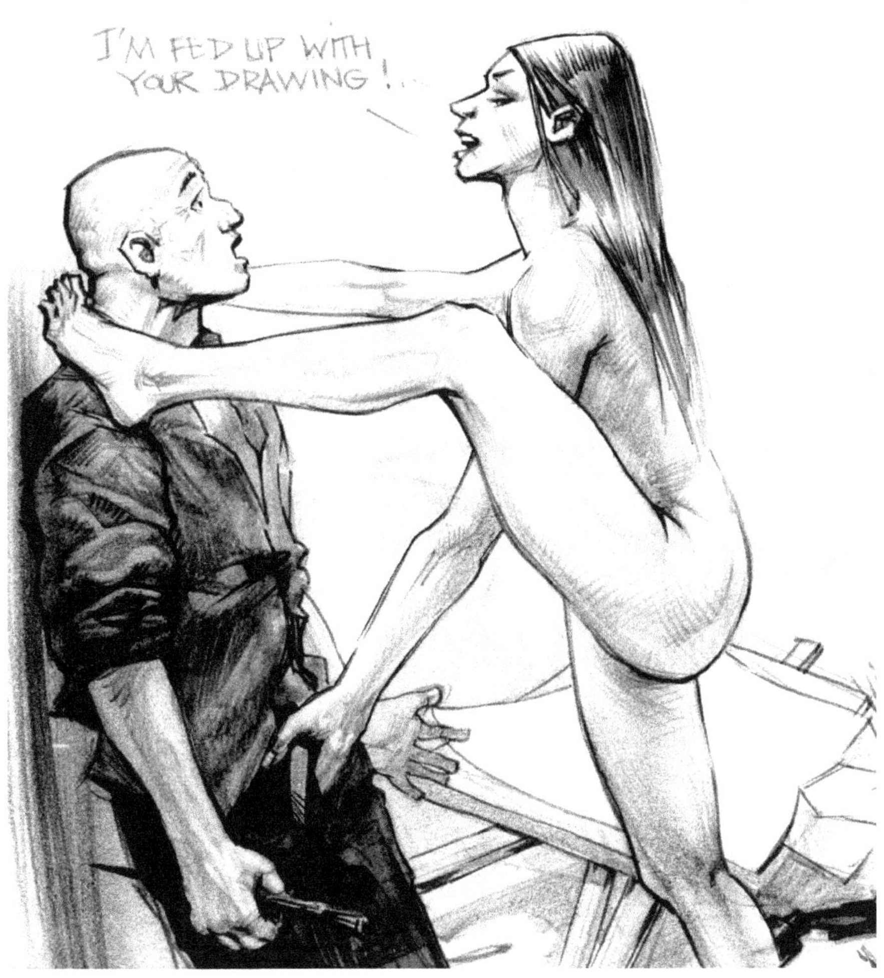
I'M FED UP WITH
YOUR DRAWING!...

SHAVE

For philanderers
Shaving is the kind option
For sensitive parts

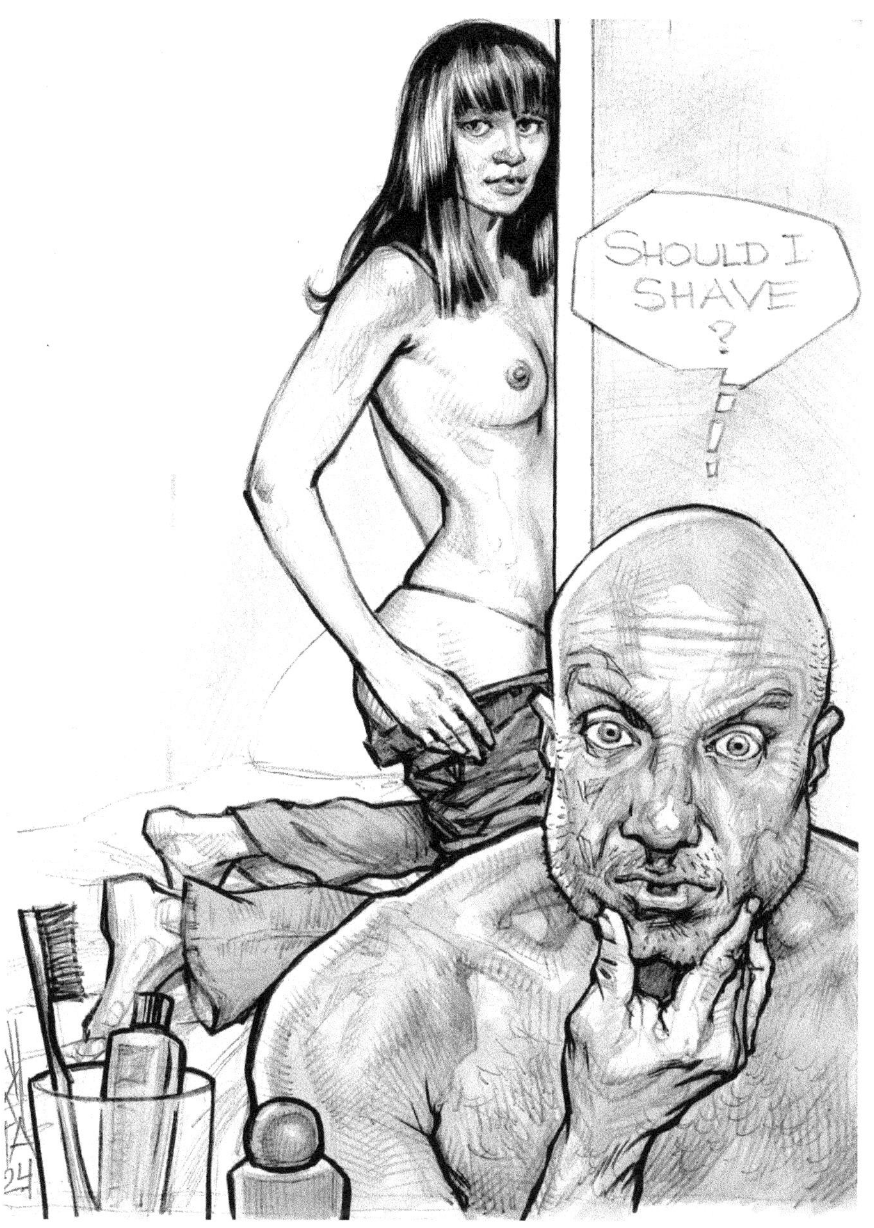
SHOULD I
SHAVE
?

UNFOLLOW

This is a warning to people like you
Who enjoy the sketches that some artists do
Of somewhat erotic young ladies undressed
Who show off their genitals and also their breasts

It is not that you don't know just what you are doing
But it's clear that corruption will be your ruin
Stark naked models seen from the front
Exposing their breasts and revealing their cunt

Nikita works hard at his creations
Serving for breakfast such titillations
So we start our day in a state of bliss
If the Facebook censor approves of this.

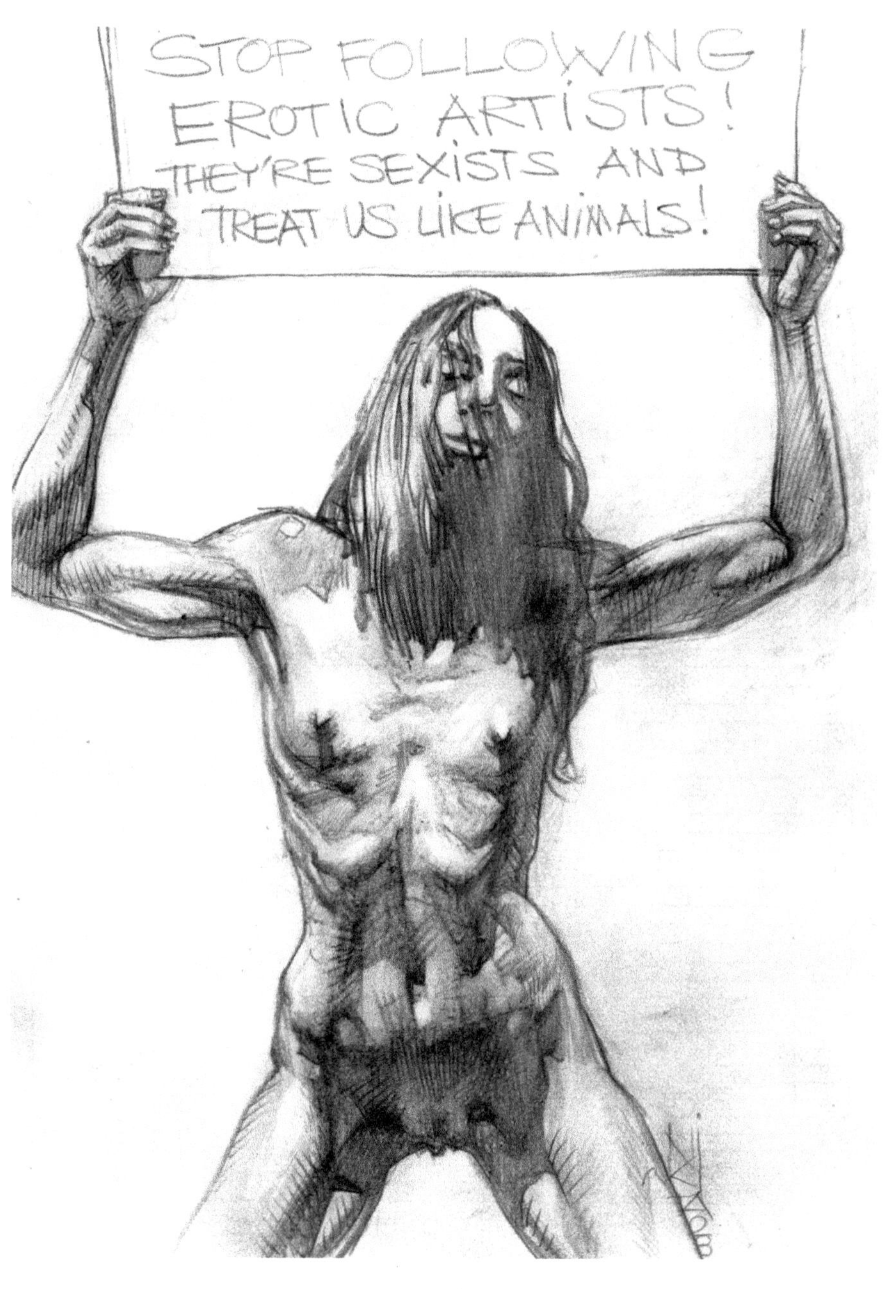
STOP FOLLOWING
EROTIC ARTISTS!
THEY'RE SEXISTS AND
TREAT US LIKE ANIMALS!

DAY OFF

Artists never avoid
Over-stimulation or
Over-indulgence

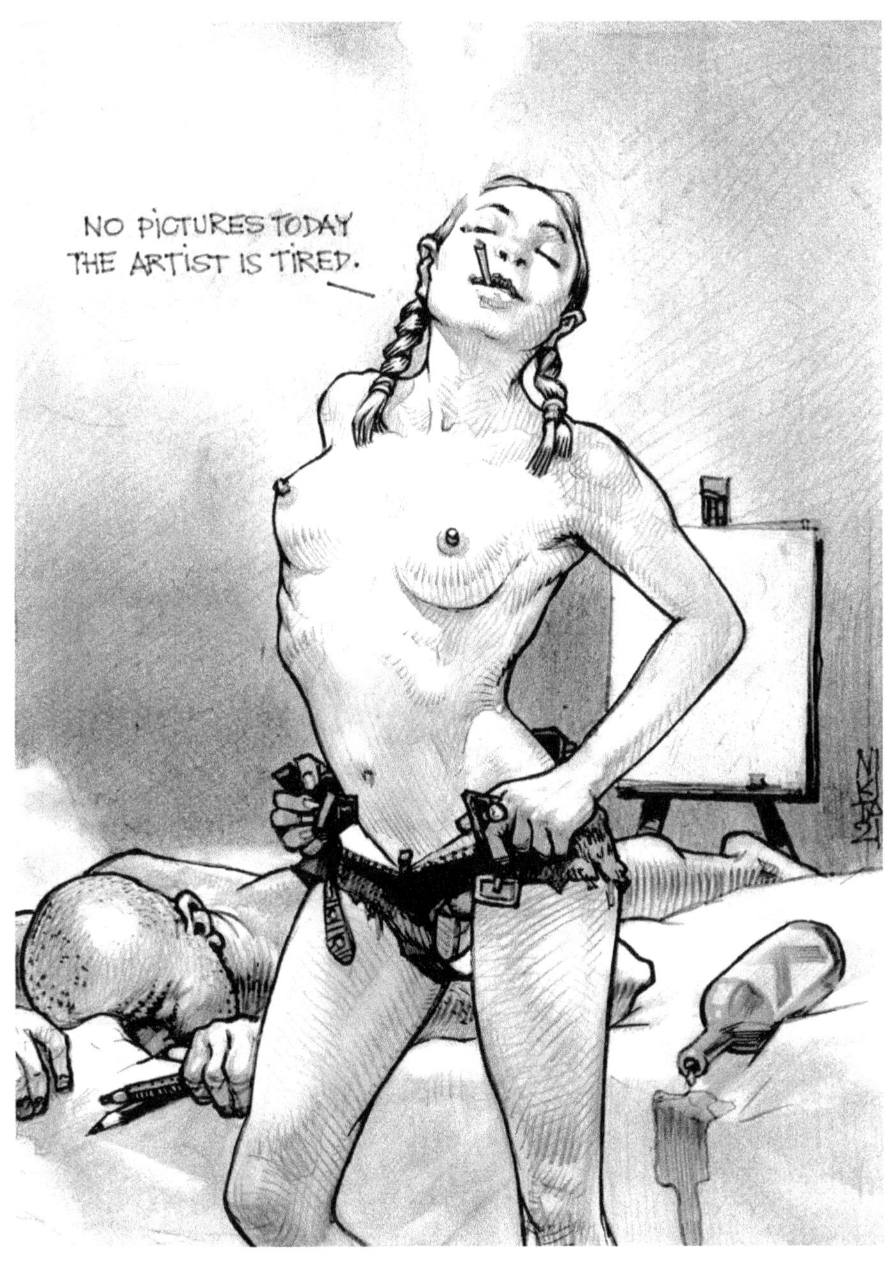
NO PICTURES TODAY
THE ARTIST IS TIRED.

ARTIST

Sometimes we may seek
To achieve things
That are beyond
Our capabilities.
This is not necessarily
A bad thing
For it pushes us beyond our
Comfort Zone.
However there is
A downside
As the results
Of our naive efforts
Especially in
The Fine Arts
May well prove
Aesthetically displeasing.

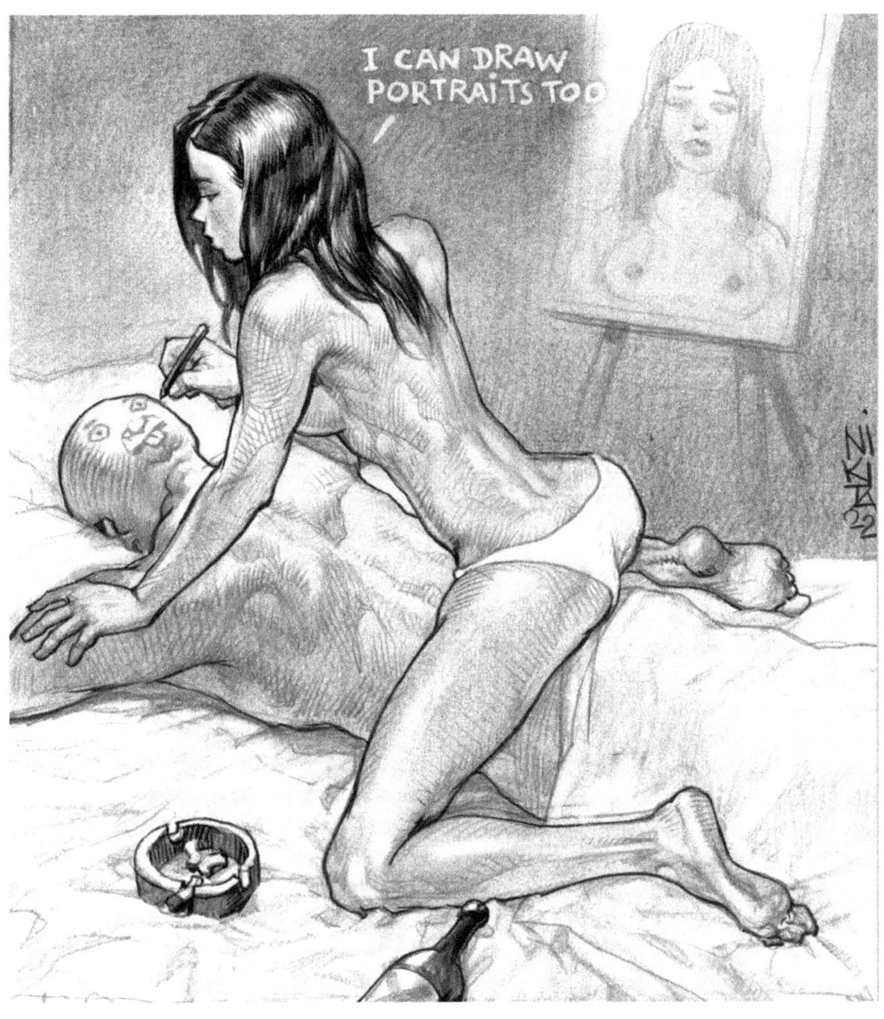
I CAN DRAW
PORTRAITS TOO

MODEL OR WHAT

Models don't only sit
Once the sketching has been done
They do Other Things!

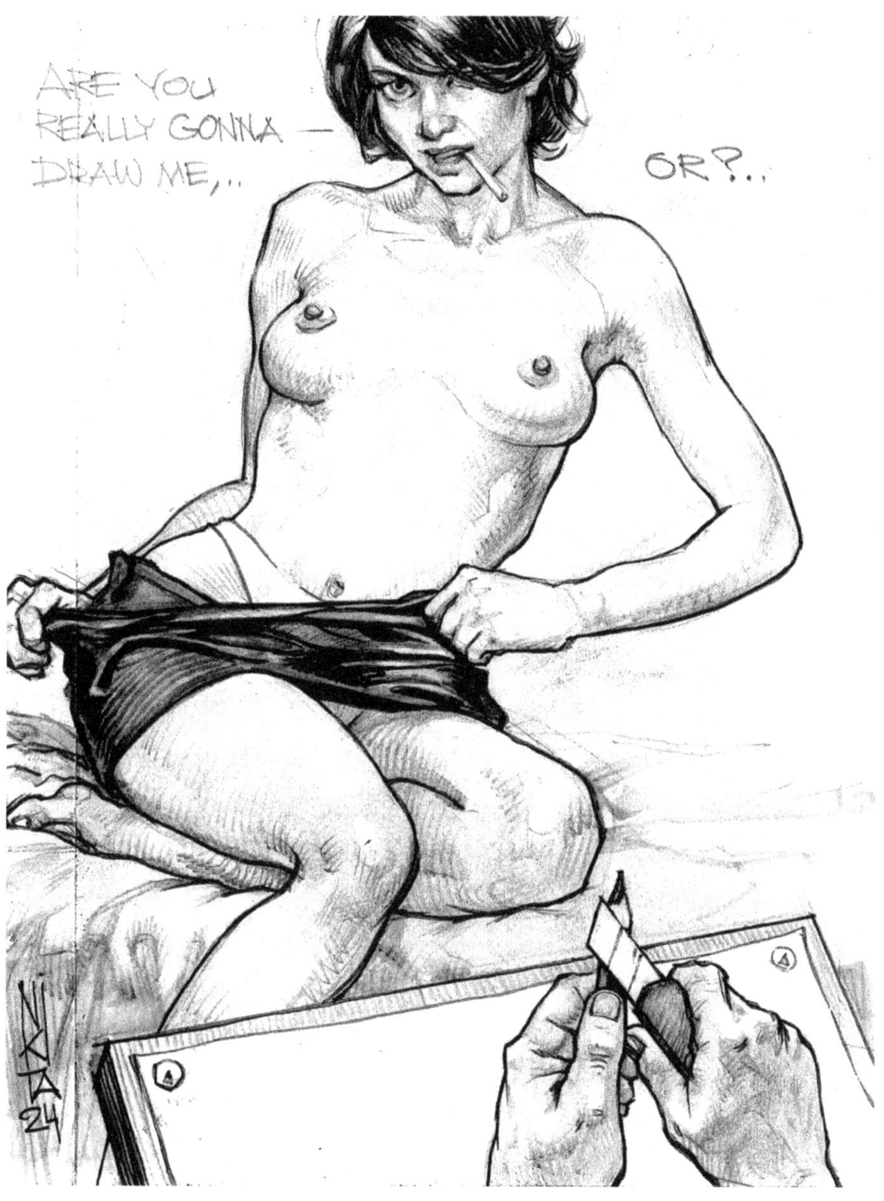
ARE YOU
REALLY GONNA —
DRAW ME,..
OR?..
NIKITA
24

GIFT

We never tell
Black lies
In fact I have never heard
Anyone identify a lie
As black.
That such lies exist
Is indisputable
But unacknowledged.
White lies are ubiquitous
They surround us
Encompass us in their
Cloying dependency.
Excuses for their telling
Are legion.
White lies, we say,
Are never intended
As a means to
Advantage ourselves
But to protect others
Our family our friends
In fact in the telling of
White lies
We can congratulate
Ourselves on being
Kind
Caring
Loving
Which of course is
Complete Bollocks!

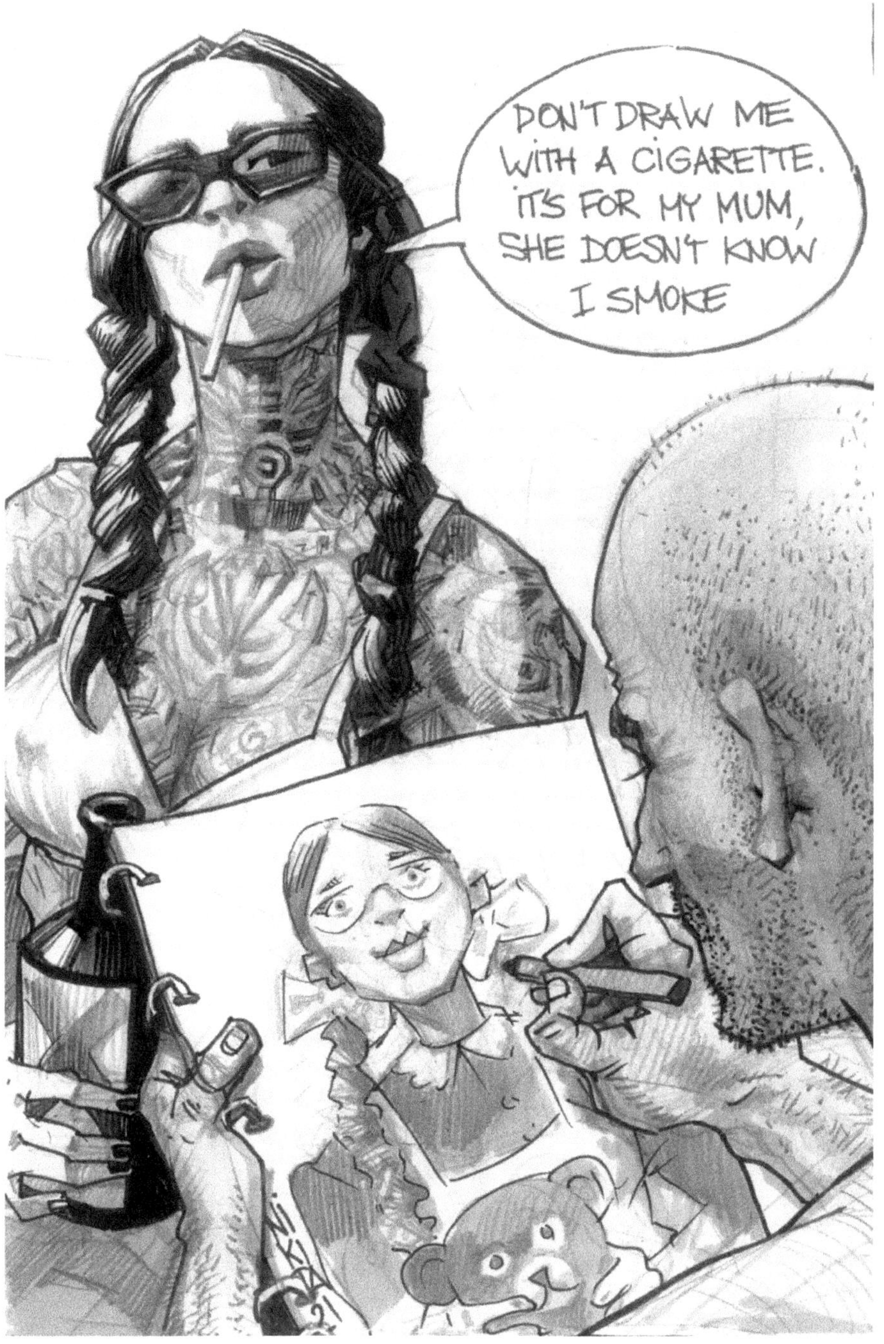
DON'T DRAW ME
WITH A CIGARETTE.
IT'S FOR MY MUM,
SHE DOESN'T KNOW
I SMOKE

BRUSH

There is an intimacy
Perhaps a special intimacy
In being
An artist's model
It might be a question of
Professionalism
For both parties
For whilst it is understood
That sexual acts
Will take place
Between artist and model
There are boundaries
Never to be crossed
Most particularly
An artist must ensure
That his model
Should never seek
To brush herself up
The wrong way.

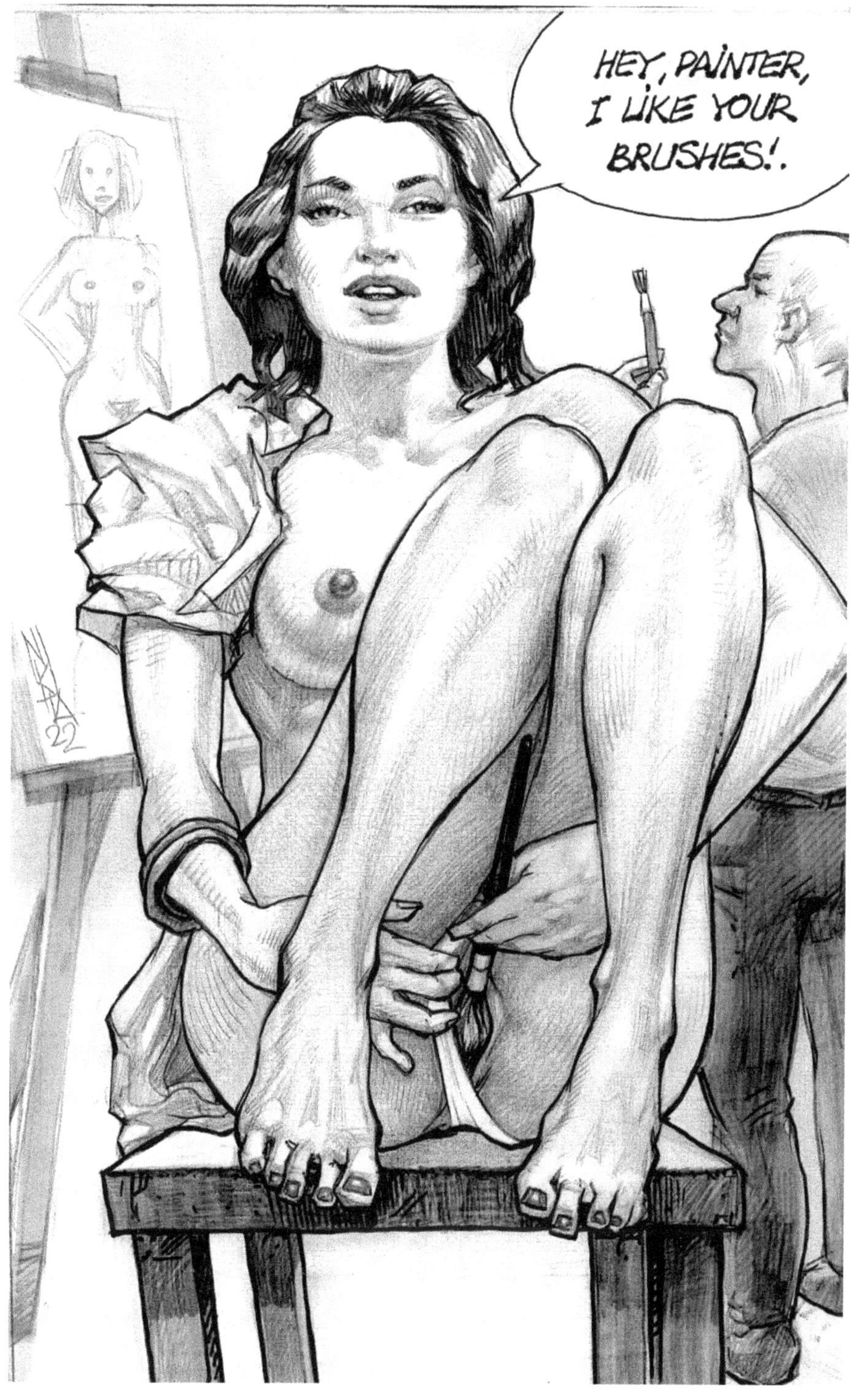
HEY, PAINTER,
I LIKE YOUR
BRUSHES!.

NIKITA'S MODEL

There is little that is as
Exciting
Aggressive
Stimulating
Depressing
As pornography.
It is all too easy for
Creative people
To be lured towards
The pornographic
Egged on by populism
But there is no 'Fine line'
For there is sexual content
In so many artistic creations.
It is us.
You and me.
Who by slavering over
The gynaecology
Turn art
Into porn.

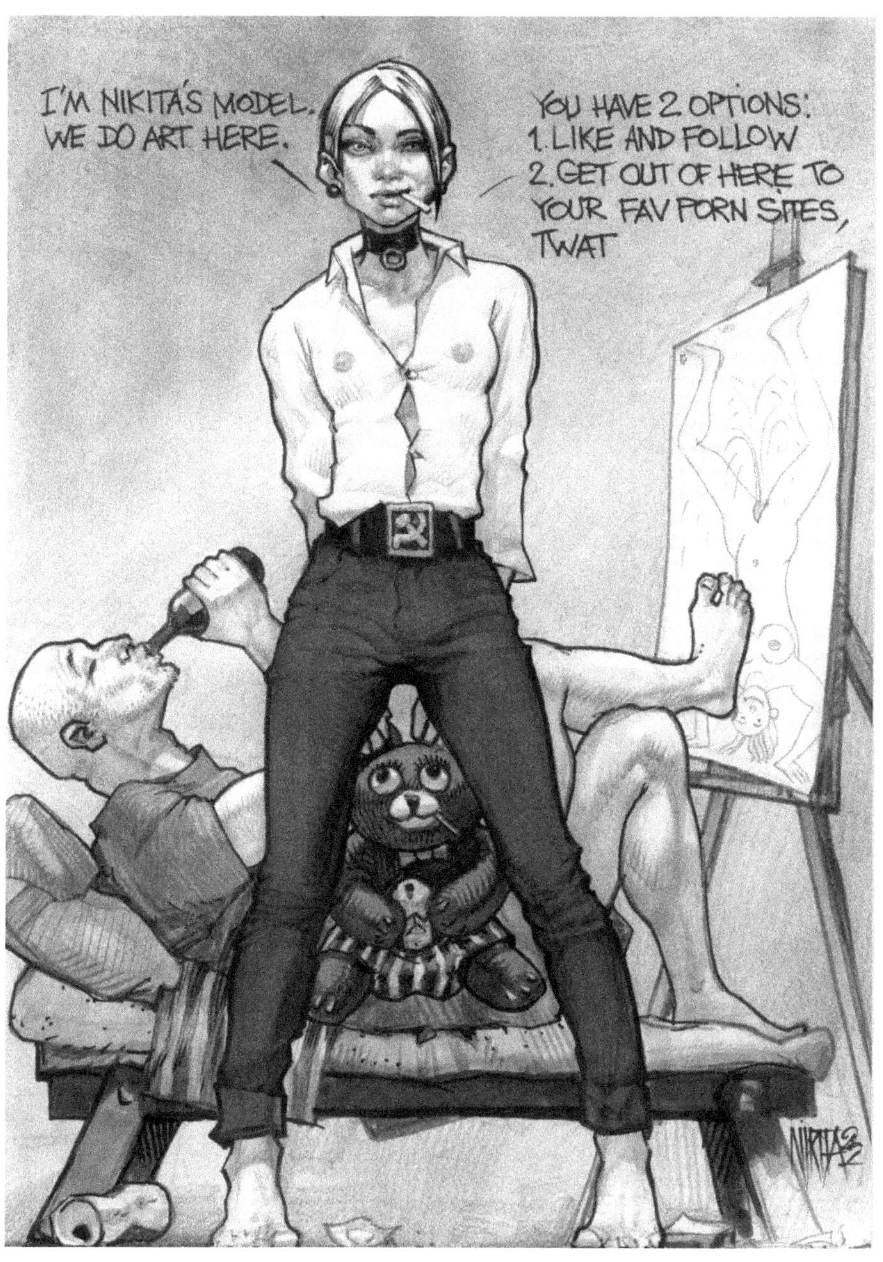
I'M NIKITA'S MODEL.
WE DO ART HERE.
YOU HAVE 2 OPTIONS:
1. LIKE AND FOLLOW
2. GET OUT OF HERE TO YOUR FAV PORN SITES, TWAT

SMOKE BREAK

Beauty just skin-deep
Inside, smoke tars the airways
Nurturing cancer.

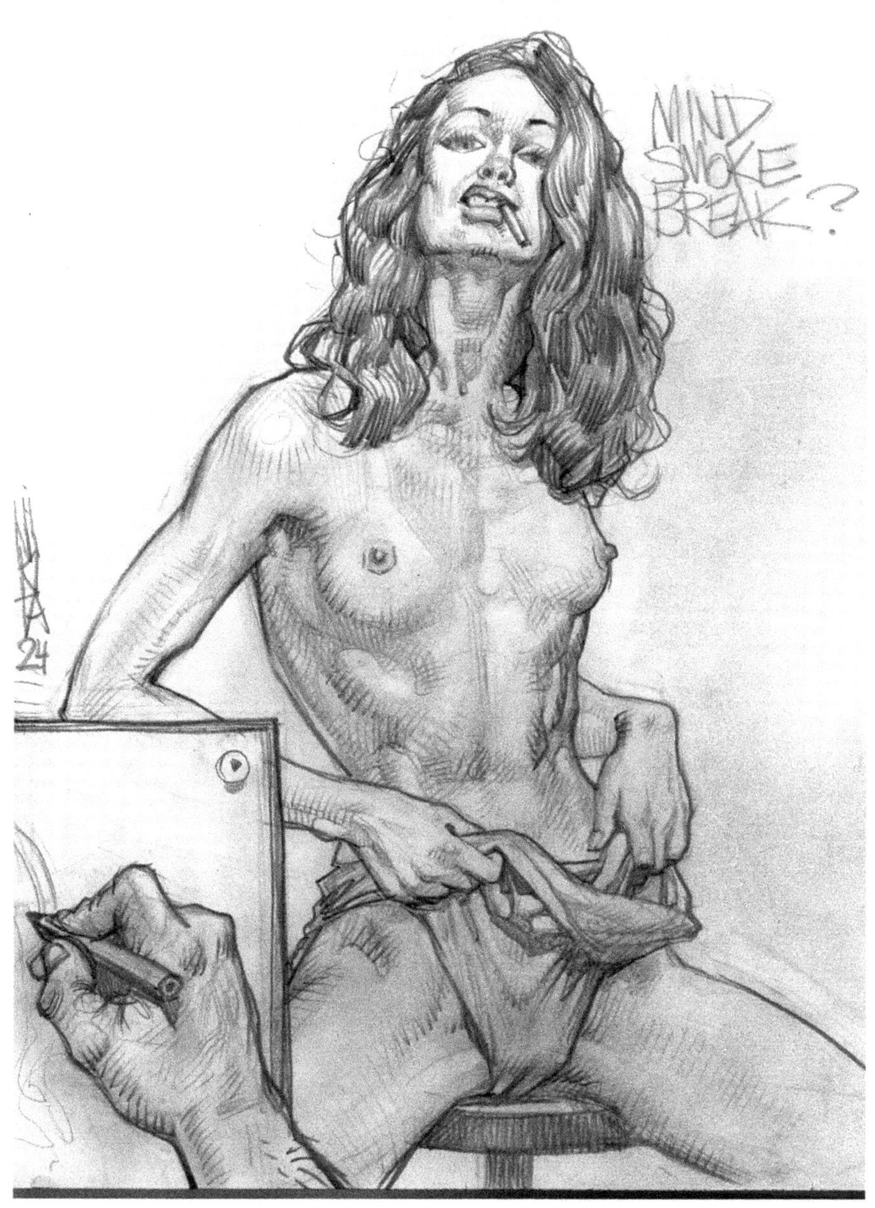
MIND SMOKE BREAK?

BORED MODEL

There was a young model called Daisy
Who posed well but was really lazy
With her portrait not done
She wanted some fun
And drove the poor artist quite crazy

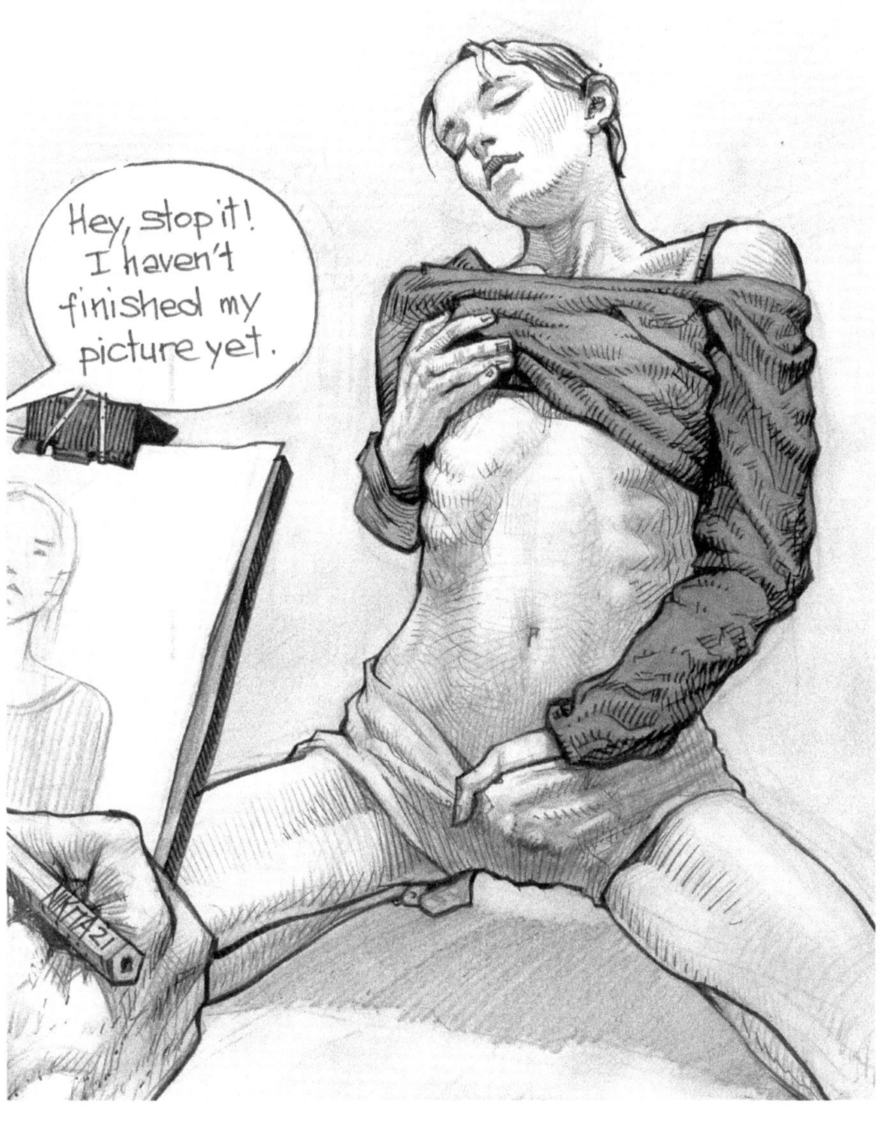
Hey, stop it! I haven't finished my picture yet.
NIKITA 2.1

DRAWING ANGEL

There was a young Angel called Pru
Whom the artist drew as she flew
It wasn't her fall
That mattered at all
But the shock of what came into view.

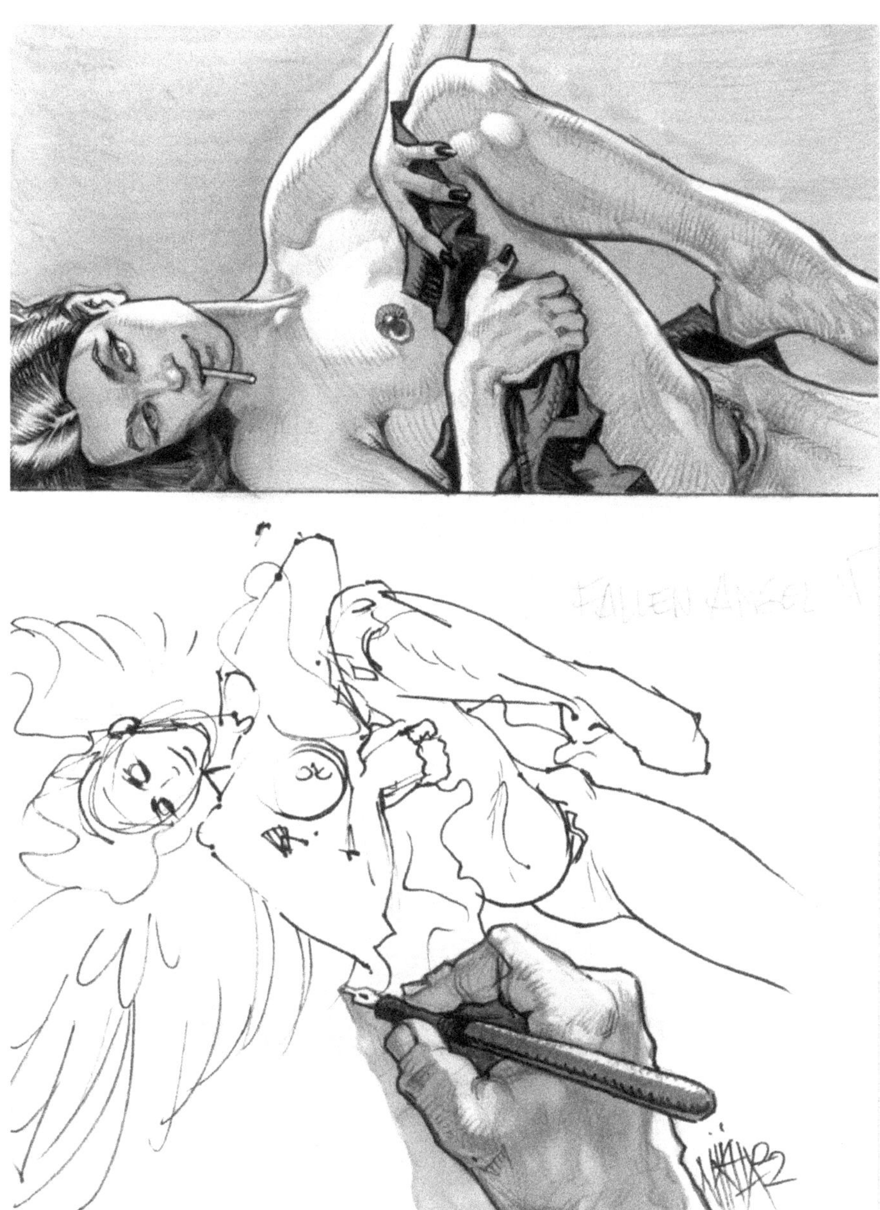
FALLEN ANGEL

HONEY

I am as sweet as can be
Made by a sweet honey bee
It is certainly true
That I'm stickier than you
But nothing is sweeter than me!

I bring you a gift from my hive
To keep your painting alive
I set your colours aglow
And then they dry out real slow
My honey helps you to thrive

When it's wet I'm not so funny
'Cos I make your pallet go runny
But whatever you do
I am working for you
Because I am your very real Honey!

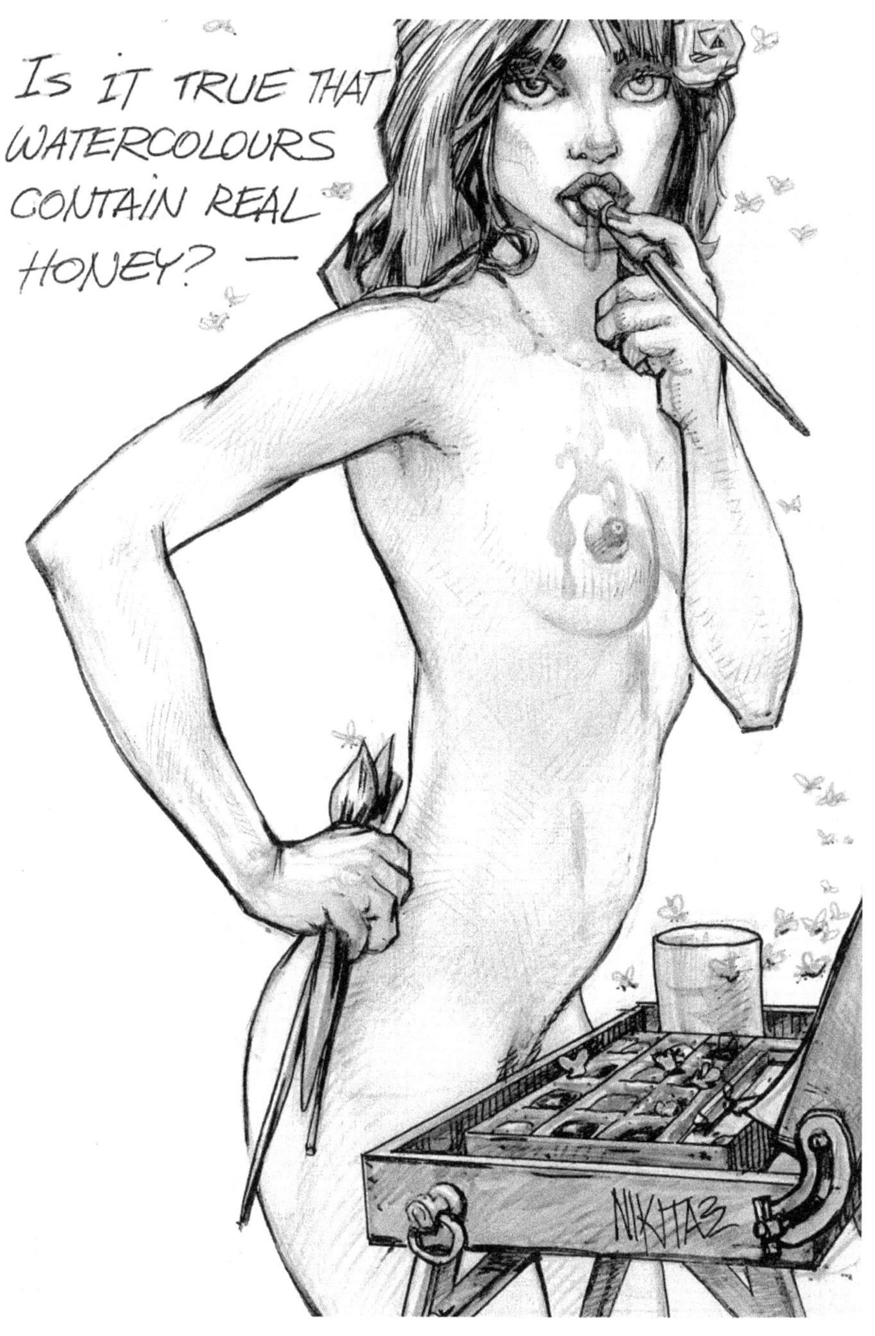
IS IT TRUE THAT
WATERCOLOURS
CONTAIN REAL
HONEY? —
NIKITA3

SATYR vs DAVID

A Satyr without an erection
Is like bacon without any eggs
A truly monstrous Member
Should project from between it's legs

If Peyronie's disease is present
The curve of said Member is great
A little bend may be pleasant
But a big one is bad for your mate.

David, compared, can't compete
For he really has nothing to hide
His manhood is shrunk and petite
Something to mock and deride

Despite his every endeavour
He can never engorge and grow
Struck impotent now and forever
By Michelangelo.

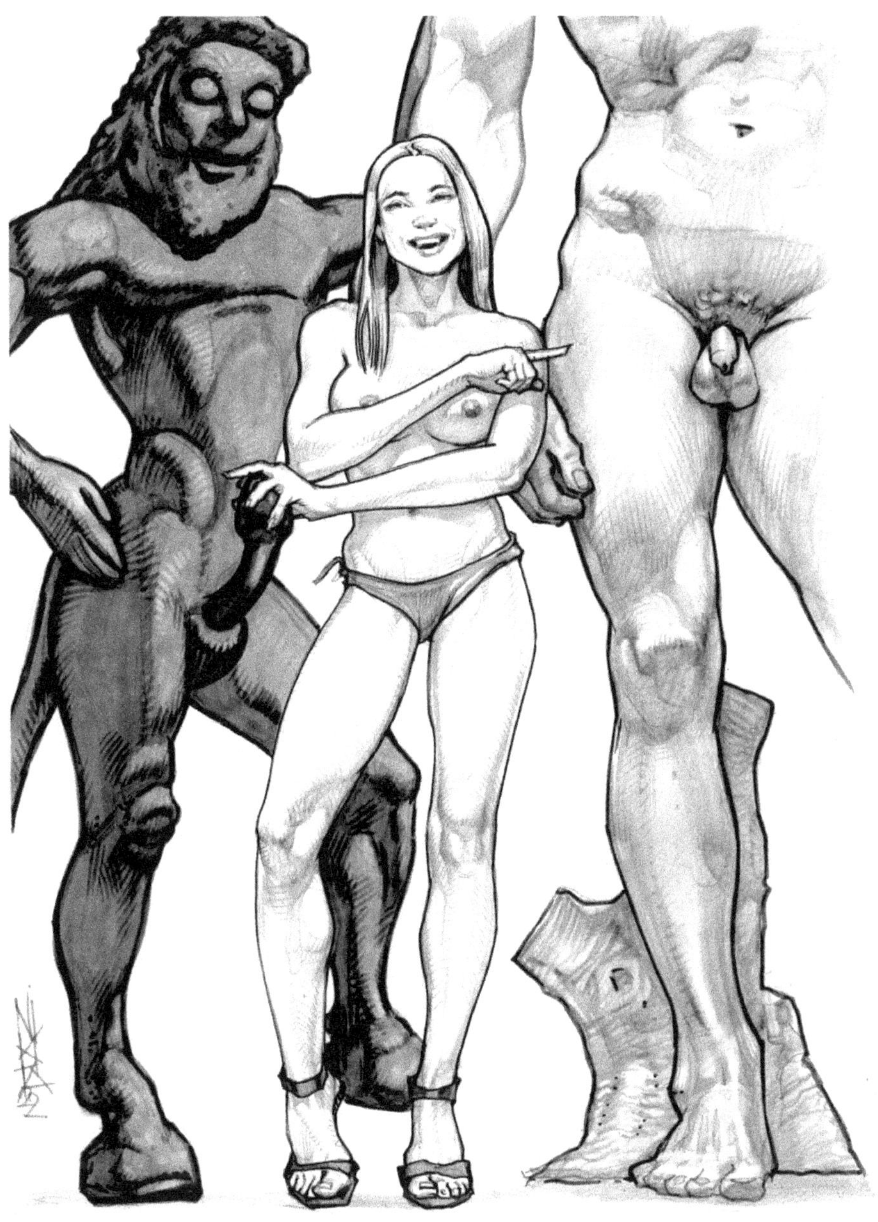

PUNISHMENT

There was a young model called Jane
Who relished the feeling of pain
When she posed for Nikita
Her husband would beat her
So she did it again and again.

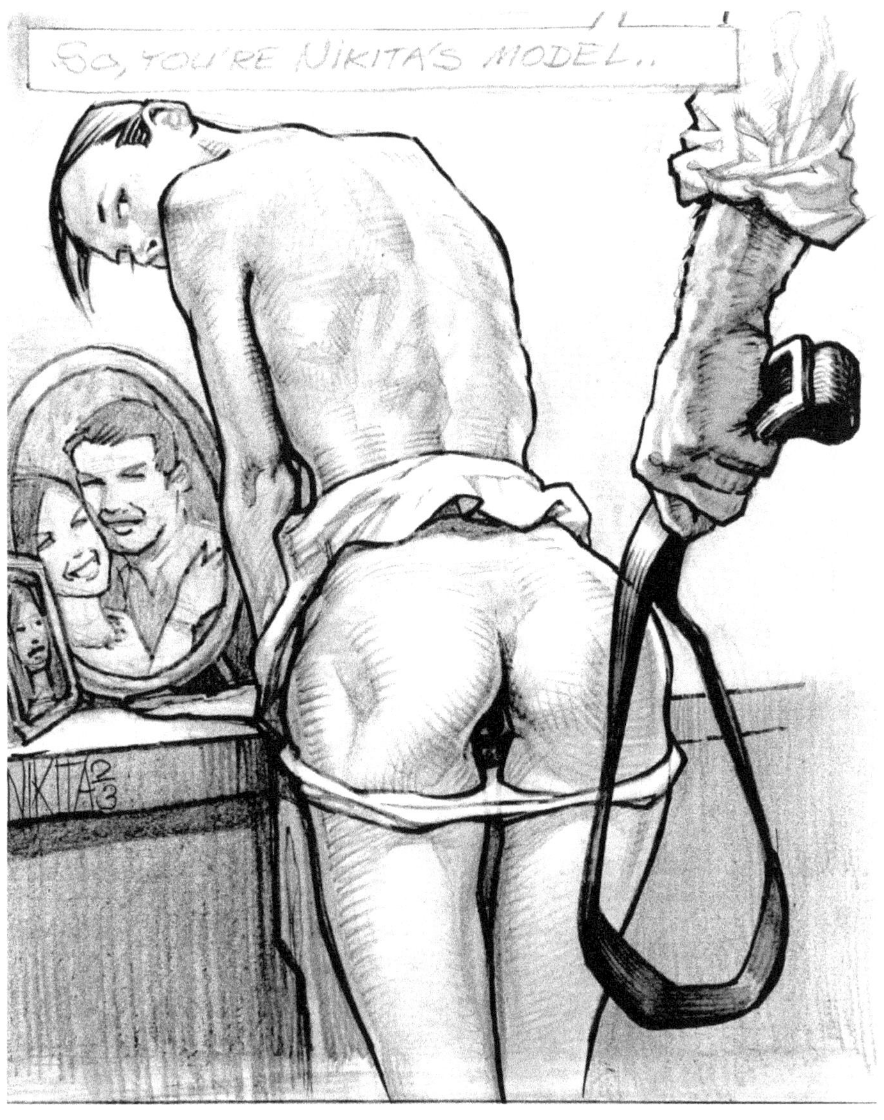
SO, YOU'RE NIKITA'S MODEL..
NIKITA 23

FB TRIAL

Facebook has ordained
Nudity is forbidden
Take fifty lashes

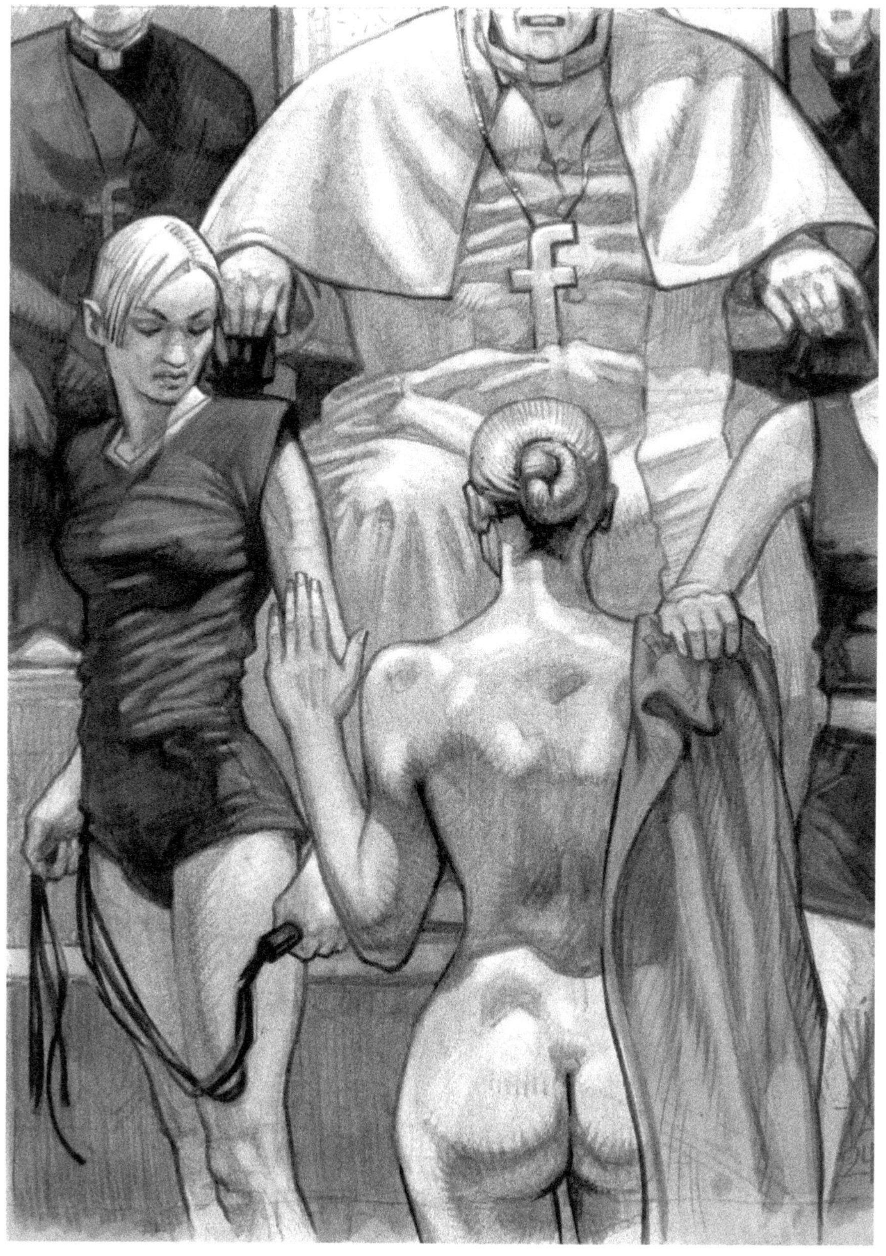

VERSINAGE

There was a young lady called Sue
Who went to a private art view
When they ran out of drink
She did not stop to think
But served up her own special brew.

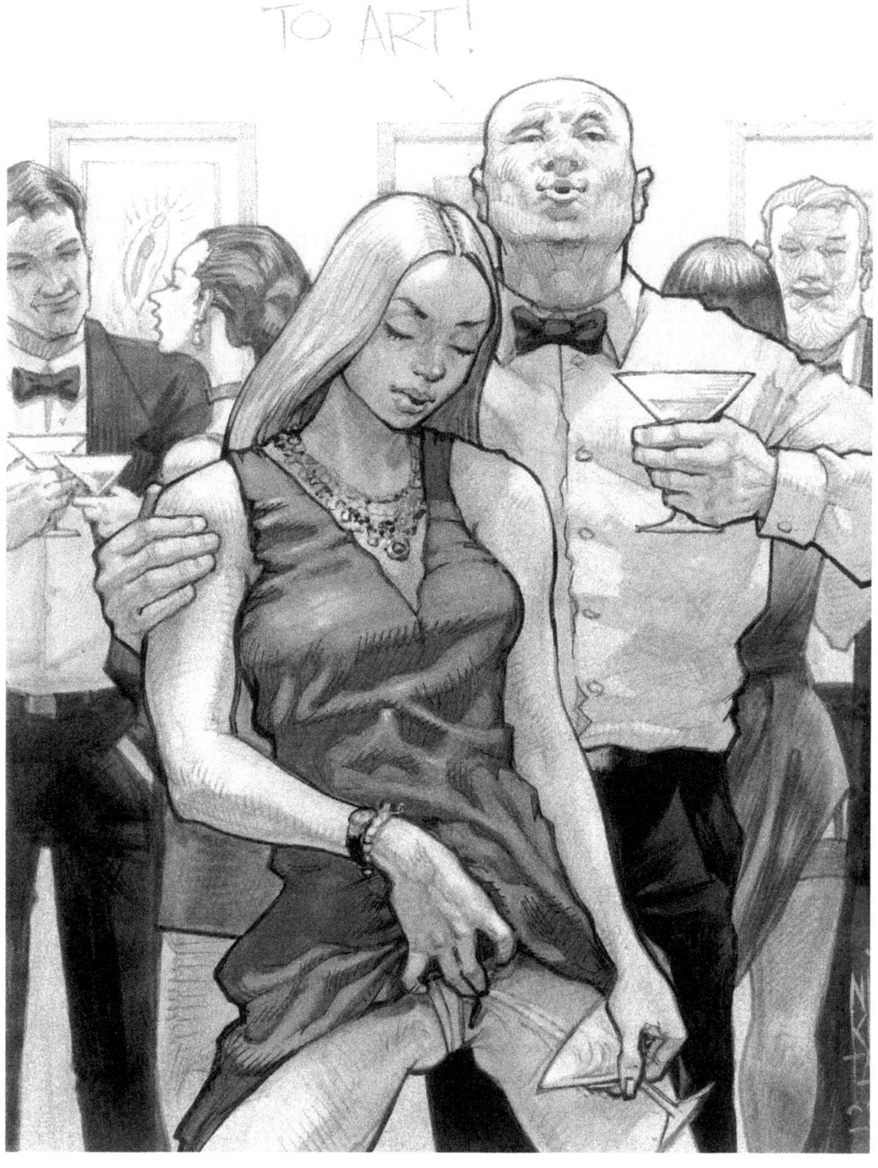
TO ART!

www.ingramcontent.com/pod-product-compliance
Ingram Content Group UK Ltd.
Pitfield, Milton Keynes, MK11 3LW, UK
UKHW062259290726
14090UKWH00017B/788